THE LIFE AND TIMES
OF BILLY PAUCH

Buffy Swanson

CREDITS

Book Design & Layout	Buffy Swanson
Copy Editor	Jim Swanson
Front Cover Image	Ken Dippel
Back Cover Image	Jack Kromer

For additional information: buffyswanson@verizon.net or 609-213-7722

ISBN: 978-0-578-37360-7
First printing May 2022
Printed in the United States of America

Dedicated to

ALFRED LEROY PAUCH

August 1930–March 2016

"Didja learn anything here tonight?
Because if ya didn't, it wasn't worth coming."

Contents

MEL STETTLER

DAN SCHAFER

Billy Pauch and NASCAR Hall of Fame crew chief Ray Evernham compare notes at New Egypt Speedway in 2002. The "play date" Billy set up for his friend saw Ray and drivers Bill Elliott, Jeremy Mayfield and Casey Atwood cut loose in Pauch's driving school cars.

FOREWORD

I've known Billy Pauch a long time. I think we met in 1976 or '7 at one of the auto racing benefits for The Matheny School, which houses and assists children afflicted with cerebral palsy. The benefits became a yearly gathering for New Jersey, Pennsylvania and New York racers, so it was a good way to meet other drivers and have a beer while doing something good for the kids.

I have no idea why or how we became friends. Billy was already winning and on his way to becoming a dirt racing star and I was driving a six-cylinder Street Stock. We just hit it off—maybe it was because we talked a little deeper about the cars and tracks than some of the people we hung out with. Or maybe we just liked the same beer. Either way, we became friends and are still good friends today.

Our conversations today can still get very technical but have become almost comical, because we can't hear from all of the years of racing and our memories of certain races just don't match up. We often talk about past races, the friends we have lost, the inevitable changes in racing technology, and family. Family has always been important to Billy.

Billy is still married to his teenage sweetheart, Barbara, and both their kids, Billy Jr. and Mandee, are involved in racing. I know for a fact that being a good dad—setting a good example and taking care of his family—was always a priority for Billy.

While Billy's path led him to become one of the most recognizable and winning drivers in American short track racing, I chose a path that found me working with and for some of America's greatest racing drivers, engineers and team owners. Although we were both busy with our own careers, Billy and I spoke regularly about racing and car design.

Having a conversation with Billy about racing is no different than having a conversation with some of the greats I've worked with over the years: Andretti, Foyt, Unser, Earnhardt and Gordon. In saying that, I mean that when you're talking with drivers or other superstar athletes who have the ability to perform at a higher level than most, the conversation is held on a different level. When drivers of that caliber describe the car, the track or the race, they describe it with a deeper degree of awareness. Roger Penske once told me the great drivers look through a bigger windshield than the others. In Billy's case, it was a dirt screen and some tear-offs.

Ray cleared his schedule to serve as keynote speaker when Billy was inducted into the Northeast Dirt Modified Hall of Fame in 2016.

Racers—*real* racers—are always looking for an edge. Even the greatest drivers are constantly working to improve the machine…always looking for a way to make it better than everyone else's. They know it takes more than driving talent to win consistently. And when you combine that attitude with great driving talent? You get guys like Billy Pauch.

Real racers are simply committed to continuous improvement—anything less is not acceptable. Everything they see, everything they think about, somehow relates to finding a way to win. The greatest names in racing all have this trait in common. Billy Pauch has had that trait as long as I've known him. Billy Pauch is a *real racer*. For going on 50 years, he has made an incredible commitment to this sport. Using his farmboy genius and the work ethic of a true champion, Billy has driven to victory lane almost 750 times.

Billy Pauch has won on dirt and pavement and he has done it in just about every type of race car that makes circles across America. Billy has done it all: big wins, hard losses, sometimes with broken bones, burns, bumps and bruises. His everyman, regular-guy personality has made him super popular with racing fans wherever he goes.

The fans who have been lucky enough to watch Billy the Kid race through the years have seen one of the greatest drivers ever to come out of the Northeast.

Great racers are noticed and respected by other great racers. And I promise you: the greatest racers in the world today know who Billy Pauch is. *Because he is one of them.*

Billy is one of the greatest I've ever worked with personally. But more importantly, he has been a shining example of what a great racer is supposed to be.

I am proud to call him friend.

RAY EVERNHAM

INTRODUCTION

Every February, when we would follow the race cars south on I-95 to Florida, the itinerary always included a detour down to West Palm Beach, to spend a couple of days with my parents.

Unlike Billy Pauch, I did not grow up in a racing family. In fact, I'm pretty sure neither Dad nor Mom had ever been to an oval track or a dragstrip or any kind of racing event of any kind—*ever*. So it took me by complete surprise, when we were saying our good-byes and getting ready to head out to East Bay in 1995, that my father suddenly announced, "We're coming, too."

So they followed us up the Turnpike and across the state on Route 60 to get their very first taste of racing: All Star Circuit of Champions 410 Sprint Cars on East Bay's third-mile clay.

They had no idea what to expect (as evidenced by my mother's white capri slacks with matching pocketbook).

Billy had just bought his first travel trailer, and he, Barbara and little Billy came down in that, hooked to his pickup truck, loaded with bicycles and toys and cooking utensils—all the necessities needed for the road trip. They had made camp in East Bay's grassy lot, parked beside fellow Flemington homeboys Ed Harrington and Kenny Saums, who had thrown a whole turkey on Ed's Holland grill early that morning, letting it smoke low and slow until suppertime.

The bird's hickory aroma was heavy in the air when we pulled up. My folks were introduced all around, a couple of aluminum lawn chairs were produced to accommodate them. It was a brilliant blue-sky day. Little Billy, age seven, was running around, and my father got up and started throwing a baseball to him, playing catch, until it was time to eat. Paper plates heaped with turkey and rolls and fixin's; open coolers with icy beer and soft drinks. Then it was time to get down to business.

Billy was in his third year driving for the Zemco Sprint team, had already aced an All Star win for them at East Bay the February prior, in '94. And he suited up, and went out. And won his heat race. And won the feature.

Bam. Just like that.

My dad was leaning back in the grandstands, taking it all in, with a can of cold Bud in his hand, under a sky devoid of any semblance of storm clouds. And he told me, "Now

I get what you like about this."

You throw the baseball around. Have a beer. Eat barbecue. Have a few laughs. And then you go out and win the big race.

How great is that?

What my father didn't understand then—and never comprehended for the rest of his life—is that it almost never happens that way.

Of the 740-odd wins that compose Billy's career, a mere handful were that idyllic, with pristine weather and pre-race picnics and predestined winner's circle picture-taking.

Blown motors. Broken pieces. Bad strategy. Cars crashed so severely you could barely cram them back in the trailer. No money for anything but patchwork repairs. Agonizing injuries, agitated politics, angry outbursts. That is the refuse that litters the long road to success.

You beat all the odds by a zillion miles if you get to 740+ wins in this business.

That Billy did it—in every kind of car he ever climbed in—is a testament to who he is.

And, to the best of my ability, here he is.

the Last COWBOY

1.

Awareness

DAVID LORENZO

John's Plain & Fancy Diner in Quakertown, PA, squarely en route back to Jersey, was always the place to stop after racing at Grandview Speedway.

It had to be after two in the morning, and Billy Pauch had already finished his filet and was leaning back in the booth as the post-race chatter died down and the waitress started to clear away the plates. It was September of 1992 and the steak dinner was a celebration: Pauch had just won his third '6er at Grandview, the track's biggest race of the year.

Little Billy Pauch Jr.—now a racer in his own right with a wife and two kids—was curled in sleep next to his dad, the adult conversation swirling over his head. Someone made a comment about how the five-year-old had followed every twist and turn of the night's action, marveling at his level of awareness, and the subject was steered to big Billy's recollections of racing, as a young boy perched in the grandstands watching his dad.

When Pauch describes anything that takes place on a race track, he talks with his hands: one in front of the other, simulating a sideways smack or a sweep into the corners. *Position is everything.* The memory he choreographed this night, his hands chopping and weaving, is a sober one.

It was the blackest blight in the old Nazareth half-mile's history. In excruciating detail, Billy illustrated just how Jackie McLaughlin was killed in 1964.

"There was something between my father and Bucky Barker at Flemington the night before, and Bucky told Leroy he was coming after him at Nazareth," he set the scene. At Nazareth, "I was sitting with my cousins in the old fourth turn, up on the hill. Halfway through the feature, they were coming off the fourth corner and Bucky slowed to try to hit the old man. Jackie was full-throttle around the outside with nowhere to go, and went over Bucky's wheel, spun sideways across the track, slid into the concrete wall and started flipping along the fence. He landed on Bobby Pickell.

"I guess Jackie broke his neck, they said. Everything got real quiet when they were taking him out of the car. I remember after, seeing the roof all bent in on Pickell's car where McLaughlin rolled over it."

Those congregated around the table in the diner sat in stunned silence. "How old were you when this happened?" one friend finally asked.

Pauch shrugged. "I think I was six or seven."

The really good ones never miss a thing. *Ever.*

Although he was just a child, Billy remembers everything about the accident that took Jackie McLaughlin's life.

JOHN REILLY

> *For some reason, he liked vehicles that move.*
> *He was probably about 4, 5, started up the tractor,*
> *got it going, didn't know how to stop it. He jumped*
> *off and the tractor went across the road. Went up*
> *the bank, across the field, lodged in a hedgerow.*
> *Guy was coming up the road at the time,*
> *just left the tavern, said he'd only had*
> *one drink. But he swore there was*
> *nobody on the tractor.*

ROY PAUCH

2.
Early Education

The late Roy Pauch recognized his eldest son was a racer before the kid even cut all his teeth.

"When he was about three, my wife took this woman to the store and she brought Billy along," Roy remembered. "Church Street in Lambertville."

The car was running while Anna Mae and her friend went to fetch the groceries.

"She looked out the store window and there was the car going up the street. Billy was behind the wheel, standing on the seat," Roy chuckled. "She had to run like hell to stop it."

Roy and Anna Mae both soon understood there was no stopping him.

Early on, Billy knew this was what he was destined for. "The old man raced; I loved racing. I knew a lot of good race drivers as a little kid. We'd be at the track all the time. It was something I knew I was going to do even when I was really young."

He remembered, as a child, drawing pictures of race cars, playing with the little plastic models in the dust in front of the grandstands, racing field cars on the family farm as soon as his legs were long enough to reach the pedals.

By the time he was in grade school, Billy and his younger brother Timmy had carved out a little dirt oval in one of the back fields, where the two boys and their friends tried to replicate the action they witnessed on the weekends, watching Roy and other locals mix it up at big tracks like Flemington and Nazareth.

"Billy was into it so much, he even built a little water wagon to help keep the dust down," Roy related.

"My father had a cornfield next to the track we built," said Billy, who distinctly remembers Roy's stern warning.

"What are you guys doing in that cornfield?" the old man would bellow. "It's two dollars a stalk if you hit 'em!"

"We made sure we stayed out of his cornfield."

In 1974, it got real. "There was a car we used to run in the fields, a '55 Chevy. I come in one day, and Billy's got the frame cut out of it," Roy recounted. "Bill, what are you doing?

'I'm going to build a race car,' he said.

"I never pushed him into racing. He just wanted to race."

It was like he had to; he couldn't help himself.

Less than a mile from Hunterdon Central Regional High School was Flemington Speedway—sending a silent siren call to Pauch as he tried to sit in class. "I remember cutting out of activity period, jumping over the back fence of the school, and walking over to the office at the track to get my pit license, for $15 or something," Billy said.

Getting to school was a marathon in itself.

On weekday mornings, Billy and his buddies would meet in Sergeantsville for the 10+ minute drive into Flemington. "Stan Janiszewski had a Camaro with a 327 in it, my other buddy had a Chevelle with a 396 in it, and I had a station wagon with a six-cylinder. And I always beat 'em to school!" Billy boasted.

"If I had to cut through parking lots, take shortcuts, anything I had to do! One morning, I was racing 'em and I come into the town, I think it was Mine Street where you turn down to go to the Agway. I come in there pretty hard, it was wet and the car got sideways. There was a big tree there and—*WHACK!*—I hit it. I'm looking in the mirror and there's stuff flying through the air!

"There was a car stopped at the stop sign, but I didn't even stop—I hadda get down to the end, I hadda cut through the parking lot, to beat whoever I was racing to school," he defended his manic mission.

"And I got to school, and I didn't even think about it. I jumped out of the car because I was always late, run into school, and I come out afterwards and I'm looking at it: the whole right-rear quarter's smashed in," Billy confessed.

"But I won!"

He managed to slip in one single time before Flemington Speedway officials got wise and kicked Billy out when he showed up to race—he was too young to run in New Jersey, so they towed their junkbox car to Middletown in New York and Nazareth in Pennsylvania, where you could race at 17.

"He had a motor he got from the junkyard and they blew that up—he didn't have no race pan on it—and then they got an old Snyder motor from a buddy of his that raced and they blew that up, too," Roy recalled. "All the kids started walking away. They found

Billy, Roy and Timmy, 1961

out they didn't know quite as much as they thought they knew."

Roy didn't want Billy to quit. So he decided to help him.

"It ain't like we had lots of money, but I let him have some ground. I helped him put in soybeans on about 25-30 acres, then we sold 'em and I give him his share," Roy said. "He had to earn this money to race."

According to Billy, the life of a farmer schooled him to drive a race car. "I was on tractors and farm equipment all my life. So I guess learning to drive and harrowing and plowing and bouncing around over plowed fields was normal, y'know?" he ruminated. "I think that enabled me to get a jump on racing."

He thought about that. "Usually, when a guy hits something, he'll get real nervous. That never bothered me. As kids, we raced out in the fields, banging into each other. It never bothered me to brush into something or to spin around or to be fearful or whatever. It just didn't."

There's a family story that both Billy and Roy have retold over the years.

"Our farm is towards Sergeantsville, and towards Stockton there was a chicken farm and they had a tanker to haul the chicken shit," Billy began. "When I was in seventh grade or so, I used to get five dollars a load to go down there, fill up a trailer and bring it back and dump it on the farm. And that motivated me: *money*."

But it wasn't as easy as it sounded. He was navigating a perilous stretch of steep, winding road.

"Coming down into Stockton, the farm was on the left and our tractor had no brakes, only a high range and a low range. So I always had to time myself with traffic to be able to make the left-hand turn—or else I'd end up in the town of Stockton, which was all downhill from this farm.

"I never once missed the driveway," Billy vouched. "I always made it."

3.

Nuts & Bolts

"I should have never been in racing. I'm a farmer. I could weld a little bit, but I wasn't even a good mechanic," Roy Pauch believed.

To be honest, almost no one would agree. In his lifetime, the elder Pauch became a sort of modern-day sage of the Modified circuit, an eccentric semi-celebrity known for his sharp wit and deft mastery of engine mechanics, with well-respected figures like motor wizard Tony Feil and legendary driver Bob McCreadie counting themselves fans of the Jersey farmer.

"My father was always a bookworm, reading up on what's working and what's not," Billy said. "He talked to a lot of people that I didn't have time to talk to. Sometimes I didn't want to listen to his stories. But he knew a lot about motors and chassis and was always trying to figure things out."

Stealthily stalking the pits, chaw in cheek, spouting philosophy, tobacco juice and a cackle of a laugh (sometimes all in the same breath), Roy could get under his son's skin like no one else could. God, he could be irritating!

But he had an uncanny knack for cutting through all the high-priced, high-tech clutter to put old-school ideas into the winner's circle. Logical. Broken down to the lowest common denominator. "De-technology," as he termed it.

At Nazareth in the Sportsman ranks, "We had a different second gear in the transmission. An old Ford transmission, had the shifter up on top and you could put a Zephyr second in there, which wouldn't turn the motor as hard," Roy said. "Come a restart, the other guy's motor would go up too fast and by the time he shifted, Billy was beside him in second—*ZZZZZZZOOM*. Put three car lengths on the guy.

"They couldn't beat him. There was one guy, Mike Geiser, I think he had five in a row, and Billy came there and just blew him off like he was tied. I remember they pumped him afterward to make sure he was legal. Guys like Tittle, Wismer, Smolenyak, all of 'em: they couldn't believe this kid—*this snot-nosed kid*—could do this."

Young Billy's raw prowess wasn't exactly appreciated by the Nazareth gang. "We hadda lot of problems with Wismer and Tittle and all those guys, trying to rough me up

"Roy is like a live computer. He can soak up more information than a UNIVAC—sort it all out and keep it on tap. He doesn't always say much, but there's a lot going on in his head.

**MOTOR BUILDER
TONY FEIL**

Drew Smolenyak (45) and Billy crash in a heat race at Nazareth in 1975. Undeterred, Billy fixed his bent car and rebounded to win the Sportsman feature.

JACK KROMER

because I was an outsider," Billy conceded. "The old man'd be standing there watching the feature with a bunch of guys. *'Is that a girl driving your car?'* they'd bust on him, because I used to have long hair that hung out my helmet."

He snickered. "I remember a couple of times, we'd be stopped on the track—I don't know if it was for a red or what—and Roy would run out and have Wismer or somebody by the neck because they were roughing me up. The old man was pretty intimidating in his day, y'know?"

Putting aside his own racing ambitions, Roy started making deals on his son's behalf.

After the first junkyard motor blew up, Roy bartered with car owner/builder Bill McConnell, trading a 396 short block he had out in the barn plus a couple hundred dollars for McConnell's Z28 302. "It was a short block with a 4-inch by 3-inch stroke," Roy described. "Ed Flemke used to run a 302—very popular back in the day. They handle so much better and they're not violent."

Larry Benson, a family friend who owned a gas station in Hopewell, not only kicked in to sponsor Billy for fuel, he also bought a set of heads and an intake and built a custom exhaust for the 302. Roy did the assembly.

Now, they had a race motor.

In 1975, Billy went out and won all eight races in Flemington's Rookie division, and another eight after he graduated to Sportsman, all with the 302. "The way it worked in Rookies, the top two would qualify for the Sportsman race—but you would start last, behind all the Sportsman consi cars," Billy informed. "I'd get up to about fourth or fifth in the Sportsman feature—which was pretty good for a Rookie. And then the first week the Rookies were over, and I was able to run a Sportsman heat and get handicapped—I didn't start in the front, but I didn't start 28th, like I had been."

"You're talking about a 15-lap feature," Pauch reminded. "You start in the 20s in a 15-lap feature, it's pretty hard to get through and win! The first week that I got to start in the top 18—*I won*."

But things weren't going quite as well at East Windsor on Friday nights. Billy struggled. Tore up lots of equipment. Roy wasn't happy.

"I was farming pretty heavy then, and after Windsor I'd have to take off Saturday mornings and help him get the car back together so he could win his Rookie race at Flemington," Roy complained. "And I got tired of that. I was pretty busy, trying to plant corn and stuff."

On a Friday night in late May, they picked up fuel at Hopewell Sunoco, ostensibly heading to Windsor. "We leave the gas station and we're going down towards Trenton, like we're going to Windsor, and the old man says, 'Turn right here…turn left here…turn right here…'" Billy accounted. "I ask him, *where the hell are we going?* He goes, 'Aah, we're going to Bridgeport'—it was called Statewide back then—'You're not getting it done at Windsor so we're going somewhere else.'"

Billy closes on Roger Laureno on his way to winning the Rookie feature at Flemington. In 1975, Pauch won every race and the track's Rookie championship.

ACE LANE JR.

It was a new world. "I'd never been to Bridgeport, never seen the place," Pauch admitted. "Pulled in there. Bridgeport was big back then—like 80-foot wide! It was the biggest track I'd ever seen, like a superspeedway! I went out, warmed up, started in the back of the heat because I wasn't a regular, qualified. Started in the back of the feature, drove around the bottom and drove all the way up and won the feature. First time I was ever there. *In 15 laps.*"

In his rookie season. Just like that.

Apparently, he made it look too easy. "This guy was screaming, *'He's gotta be illegal!'* 'cause I guess he was standing on his feet and he still got beat. So they pumped Billy. They got him at 287; it was a 302. That's the story," Roy declared. "Won the first time there. Never seen the track before in his life."

However, the 302 was a little underpowered for the Jersey tracks, where 339 CID was the limit in the Sportsman class. So Roy cut another deal with Bill McConnell for a 327. "It wasn't what you'd call a cherry motor," said Roy, explaining that this piece was a warranty motor, a discard from a dealership. "If you had a bad motor in your car, the dealership would change it under warranty. Then they'd scar it up so it couldn't be used— hit all the pistons with a hammer, break the block, like that."

Roy repaired the block on the 327. "The pistons still had dings in 'em, but it didn't hurt it," he determined. And he built it out to 339.

"We won all but one race with that motor in '76—27 out of 28 wins with the same motor," said Billy, who also won Sportsman championships at Flemington and East Windsor that season. "Broke Dusty Malsbury's record for most wins in a year at Windsor: he had 15, I broke it with 16. At Flemington, I had 10 wins; one win at Reading; and one at

ACE LANE JR.

Pauch took it all in 1976: the Flemington Sportsman 100, division titles at both Flemington and East Windsor, and the NJ State Sportsman championship.

As hard as it ever got, Billy never give up, he just kept going on. And he figured out how to win races. He's a funny driver. If you beat him off the turn, you might pull him off the turn—but when he gets to the other end he's going to hang his balls out the window and get you back.

ROY PAUCH

Nazareth in the beginning of the year with the 302. It was a big year."

"He didn't really have as much as a lot of people but his driving ability made him," Roy decided. "If you ever watched Billy race: if he don't get you coming off a corner, he'll get you going in. He'll come down the straightaway behind a guy, wait for that guy to lift, and then just sail right through there, all the way out at the fence. Even back then, he was passing three-four cars at a time. Doing Modified times in the Sportsman."

The Kid was good. So Roy brought him to where the big boys raced: Reading.

"I remember him being out there at Reading—broke a crank and blew the whole back of the motor out. Reading was known to be a baja—a lot of traction, drag tires and the motors used to crack over the mains, in the back where the clutch and flywheel were over the top," Roy talked about the toll on their meager equipment. "Billy had one won in '77: Dave Kelly was running second, and the motor started leaking oil on the clutch. The clutch started slipping and he got second. Brought it home, took the transmission down, the flywheel down, washed it all down. Had some kind of pretty good glue, an epoxy, and patched it back up with that and finished up the year. Finally went and got it welded."

By '78, Billy was only running Modifieds, after claiming three championships and 47 wins in the Sportsman ranks. Jimmy Horton was the man to beat at East Windsor in the Statewide 3. "Jimmy had a Weld car; I don't know whose motor it was but it was injected," Roy said. "We had backwoods stuff."

Roy had a big manifold laying around ("looked like a gorilla manifold, they call 'em log manifolds") and put it on Billy's motor with a vacuum-secondary carb—*cheap traction control*. "Nobody could ever make that manifold work—when you set the points throttle, the air all slows and it backs up and starts gagging. But by choking it, and with the vacuum-secondaries on two barrels, you get the air going fast enough and then the backs come open," Roy detailed. "It cured everything. That thing was working better than when I had injectors on it."

Promoter Lindy Vicari and starter Tim Kirsch congratulate Billy after winning a Wednesday night Sportsman special at Reading in 1976.

BRAD BARMORE

When they towed into Windsor, another competitor sized it up, puffing on his pipe, and scoffed at the setup. "That went out with high-button shoes, Pauchie."

Roy got the last laugh. "We pulled Jimmy off the corner the whole race—a car, car and a half. Then after the race, they had to make some big excuse for not winning."

Once he went Modified, Billy didn't cross the river to run Nazareth a lot. But in the fall of '84, promoter Charlie Bray was running a twin 20 card for small-blocks. Only problem was: Billy didn't have a motor.

"He had to borrow one—we never had nothing, not the big bucks," Roy recalled. "Bob Travagline had this short block but it was wore out; the bore's wore out, the rings are out of it, the engine guy Bitner tells 'em he can't do anything with it anymore. So Billy brings it to me and tells me, 'I borrowed this short block. Can you put heads and an intake on and get it ready for me to go to Nazareth?'"

Roy groaned. "I hadda buy a pan. Bought that off of Chip Slocum, $90. And we had an old set of heads—they were getting kind of rotten, but they were all right. Vacuum-secondaries, 850 alcohol carburetor. There was a cam that came from Karl Freyer. It wasn't bad. It was real driveable."

But when they got to the track, the car was so tight it wouldn't turn.

Billy badly wanted to race, so he kept tinkering with the car, a copy of a Troyer he'd built himself. "Whaddaya think, old man?" he finally asked.

Roy spat, "Well, you oughta put that 310 Carrera on the left-front."

Pauch went out there, ripped right past Doug Hoffman, the King of the Small-Blocks, and beat him by a whole straightaway.

"Billy goes, *this ain't right*. He asked Hoffman, 'What's the deal here, something happened to your motor?' Nope, nope. Then he went out and beat Hoffman again in the second race," Roy related. "The guy who did Hoffman's motors—Butch Sentner—got Davey Hoffman to write out a protest, made us take the head off. I got them believing it was really illegal. *Heh, heh, heh.*"

Track tech inspector Chet Crane and Sentner went down the motor. "It was legal—you could see, nothing but oil slopping all over!" Roy roared. "It was junk. They got beat with shit!"

The borrowed short block was returned to Travagline, who took it to a machine shop to have it bored. "That's when they found out the main cap was broke off and the other one was cracked. It coulda blew up anytime," Roy revealed.

For Roy Pauch, it was always about nuts and bolts. Parts and pieces.

Billy after his twin 20 sweep at Nazareth in 1984, flanked by his mom and Barbara.

MEL STETTLER

That's something a guy like Bob McCreadie could relate to—and why they became friendly. When Bob was going great guns at Weedsport and Rolling Wheels, Roy ferreted out the fact that McCreadie was running an uncommon camshaft. He wanted it.

"I liked Roy, always respected him. And I wasn't racing against Billy," Bob said. So he had no problem sharing his secret.

"McCreadie was coming to Middletown so I picked it up there," Roy remembered. "Very short duration cam; a lot of bottom end. But they put it on a long center, like street cars have. Holds the valves open longer," he explained.

"Anytime you put that cam in the car, you were a winner," Roy enthused. "When

Billy was driving for Trenton Mack, I put my street manifold and that cam in the car. He started 16th and it only took him three and a half laps to get the lead. So driveable! He could just drive right on by."

The conversation sparked a memory from farther back, in 1981, when Billy was driving for the Liedl team with Tommy Cimpko turning the wrenches. "Truppi built this motor for Ken Brenn's kid. Beat us two 20-lappers in a row at Flemington. Billy couldn't even hardly run with him," Roy recollected. "I had this cam I got from Comp Cams—I got it by mistake, that's another story. But I knew it was good, Timmy had run it a little bit. I talked Cimpko and Billy into putting it in. Put that cam in straight up: didn't advance it, didn't retard it.

"They went out and won 10 straight at Flemington," Roy stated for the record. "Won 14 total there that year with their four-bar car."

"I swear he was in the Cam of the Month Club," Billy said of Roy. "Back in the '70s, he'd be changing the cam almost every month! *What the hell!?*"

And Roy's monkeying around wasn't just limited to camshaft R&D.

Davey Hoffman, who worked for Billy and car owner Bob Faust in the mid '90s after splitting with his brother Doug, remembers the ongoing battles between father and son.

Roy doing his thing, 1996.

BOB YURKO

BOB YURKO

"Some things Roy would do were just totally insane," Hoffman figured. "Billy would come into the shop and say, 'What's that carburetor you got on my car?'"

Roy would take his measure, spit out an old success story. "Well, we ran this carburetor back when we beat Hoffman in the twin 20s at Nazareth. And that guy right there is the guy that had us tore down!" he enforced.

Both the driver and the crew chief didn't think much of that. "Yeah, Dad, that was *15 years ago!* I'm not running that thing!" Billy made it clear.

"He'd just smooth it over: we'd go to the track with that stupid carburetor on the car and then we'd take it off," Hoffman recounted. "After hot laps, Billy would say, 'Get that piece of junk off my car!'

"But there were times he'd let Roy do his thing. It was still his dad, after all."

They certainly had their share of standoffs, especially in Roy's final years. "There was one time he thought I wasn't home or something, and he had my race car running, and he's playing with the carburetor." Billy was incensed that his father was making changes without his knowledge or consent. *"What are you doing?"*

"I'm doing what I want to do!" Roy barked back.

"It don't work that way no more. Y'know, I ain't a little kid no more, old man!" Billy shouted, then banished Roy from the shop. "We got in a lot of skirmishes at the end there. A lot of disagreements."

Billy paused, took a breath. "If you ask me who was the biggest influence in my career, it would be my father. He helped me through most of it. But when you get to a certain age, when you're over 40 years old—you don't need your father telling you what to do all the time. *You gotta give up the wheel at some point and let me steer the ship.*

"That's just the way it is."

4.
Breaks...and Breaks

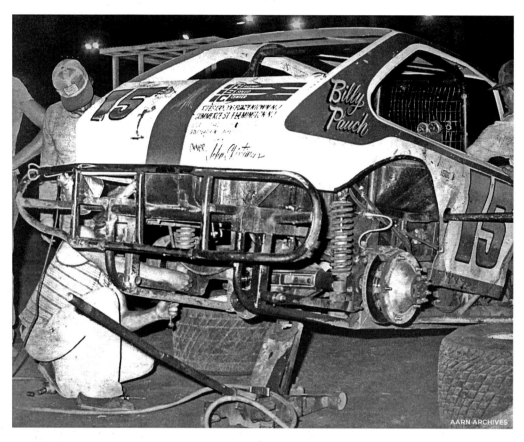

AARN ARCHIVES

Billy was first dipping a toe in the Modified pool in 1977, had a couple seconds at Reading. "If you could finish second with those guys, out at Reading, you were a pretty good racer," Roy reckoned. "I remember after '77, it kind of opened things up. *This kid's getting good, we've got to get hold of him.'* You see how it works in racing: owners always like to hire somebody who's gonna make them look good."

Actually, there were those who started to sit up and take notice after Pauch annihilated the Sportsman class the season prior.

John Skistimas, proprietor of Raceway Speed Center in Bordentown and a sometime promoter at East Windsor, was quick to single out Billy. Pennsy star Glenn Fitzcharles was dominating in an Ebersole-built car at the time; Skistimas was a dealer for the chassis. So for '77, Pauch drove an Ebersole car, with John's support and sponsorship.

Skistimas had actually brought Billy to Terry Ebersole's attention the year before. In 1976, Fitzcharles was winning in the Verona-McCabe Ebersole Gremlin, but couldn't seem to get around in a new Chevette-bodied car that Ebersole had designed.

"So they put me in it one night at Flemington, to see what I thought," Pauch related. "I remember driving it in the heat race. And I came in and Terry Ebersole was standing there, talking to me. I was explaining what I thought of the car, and Glenn came over."

Fitzcharles had barely entered the conversation when car owner Jerry Verona lit into him. "Get the frig outta here!" he hollered. "I don't wanta hear what you've gotta say!"

"I was like—*whoa!*" Pauch was dumbfounded that his opinion would be valued over that of Fitzcharles, the defending Flemington champion. "I guess he didn't want Glenn to influence what I was thinking. He wanted to hear a separate view of the car. But I was just a kid!

"Then I went out in the feature and John Scarpati wrecked me. It was a one-night thing," Billy shrugged. "But I guess because I was so good in the Sportsman in '76, Ebersole wanted me in one of his cars. And Skistimas was selling 'em so they worked out a deal, so I would get one for the following year."

Flemington Speedway, July 2, 1977: Billy in the Raceway Speed Center Chevette and Glenn Fitzcharles in the Verona-McCabe 23. Fitz would go on to pass Pauch for the win.

JACK KROMER

Skistimas was the first to perceive the promise and promote Pauch. "I saw he was a good kid, a hard worker who maybe needed a little help," he recalled. "No question, he had talent. What made him so good is he could recognize the small nuances and changes that needed to be made to go faster. He absolutely understood the cars—and Billy wasn't afraid to make changes."

It was a learning year, with a lot of ups and downs. Before the Ebersole Chevette was ready to race, Pauch quickly banged out three Sportsman wins in his own car at Nazareth in early spring—his only scores all season.

But they had high hopes: Skistimas paid for a Fred Bitner-built big-block to run the Super DIRT Week classic at Syracuse, and that fall they headed upstate.

"I probably shouldn't have went," Pauch said in hindsight. "There were like 150 freakin' cars there, and I didn't make the race. Might have been the first time in my life I didn't qualify for a race. So I'm riding home, all dejected, and I'm listening to the CB radio—remember those?—and people are talking. 'That Pauch kid will never make it as a Modified racer. He's a good Sportsman racer, but he ain't gonna make it in Modified…'

"I didn't reply to 'em—but hearing something like that always gives you a little incentive. *Pissed me off!* That's one thing you never want to do."

Rookie Pauch and rim-rider Kenny Brightbill sandwich Jim Keppley in a 1977 thriller at Reading.

MIKE FELTENBERGER

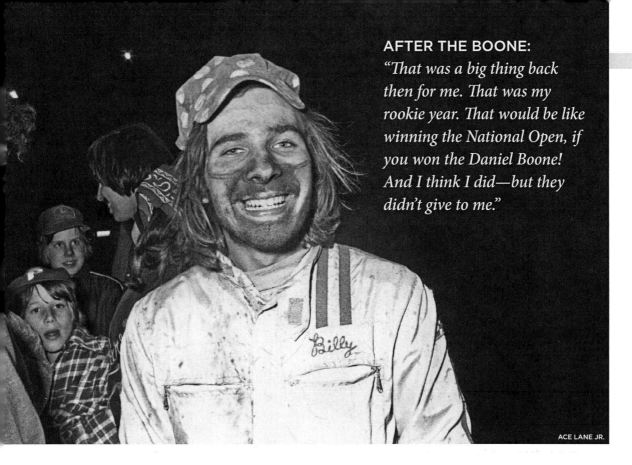

Reading's annual Daniel Boone 200 was the Pennsylvania counterpart to Super DIRT Week for the Mods—a big established race that everyone and their brother entered. "We had a lot of tires we didn't use at Syracuse because we didn't qualify, so we went to Reading for the Boone," Billy said.

Still stinging from the Syracuse shutout, Pauch put the Raceway Speed Center Chevette soundly in the field. "I'm pretty sure back then we didn't pit—we just had a big tank in the car with 40 gallons of fuel, and ran the same tires the whole race. They were running drag tires back then, but we had the low-profiles we bought for Syracuse. We didn't know nothing! The old man was the coach, he made the calls—the gear, the tires and all. And we just rode," he reviewed. In the later stages of the event, "Osmun was leading in the Ferraiuolo 73 and his radiator mount broke and went into the fan. He dropped out."

And all of a sudden, Pauch was out front. A novice from New Jersey was leading Reading's biggest race of the year.

"With five to go, Brightbill passed me. By that point, my tires were bald," Billy said. "And I finished second—which was big, y'know? Because I was just a rookie."

The next day, Billy got a phone call from Frankie Schneider. "You know you won that race," Schneider flat-out told him. "Brightbill was in a skirmish there in the third turn. You went by him, put him a lap down. You won."

"A little late now," Pauch acquiesced. Kenny Brightbill was the all-time winningest driver at Reading, a local god to Pennsy's rabid racing fans. "It's Reading and it's Brightbill," he was resigned. "Whaddaya gonna do? You're not going to argue with that."

BOB YURKO

But that performance put Pauch on everyone's radar, led to other opportunities.

When John Skistimas became East Windsor's promoter in '78, the deal with Billy ended. "He said, 'Look, I'll sell you the car for a good price.' So we ended up buying the car." Pauch switched the back coilovers on the Ebersole to leaf springs, and swapped the Chevette body for a Gremlin. "I wanted that motor so bad! It was a good motor, but we couldn't afford it," he bemoaned. "And Scarpati got the motor. Which was a waste because he couldn't drive."

They made do with what Roy could piece together.

Horton and Pauch size each other up at East Windsor in 1979, with Pauch persevering for the win.

ACE LANE JR.

On June 4, 1978, he recorded his first Modified win at Windsor; the following week, he was in the winner's circle at Flemington.

Pauch's first win for an owner came in an early July 100-lapper at Flemington, for Hall of Fame mechanic Sonny Dornberger. Radiator builder Fred Orchard got them together.

Billy's first win for an owner came in a Flemington 100 in July 1978 for Sonny Dornberger (right).

ACE LANE JR.

"Osmun was getting out of the 99 so Dornberger gave me a shot at it," Billy remembered. "We ran Windsor that Friday, I finished second to Horton. Horton was dominant at Windsor in '78—he won like every race. Went to Flemington for a 100-lapper, won that. Went back to Windsor on Sunday, finished second again.

"Then the following week, I was running it at Flemington and clipped the inside wall and broke the steering, hit the outside wall and totaled it," Pauch confessed. "And that was the end of my ride with Sonny Dornberger. My first ride for somebody else."

That fall, he got the nod to drive John and Tony Norcia's infamous Black Horse Racing 81, finishing out '78 as a teammate to Sammy Beavers. "Then Beavers left, went back with old man Horton. So I started the year out with the Norcias in '79," Billy detailed.

He won a single race for the team at Flemington in May. "The car was good—I'd get it up front all the time. And it would break…and it would break…and break," sighed Pauch, who rapidly became disillusioned. The Dornberger car…the Norcia car…These were high-profile rides.

"I'm getting in the car, Osmun is getting out. I'm getting in the car, Beavers is getting out. I didn't know any better—why're these guys getting out while I'm getting in?" He came to the realization. "They're *leaving*. They weren't *fired. They were leaving!* You think you're getting the hot setup there, but…*aah,* I guess it's just like all teams. They get sour, they need a change—driver, mechanic or something."

ACE LANE JR.

Pauch leads the way at Reading in the Black Horse Racing Team 81.

Billy had had enough. "It just didn't fit well with me. I don't like breaking; I like to finish. I was trying to do it for a living, and when I don't finish, I don't make money."

Driving for the Norcias, Pauch would always bring his own car to the track for a backup. When the 81 overheated and broke in warmups on June 2nd, he pulled his car off the trailer. "And I won the feature. So that week, I called 'em, told 'em I'm just gonna run my own car," he decided.

"Can't tell ya how many races I won that year, but that was my first Modified championship at Flemington, in '79."

The only lasting legacy from Billy's brief stint with the Norcias? Their gleaming black and gold Gremlins, the iconic rearing black stallion emblazoned on the back quarters, were wrapped in a Wild West mystique, conjuring the countenance of a black-hatted cowboy saddled up for a showdown, a stampede to the front of the pack.

He wasn't with the Black Horse Racing Team very long, but the nickname stuck forever: *Billy the Kid.*

5.
The Staten Island Connection

"What am I getting myself into?"

Pauch posed the question to fellow driver Roger Laureno back in mid '79, after asking for directions to Joe Scamardella's Chrysler-Plymouth dealership in Staten Island.

Billy had reason to be apprehensive. For a farm boy from pastoral Hunterdon County, Staten Island was like a foreign country—a bona fide borough of New York City where residents spoke with a fast-patter, attitude-edged accent and screeching police sirens scored the soundtrack to everyday life.

Laureno, born and bred, was a member of the Island's auto racing scene which centered around Weissglass Stadium until that track closed in 1972, sending many of its cars and stars across the Arthur Kill and into New Jersey.

Scamardella's father, also Joe but nicknamed Pippy, had raced stock cars at Weissglass in the early '50s, back when the track was running under NASCAR sanction on Thursday

Promoter Joe Scamardella congratulates Billy following his big win in the 1979 Syracuse qualifier at Acella Speedway (aka East Windsor). In 1980, Billy drove for Joe.

AARN ARCHIVES

nights. With drivers like Red Hamersly and Howie Brown, he crossed the river long before Weissglass went under, competing at Wall, Old Bridge and other Jersey joints throughout the '60s.

When young Joe came of age, he started his own team, first on pavement and then on the dirt tracks. Scamardella got hooked up with driver Mike Grbac and mechanic Tommy Cimpko, out of Franklin Township where the cars were kept: the King Chevrolet racers, named for the Staten Island dealership Joe managed and carrying the numbers his dad ran—7, 121 and 122.

By the late '70s, Scamardella opened the Acella Chrysler-Plymouth dealership on Richmond Terrace and the race car fleet—by then, a genuine King and a King copy built by Cimpko, kept at Cimpko's—bore that marque. Sammy Beavers, Fred Dmuchowski and Billy Osmun were the line of drivers after Grbac.

Which brings us to Billy Pauch, trying to find his way to Staten Island.

In 1979, Pauch was coming into his own. After a very short turn with the Norcia team that produced one win at Flemington, Billy won another nine in his own Ebersole

BOB HESS

Billy ran well but had no luck at Middletown. After officials took a win away, Pauch was able to convince Scamardella to return to Flemington.

Billy edges Sammy Beavers in the nailbiting final laps of the 1980 Flemington 200. It was Billy's first 200-lap victory. (Below) Tommy Cimpko, Nick Lombardi, Barbara and crew at the finish.

ACE LANE JR.

DAN GOLDEN

Gremlin, including a shocker in Albany-Saratoga's big 79-lap Shootout in his first-ever appearance at the track. He would also ace a pair of 100-lappers, at Flemington and Windsor, and was well on his way to cementing the first of his eight Flemington Modified championships when he met with Scamardella to apply for the 121 ride late in the year.

"Joe was the first big-time guy I drove for," said Billy, who thought he was all set. He was Flemington's 1979 champ. He would return to defend that title at his hometown speedway in a top car for a top team, wrenched by a top mechanic.

It was all looking like champagne and roses.

But before he even attempted to strap in, Billy was sucked into a Staten Island-style soap opera with more provocative plot twists than a Scorsese screenplay.

In mid-August of '79, Scamardella was at the center of one of the biggest scandals to ever rock New Jersey racing when he partnered with Lindy Vicari, late of the liquidated Reading Fairgrounds, to wrangle East Windsor's lease from the promotional team of John Skistimas, Harry Dee, Howard Fosbre and George Nessler.

Immediately, Joe changed the name to Acella Speedway, after his S.I. dealership— and proceeded to publicly provoke Flemington promoter Paul Kuhl.

At the first drivers' meeting, Scamardella announced that they were severing any ties with Flemington Speedway and the NJ State Championship, which was Kuhl's baby. Fuel was thrown on the fledgling feud when Joe had the audacity to step on some of Paul's sacrosanct Saturday night dates at Flemington. Kuhl went wild.

By the end of the year, it was an inferno. Acella had adopted Reading's old model: racing into November with the long-established Daniel Boone event serving as a grand finale. For spite, Kuhl extended Flemington's season and scheduled the crowd favorite Mod four 20s against the Boone.

LENNY H. SAMMONS

In spring 1980, Scamardella and Kuhl publicly shook and made up. Three years later, all hell broke loose.

It was all-out war. And an unwitting Billy Pauch was about to become its first casualty.

Instead of returning to his home track in 1980, Billy was banished to Orange County Fair Speedway in Middletown, NY.

"Joe was pissed at Kuhl and he wasn't going to support him. So he made me run Middletown. And I hated it," said Pauch, who keenly recalled the weekly agony of being forced to drive right past Flemington en route to New York. "It was hard for me to run Middletown because I loved Flemington so much. Driving past Flemington to get to Middletown—I thought, *this is stupid!* Flemington's 15 minutes from home and I'm riding two hours to go to Middletown! It didn't set right with me.

"Flemington was my track."

The team actually showed well at Orange County, "but I didn't have any luck," Pauch conceded. "We had a 100-lapper won there, and the brake caliper fell off or broke or something, and we dropped out with 10 laps to go. And then I did win a race there and they took it away from me for going under the yellow line. Which was a bunch of bullshit."

After all these years, fans on Facebook forums still heatedly discuss Billy's controversial DQ that night, concurring that he was robbed. "He got below one of the tires on the infield, but it was done every week by the regulars. They took the win away for that reason," one eyewitness argued. "After Billy O dominated the '78 season after missing three races, the track didn't want another outsider doing it again."

Noting, "I never liked Middletown after that. It soured me," Pauch convinced Scamardella to come back to Flemington for the annual Memorial Day 200. He clearly remembers that homecoming.

"We had a 427 Chevy motor that I only ran once a year in the 200-lapper because it didn't have no power—you'd just get it wound up, like a rubber band, and it would go, go, go, go, go. They'd run out of motors on the 121, so we took it out, put it in that car," Billy said. "Me and Beavers were running head to tail, back and forth for the lead—Beavers was in Horton's car and I was in Joe's car. And I won the race. My first 200-lap win."

The next thing you know, Paul Kuhl and Joe Scamardella were shaking hands, posing for a photo op on the frontstretch. "And I came back to Flemington and went on a tear," Pauch proclaimed. "Won five or six straight with the 121."

All was finally right with the world. For about two seconds.

Back on Staten Island, Scamardella's partner in the dealership, a doctor, had run into some trouble and needed money, about $30K. So Joe borrowed half of that from Tony Sesely, another Modified car owner from the Island contingent. When they stopped making payments, and the vig got too high, Tony rolled his flatbed up to Tommy Cimpko's shop and took both race cars, stashing them at Glenn Fitzcharles' place in Pennsylvania.

You can't make this stuff up.

So there was Billy Pauch, helmet bag in hand. And no car to race.

MEL STETTLER

Four wide at Flemington.

"I wound up driving for old man Horton that night," he said. "Then Joe got pissed off at me. I told him, 'What did you want me to do? I was there, you didn't bring me a car.' Joe said, *'You shouldn't have run!'* It was a mess."

The high drama continued. "The rest is ugly," Tony understated. When "the boys from Brooklyn" showed up, making sure Sesely understood that it would be in his "best interest" to return the race cars, he obliged, with the agreement that he would get all his money back.

Flemington promoter Paul Kuhl put a $500 bounty on Pauch's head after he won four in a row in 1980. Billy stretched his win streak to five and collected the extra cash.

When Tony didn't get paid, the second chapter in the Staten Island saga was staged.

Scamardella had commissioned a top-shelf asphalt Modified for Pauch to drive in the final race at Trenton Speedway, but the car wasn't completed in time. They had thoughts of bringing it to New Smyrna in February '81; but until then, the untouched Troyer car—Jack Tant motor, Pauch's name lettered on the roof—sat on display in the Acella Chrysler-Plymouth showroom.

When Sesely took that car, right out of Joe's dealership, he figured they were even.

Square and done.

Incredibly, over the winter, Scamardella's Staten Island car dealership burned to the ground. And that was that.

Billy only ran the 121 a single season: hard to believe when that year was packed end to end with more lurid plot lines than a sequel to *The Godfather* (part of which was filmed on Staten Island).

Tommy Cimpko paired Pauch with the Liedl brothers for '81 and he picked up where he left off at Flemington. Two years later, Billy contacted Joe about the possibility of funding a run on the USAC Silver Crown series. Scamardella was interested.

"We did a season with the Champ Cars in '83," Pauch said. "I was lucky—I finished second to Bettenhausen in the opening race at Nazareth in March, and made enough money to kinda finance the deal to run through the year."

Billy runs outside Keith Kauffman en route to a runner-up finish at Nazareth National in March of '83.

CHARLIE MELICK

At the end of May, Pauch pulled into the mile dirt track at Indy—and was met by police and car builder Grant King. "I had my Nance car, not a King car, but this was Indianapolis, where Grant lived. He had a lien or an injunction or something. And he had the cops there to confiscate my race car, right at the gate," he reported, flabbergasted.

The backstory was this: "In 1979, when I ran the Modified at Syracuse for Joe Scamardella, we broke a transmission. So he got a transmission from Fast-Lane—what was it, Billie Harvey? And it was Grant King's stuff. So King sent Joe a bill for $1,200 for his transmission, and Joe says, 'Screw him! That's way too much money, I'm not paying him.' And Joe never paid him for the transmission. So when I pulled into the Indy Fairgrounds—they were sitting there waiting to confiscate Joe's car."

More drama.

"Is this Joe Scamardella's car?" the sheriff asked.

Pauch knew the right answer: "No, it's my car."

King doubled down, "This is Joe Scamardella's car!"

That's when Billy produced the entry form. "For some reason, I put my name as the owner—and that kept me from getting my car confiscated," he said. "Grant King was livid! He was pissed that we got one over on him. But there was nothing he could do because they had no proof that the car was Joe Scamardella's."

Billy couldn't believe it. "I almost lost a race car again, after the incident with Sesely taking the Modifieds. *Jeez*."

"Hey, I was just a nice guy from Staten Island," Tony demurely defended himself. Weren't they all.

As a postscript… The feud between Scamardella and Kuhl didn't end when Joe and Lindy handed East Windsor's keys back to Don Jones at the end of 1980. In many ways, it was just beginning.

Cut the scene to the Flemington Speedway awards banquet in November of '83. A long black limo with New York tags pulled up to the Flemington Elks Club, and out stepped Joe Scamardella—always a sharp dresser—and a crew of his associates. He'd come to deliver a bombshell: Frank Bohren, the second biggest shareholder in the Flemington Fair & Carnival Association (aka the Fairgrounds Speedway), had sold his percentage of the operation to none other than—get ready for this—Joe Scamardella.

Paul Kuhl was apopletic, grabbing the microphone to announce, "There is no way I can work with this man," pointing to Joe, calmly sipping water as he sat at his table, "and therefore, you have seen your last stock car race at Flemington Speedway!"

Enraged, Kuhl swore to close the track, wildly threatening to summon federal authorities to investigate the transaction.

The future of racing remained in limbo, with Kuhl and Scamardella going tit for tat in the newspapers for weeks, until it was all ultimately resolved in a Flemington attorney's office: Joe sold his speedway interests to Paul and the two shook on the deal. Nice as pie.

Unlike almost everything that came before, "it ended well," Rick Kuhl pronounced.

6.
Goes Like L

ACE LANE JR.

The deal went down during a December deer drive, at a hunting club in Hillsborough.

"If you Liedl boys ever want to get into racing this is going to be a good year to do it," Tommy Cimpko tossed that out to Leon and Gene Liedl as they flushed the woods for whitetails. "It doesn't look like Joe's gonna go racing because he's in so much trouble, with the fire and the dealership and all. Billy keeps calling me, asking, 'What's going on? What's going on?' I don't have no answers for him."

After owner Joe Scamardella's car dealership went up in flames, and the race team all but disbanded, builder/mechanic Tommy Cimpko was stuck. He had a hot-property driver in Billy Pauch—and nowhere to put him.

The Liedl brothers—Leon, Gene, Joe and Art—were fans in the Flemington grandstands. Of course, their father and uncles had fielded stock cars back when the elders had a gas station in town. But that was decades earlier. Now, the family business was well drilling. The boys loved racing, never missed a Saturday night, but they'd never even set foot in the pits.

"We came home, talked to Joe, Art and my father," Leon said of the sudden opportunity to become car owners. The consensus: "Let's do it. Whadda we gotta do?"

The first order of business: get a car. Racer Kim Trout was selling out so they bought his operation, which included a Harraka-built Mod that Cimpko immediately and completely revamped.

"We bought that car and put it on the table and Tommy cut it all apart. It was a beautiful car, and he cut the whole front off, the whole tail out of it—he didn't like where the torsion rack was or nothin'," Leon said, appalled. "I thought, *this thing'll never run again!* You take a torch to a brand new chassis—*are you kidding me?* But Tommy knew what he was doing. And it was a beautiful race car when he got done with it."

With Cimpko at the helm and Pauch's input, the L car made its debut in 1981.

"It was a learning curve for us," Leon described the team-building effort. "We're in the well drilling business. We fix all our own equipment, it's all nuts and bolts—but a race car is a lot different." Yet, the Liedls had every faith in their crew chief and driver. "We had the greatest mechanic I've ever known: Tommy Cimpko. We all went to his shop, built a race car and went racing."

Pauch caught Billy Cannon right at the line to sweep a four 20 card at Flemington on August 22, 1981.

GEORGE GORDON

They found out right quick that it wasn't as easy as it looked from the grandstand seats.

"We struggled the beginning of '81," Billy remembered. "Bitner built the motor and we had a lot of problems—it wouldn't run…wouldn't run. We were on injectors with a drop tank in it, and we couldn't finish a race."

Frustrated with the unfounded motor issues and all the DNFs, the team finally decided to abandon the alky injection setup and put a carburetor on it in late May or early June. "So they took the drop tank out to put a fuel cell in, and when they set the plastic drop tank down they heard something tinkle in it," Pauch related. "They opened it up, looked in there and found a rock that was jammed up in the pickup. That's why the motor wouldn't run.

"So we left the injectors on, and went on a winning streak."

It wasn't any flickering streak—it was a full-blown nuclear strike. From August 8th through September 12th—six solid weeks—Pauch and the L team monopolized Flemington's victory circle, winning 10 straight—nine in the Modified, and one winged Mod Sprint.

Included in that string were Billy's fabled "four in one night," a feat rarely accomplished anywhere in the Modified world—and never before at Flemington.

"It was a rained-out 30 and three 20s," Leon relayed. "They ran the 30 first. I think that Billy was up to fifth or sixth when the rain came," so that's where he started when they picked it up. "He was just cruising out there. We won that one for fun," he chortled.

"Start the three 20s. Won the first two." Now they were three for three, going for an unprecedented quartet. "In the last one, Billy was gone. I guess he thought he'd back off it a little bit, and when he did, he hit the wall," Leon grimaced. "Broke the radius rod off the right side. Come in, Tommy told the welder just to lay a bolt in there to hold the rear in and weld it up. Never got it right in there; Billy just had to hang on.

"Now, we had to start in the back and come through again," Liedl said of the nail-

ACE LANE JR.

ONE LAP

"You want me to put a show on? Take 'em one at a time or two at a time?"

Leon Liedl remembered Billy needling Tommy Cimpko, breaking balls before a feature at Flemington, when they were stringing together 10 wins in the summer of '81. As such, the L would be handicapped way back in 18th.

"And Tommy said, 'No. One lap!' And when Billy'd come around to the flag stand," Leon contended, "in one lap, he'd have the lead."

Memory has a tendency to mutate facts—especially after 40 years.

"I did it in a heat race," Billy corrected, trying to pinpoint the comment. "I can't confirm that I said that. Aah, maybe I did. I was always joking with Tommy: 'Do you want me to win this in one lap? *Heh, heh.*'

"I do remember I started in the back of a heat one day, went to the outside and in one lap in the heat race I got the lead. Back in those days, there were probably 12-14 cars in a heat! But it wasn't a feature," Pauch stated.

"The best I ever done in a feature was at Windsor, where I'd start 18th and in three laps I'd have the lead. But that's when we were so dominant there. That's when we had the injected Shaver motor. We just outclassed 'em," he said of the 1991-92 effort in the Tabloid Graphics car.

"If my memory serves me right, that was the best I ever did in a feature—three laps to the lead. But not at Flemington. At Flemington, it was in a heat race. *One lap.* And they were all stunned that I did it.

"And I was stunned, too!" Billy underscored the accomplishment. "That's pretty impressive. At the least, I started 12th; at the most it was 14th. So I passed like 12 cars. In one lap!"

biting final laps. "And he did, like it was nothin', and won it. Caught 'em right at the checker. That was a big accomplishment—four in one night."

Pauch recalled his do-or-die drive, carrying a crippled car across the line to score the Texas hat trick. "I seen a picture of it and saw how I was messed up," he accepted. But that didn't hinder him. "Billy Cannon was leading and I rolled around him coming out of four on the last lap and beat him by half a car length at the start/finish line."

It was a sterling example of Billy's steel-willed mindset: *never, ever give up.* "They pay you at the checker. On the last lap—you better get it done or it ain't gonna happen," he laid it out. "I don't wait until the end, but…if you watch a race, if somebody's gonna choke, they choke on the last lap. And if you're in position, that's when you're gonna get 'em. They always get nervous at the end of the race. That's when you can get 'em."

Gene Liedl and Nick Lombardi hoist Billy after a big win.

GEORGE GORDON

What was more remarkable than the team's 10-in-a-row late-summer rout? They won all 10 races on the same right-rear tire— an M&H 330 low-profile.

Leon Liedl explained how that was possible. "Tommy was a stickler on running an inch and a half of stagger. You tell people today about putting an inch and a half of stagger in anything, and they'll tell you *you're nuts!*" he conceded. "But it's sure-footed. When Billy went to the corner, he'd turn to the left. Guys go in the corner now, they turn to the right. You know how hard that is on the tires? Billy would turn to the left, and then once she started coming around a little bit he had to counter-steer to get himself around the corner. But with an inch and a half of stagger: there's no wear on tires. *None.*"

Looking back, Pauch still can't believe it. "I don't know how we did half the stuff we did. Ten straight wins with the same right-rear feature tire!" he snorted. "Let's see if Stewart Friesen can do that today!"

They had it figured out, all right. And they were on top of the world. During that winning spell, the team was the focus of all attention in the Flemington pits.

"They'd interview us, with video cameras and all. 'What do you expect to do tonight?' My brother Gene told 'em, 'If we don't break, we're gonna win!'" Leon set the scene.

"That's awfully cocky," was one reporter's cutting comment.

"It's not cocky—it's true," was Gene's comeback. "That's what we're here to do."

Leon doubled down on his brother's statement. "We felt we had the best driver. Tommy Cimpko built the best chassis. It was simple. *We're gonna win.* And we did."

They were all having a ball.

"It was unbelievable! I'm so glad we did it—for Billy's sake and for our sake. My mom and dad couldn't wait to go to the races! They loved it," Leon exclaimed.

"After the races, sometimes we'd be there for two hours or more with the fans. They hadda chase us out of the track! *'We're shutting the lights off! Can you leave?'* Billy's like, 'Shut 'em off! We'll still sit here!' Everybody'd be bringing him a beer."

And the party didn't end in the pits: Billy's cemented big-winner status earned him a standing invite up to the Purple Room, above the track office, where promoter Paul Kuhl hosted a weekly post-race shindig.

"We were never invited up there. Only Billy. From what I understand, it was a party: drinks, food, every muckety-muck that had anything to do with racing was invited up there," Liedl said. "We loaded up—we hadda go to work the next day! Billy would go from

MEL STETTLER

there to the Union Hotel on Main Street," where the Flemington revelers would close down the bar.

Also in 1981, seemingly out of left field, Billy became a Friday night regular at Albany-Saratoga, some three and a half hours from home, driving for a start-up team—against formidable track favorites Jack Johnson, Dave Lape and C.D. Coville—with a lot less success. In fact, none at all.

AARN ARCHIVES

There were five partners in the car: Bruce Schell, Mark Picarazzi, Rick Beckmann, Paul Galbraith and Walter Kippen. "A white 24S. Buncha young kids," Pauch remembered. "I'd drive my balls off and could never win a race for those guys. Just didn't have the right combination."

At their wits' end, the team brought the car to Flemington one night, for a triple 20 program, and put Billy's brother Timmy in the seat. "We wanted to go down and see for ourselves why Billy was so successful there and we weren't successful at Albany," Schell said. "Timmy was a pretty good wheelman and we figured we'd get him in the car, with Billy there, and maybe we'd get a second opinion. We were just trying to get some data on why we were missing it. Unfortunately, the car got destroyed in the heat race."

"It was a shame. It was a Grant King copy, painted and lettered to the nines," Leon Liedl said. "They were real nice guys, not wise asses or anything. Tommy could've helped them. But I guess that one guy who'd been with Coville figured, 'Oh no, we'll get it.' *Are you kidding me?* You already ran half a season and you're not going nowhere!

"Then we bring the L up there and we blow the field away," Liedl validated.

Albany's late September "run-watcha-brung" Super Shootout featured four 50-lap races—three for big-blocks, one for small-block Mods. Driving the L and Don Arnold's 57 SBM, Pauch trounced to take half the card.

Which was a relief, after all those winless Friday nights. "OK," Billy breathed, "it wasn't me."

If 1981 was an idyllic honeymoon, '82 was a dose of reality. It takes money to win races on any consistent basis—and the Liedl brothers aren't the Walmart Waltons.

They were particularly piecing together the pricey under-the-hood stuff.

"We didn't have no expensive motors," Leon admitted. "Toward the end there, Tommy would take 12 pistons and 12 rods to Tony Feil and told him to pick the best eight rods and the best eight pistons and put it together. That's what we raced with.

"We didn't buy nothin' new. We were just well drillers, trying to go racing. Tommy didn't care—he said, it'll work, no problem."

Until it didn't.

It was early in the year—May 15th—"and Roy Pauch built a motor for us to try," Liedl said. "Went out in warmups, everything was good. The last three laps of the heat, the motor started laying down. We brought it in, pulled the plugs out. Burnt a hole in the piston."

Billy was running Don Arnold's small-block car that season, at both East Windsor and Penn National. "So Billy called Don, who was laying in his living room, watching *Wheel of Fortune* or something. And Billy said, 'Where's the car?' Don said, 'Well, you got lucky—after Windsor, I normally pull it apart and wash it, get it ready for the next week. I didn't do nothin' because I got busy at the service station. It's still on the roll-off.'"

"Bring it here!" Billy told him.

Making the 40-minute drive from Piscataway in 25 flat, "Don Arnold had three cops

FIRST FLIP

With its odd shape and its unforgiving board fence and the no-brakes driving style you needed to use to really get around the place, Flemington Speedway was notorious for destroying equipment. *"Flippington,"* they called it, as car after car barrel-rolled or end-over-ended or completely crashed over the wall. Not once in a while: *every single race night.* "How could you tell if Flemington got rained out?" journalist Jim Donnelly posed the question in *Hemmings Motor News,* before giving the tongue-in-cheek answer: "There were no photo sequences of flips in the next week's racing papers."

Almost five years into his career, going into 1981, Billy Pauch was one of the few who had never flipped at Flemington. Oh, he'd ridden the wooden fence a time or two—how could you not, when it would suck you up with all the power of a high-end Hoover? But he'd never actually gotten on his lid.

Until this night.

It was June 27, 1981, the 100-lap Mike Grbac Memorial. It was only lap 8 and Pauch was charging through traffic in the L, when a lapped car got into him going into one. That was it: he went up and over, with Glenn Fitzcharles and Mike Grombir also along for the ride.

The driver who triggered the incident continued around to turn three as the field stopped for the red and the track crew headed to the scene. Pauch exited the wrecked racer, but instead of assessing the damage or collecting his bearings, he took off at a

behind him as he was coming through the gate. They hadda throw the yellow in the Sportsman consi so he could cross the track," Leon narrated. "We unloaded it, pulled the drag tires off, put our tires on. Tommy had to remember what to do without scales, to lower the car down for the low-profiles."

Pauch started 17th in the Mod feature; in less than five laps he was running third with a car that could've legally competed in the Sportsman class. "A baby 318 small-block!" Liedl wondered. "He never lifted, wound it all the way around."

The screaming small-block ultimately broke a crank. *Done.* Overnight, Arnold popped a big-block under the hood, returning to Flemington the following afternoon for a MODCAR 50-lapper. Billy dominated that day, lapping all but six cars in the talent-deep field, to notch his 100th career victory.

In between wins at Windsor, Billy aced another at Flemington in the Arnold 57 before returning the Liedl L to victory lane on June 26th. But it was getting harder and

dead sprint across the track.

"It was Jules Szestak, number 37," he fingered the culprit. "I hadda run all the way around the track until I found the guy!"

The L team was parked along the frontstretch in the pits, the crew standing in wait for what would happen next. "As I was running by, I threw my helmet over the fence to 'em — I was so pissed, it was the first time I ever flipped at Flemington! I *never* flipped!" Pauch was wild. "And that's big at Flemington — I mean, *everybody* flipped! I was so mad because the guy flipped me. And I never flipped at Flemington. I had a perfect record until then."

Leon Liedl has a clear memory of the night. "Destroyed the car. Billy jogged all the way around the track, went to grab Szestak and his firesuit was so old, it ripped right off him!" he retold the story.

Jules Szestak hung up his helmet not long after the incident that put him in the crosshairs of controversy with one of the speedway's most popular drivers. Billy's unblemished record was scarred for life: he had flipped at Flemington, just like any other mere mortal. The grudges, on both sides, were chiseled deeply and held forever.

"We used to drill wells for him, and after that incident he didn't use us to drill wells anymore," Liedl said of Szestak.

"We didn't care. Racing was more important."

harder to shoulder the effort.

"We'd been racing with our own motor. But Billy always said he could use a few more horses getting down the front and backstretch. Roy said, 'Put this motor in there. I done my homework on it.'"

But there were problems, possibly with fuel distribution: burnt another piston. "He did that all the time," Billy said of his father. "He liked to make things rich and then he couldn't get enough fuel to the motor so it would lean down and burn."

Leon recalled the mad scramble that night. "So Billy, Bobby Burns and Dave Zyck went with Bobby's truck up to Roy's to get a Bitner 427 that was a basic motor, probably had 10 races on it, that Billy used to run," he said. "Pulled it out from underneath the bench, rode it back to the track, put it in the car. And blew the field away that night."

Billy and Leon Liedl toast a 1981 MODCAR victory.

ACE LANE JR.

Haphazardly changing motors at the track: it's not the way you want to win races.

"We were like phenomenal the first year, in '81. Then in '82, everything started falling apart because it was all worn out and blown up and used up," Pauch admitted.

The Liedls had ridden in on Joe Scamardella's coattails, flying high with Tommy Cimpko. But by the end of the second year, the joyride was over. Billy won the big Flemington 200 finale in his own car, with his trusty fallback 427.

His last win in the L was the Tri-Track 100 on September 11th—a crazy day that began for Pauch in a Champ Car at the Indy Fairgrounds, and included a frantic flight back to Flemington, a heat-race penalty that put him in the consi, culminating with a peevish push to the front that had him almost lapping the field—*twice*. The Liedl brothers turned the wrenches for their last win with Billy: Tommy had traveled to Pennsylvania to get the hunting lodge ready for big game season.

"To run a 200-lapper—the motors were getting tired, it just didn't come together,"

Tommy Cimpko, car owner Don Arnold and Miss MODCAR Debbie Rio (now Mrs. Fred Rahmer) join the winner.

ACE LANE JR.

said Leon, who also weighed the family's work commitments. "Towards the end of the year, we get really busy. In the winter, it's hard to drill so you gotta catch up on your jobs."

It had always been a stretch, let's be real—but Lord, it was fun while it lasted.

"We didn't even have a hauler—we borrowed a truck from another guy in the crew, Cliff Welton. He had the newest truck of all of us so that's the truck we used," Liedl acknowledged. "We weren't sponsorship-savvy, like Brett Hearn. We didn't know how to go out and talk to people. It was all our own money. Every dollar. Motors were getting more expensive. At that time, they were talking about $10,000 for a motor. We're like— *whaddaya nuts??!* We were lucky we had $4,500 in these motors—and that was a lot of money."

Leon and his brothers understood their driver was destined for bigger things. It would be unfair not to let him go.

"Billy wanted to do more. He wanted to go to Syracuse. What with working, and the business…I got married in '82, we were all building houses… It was a lot of work! Flemington was home, 12 miles from us. We really didn't want to go any farther.

"It just got to be a lot. Of course, Billy was the star—he wanted to keep rising!" Liedl reinforced. "I don't blame him whatsoever."

One telling fact that Liedl pointed out about the team: the close relationship between Pauch and mechanic Tommy Cimpko was the glue that held everything together.

"He was like my second father," Billy characterized the bond between them. "We just hit it off good. I was getting away from the family car, going somewhere else. A lot of stuff he did was different to me. Like an inch and a half of stagger—ain't no way that should work, but it did. I think he just had the car so stiff that it worked."

It was all a new view for Pauch who, up until then, had seen everything through Roy's eyes.

"Tommy was the main reason, between the 121 and the L car, that we won all those races. We just clicked—like a pitcher and a catcher or whatever. We understood one another. He understood what I needed," Billy determined.

"I'd tell him what the car was doing, he'd set it up and we'd go out and win races."

Pauch thought enough of Cimpko that when he died in 2019, he had his current Kevin Bifulco Modified painted like the 1981 L car, as a one-night tribute to Tommy at Bridgeport.

According to Leon Liedl, Cimpko felt the same way about Pauch.

"Tommy Cimpko had four daughters. He always wanted a son to make a race car driver out of him. Well, Billy Pauch was Tommy Cimpko's son. He told Billy that many times," Leon divulged.

"When we had Larry Kline drive for us in '83, Tommy would scale the car in the shop but he never went to the track. 'Why would I go backwards?' Tommy would say. 'I had the best race driver who ever walked.'"

After acing a big shocker in Albany-Saratoga's 1979 Shootout in his own car, Billy was tapped to drive there weekly in '81. The team had all good intentions but never won a race.

ALBANY

All of it, from the start, was a long shot.

Five kids from the Capital District, who'd kicked around in the pits a bit with the likes of Mert Hulbert, Dave Leckonby and Mark Fluery, figured they were ready to field a race car.

"It was all Lebanon Valley guys with the exception of me," remembered Bruce Schell, the ringleader of the group. "We were helping Mark Fluery and he had a Grant King car. We were young and foolish: we figured we could build a Grant King copy and get a driver for it."

So in early 1981, they put their limited dollars and their limited knowledge together to construct the Ribley & Harppinger-sponsored 24S at Bruce's father's fabrication shop in Schenectady.

And as young kids itching to make some noise, they picked Jersey boy Billy Pauch to drive it.

Previously, Pauch had brought his own Ebersole Gremlin to Albany-Saratoga's 1979 Shootout—and pulled off a major upset. "My first big win in New York, outside of Flemington or Nazareth," said Billy, who recalled getting lost on the long ride home. "Dave Zyck was driving, and we looked up and we were going past Yankee Stadium."

That stunning victory was still fresh in their minds when the kids contacted Pauch.

"Anytime he came up to Malta, he would kick everybody's butt," Schell pointed out. So the group approached promoter C.J. Richards with a proposition: "If we can get Billy Pauch to race here every week, what would you do for him?"

There was some back and forth before the deal was done. "The way it worked out: my dad's business was kicking in $100 every Friday night; C.J. was kicking in $100 and giving Billy a room to stay. And he would come up every Friday night and race the car," Schell explained.

As it went, the team never fully coalesced, never won a race all season—the only season they were together. One and done.

"We were running against Jack Johnson, C.D., Dave Lape, Chuck Ely, Butch Jelley—it was a pretty good field there on Friday nights," said Pauch, who at the same time was racing Kenny Brenn, Glenn Fitzcharles, Kenny Brightbill, Sammy Beavers and Fritz Epright at Flemington—and winning more than his share every Saturday.

"I drove all year for those guys and never won a race for them."

But it was still a great memory.

"That was a lot of fun," Billy looked back. "Get up there to race, then go to the bars—they didn't close until four in the morning. Sleep 'til noon. Then stagger back to Flemington and win about 10 straight," he deadpanned.

7.

Al, Dave & Christine

With his masterful proficiency and passion for the place, it's no shock that Billy Pauch is the winningest driver in Flemington Speedway history.

But here's the surprise: the team that got him into victory lane the most was not Glenn Hyneman's big-budget Keystone Pretzel effort, with its gleaming red rig and fleet of Olsen cars. And it wasn't the Barker Bus outfit, powered by Pete Chesson's lust for competition and carte-blanche checkbook.

The biggest chunk of Billy's 114 dirt Modified wins at Flemington—29, to be exact—were taken down by a Troyer owned by Al and Dave DeBlasio, the unassuming sons of a local mechanic and gas station owner.

And the car's name was Christine.

She was Mud Buss #47, purchased through Lawrence Engineering just after Memorial Day in 1982. Standard-issue Troyer: coils on the front, torsion on the rear. The DeBlasio brothers spent the summer putting her together, Wally Marks supplied the smoke, and they got Frank Cozze in the seat that September. He stayed on through '83, picking up a pair of wins at Flemington.

Al DeBlasio (CAM2 shirt) and brother Dave (holding flag) celebrate with the crew after a 1984 SDS victory at Flemington.

MEL STETTLER

ACE LANE JR.

"Billy did drive for us one time in '83—we went up to Middletown for that spring 100-lap race when Cozze was taking his own car. Wally Marks was pretty friendly with Roy and they got us together," Al recalled. "We really didn't do too much that day but that's where we first got to talk to Billy, at that race."

In February of '84, a deal was struck and the DeBlasios' Buss moved from Al's Sunoco, at the blinking light in Pennington, up to Billy's shop on his father's farm in Stockton.

The next three seasons were mythical. On July 11, 1984, the team took Flemington's Super DIRT Series event, then swept triple 20s at the square three days later. In a September special, the car was so uncanny that Billy was able to lap the entire field, finishing the 100-lap distance alone. They ended the season with 11 wins and the 1984 New Jersey State Modified championship.

The 1985 season was even better, starting with three wins in Florida, where (1) DIRT wasn't running the show, so (2) the rules were wide-open. As such, Billy built a wedge-shaped body as wide as a king-sized bed around Christine, which effectively kept her planted on the slick surface where all the other cars couldn't stick.

"That was the only time Billy dominated Florida," Roy asserted. "The guy who hauled with the bus, Marcel Lafrance, told him afterward, 'Billy, you could smoke a cigarette out there!'"

Back north, the team took two at Fonda, and continued to control Flemington where they hit for a pair of 100-lappers in April and September, three of four 20s in August, and the Flemington Modified track title. Christine underwent some necessary alterations to make that happen: a hole in the firewall and hand controls so Billy could drive her after dislocating his kneecap in a hellish wreck in D.A. Hanson's car at Penn National. That they were able to pull that off, and still win the Flemington championship despite missing a month's worth of point races, falls in the sphere of the supernatural.

But that's how she got her name—"Christine," after the possessed 1958 Plymouth Fury featured in the Stephen King novel. The car that refused to die.

In late summer of '85, Christine got a sister of sorts: a long-track Troyer purchased specifically for Syracuse, where it timed well but ultimately blew a rear. They started out '86 with the new piece, but at Flemington "the motor-forward car was a piece of shit," Billy determined.

So Christine was resurrected.

"We had moved the motor mounts back to run the short tracks, but never had the same results with the new car. Maybe we didn't work with it enough because we knew what we had in reserve," Dave considered. "To keep racing, you gotta do what you gotta do. So we went up in the barn and pulled Christine out."

She was good for another DIRT series win at Flemington and a second consecutive Flemington Modified crown.

"Of course, anything Billy got in went good," Dave hastened to assure. "But this was our special car. We gave it that name, that personality, and it always seemed to work wherever it went. Florida…Fonda…Flemington… There were other Troyers out there—but Christine was special."

She had a helluva run.

"Even back in '83 when we won twice with Cozze—it was pretty fantastic, winning *anything* on the shoestring we had," Al said, amazed.

"There was certainly something to that car."

8.
Autumn in New York

The week started off on a high note, with a big win in Fulton's inaugural Victoria 200.

KEN DIPPEL

The October schedule was always crammed to the corners, what with Super DIRT Week and all, and Pauch—never one to leave a purse untapped—was committed to almost all of it.

But what he took on in nine days in the fall of 1986 was a lot, even by his over-achiever standards.

On Saturday, October 4th, Billy won his sixth of the season and wrapped up his second consecutive Flemington Modified championship in the DeBlasio brothers' "Christine" (the car that never died), all the while fretting that he was missing the preliminaries of the very first Vic—the passionately-promoted small-block spectacular that Bub Benway was throwing at Fulton Speedway. Conveniently, Fulton lost that day to heavy rain. So Pauch flew to upstate New York early the next morning, climbed in Jerry Becker's 41a, won his heat, drew an 18th starting spot for the 200-lap Monday event, and put on a show for the New York fans that they talked about all winter, hanging the car off the cushion to beat fellow Penn National runner Ronnie Tobias to the checker.

KEN DIPPEL

The SDW Modified pole award was worth $1,500.

Meanwhile, back in New Jersey, Pauch's Syracuse-bound Modified (due at the mile track on Wednesday A.M.) was only partially assembled. It was, by Syracuse standards, no big-deal effort: last year's long-track Troyer frame had been dragged down from the top of the barn some three or four weeks prior and gone over. Billy fabricated a new sheet-metal shroud for the car, sent the '85 Bitner-built motor to Tony Feil for a redo, and that was about it.

"We're not a big-bucks team," said Dave DeBlasio, who jointly owned the Modified with his brother, Al. "In fact, we're thinking about passing the collection plate to pay for the motor rebuild."

However, neither Dave nor Al wound up pulling the old tin-cup-on-the-corner routine to pay off the Syracuse motor. Pauch, who flew home after the Fulton victory to finish up the car, unloaded it at the Fairgrounds on Wednesday, took to the track and immediately began turning some of the fastest unofficial times of the day. It was no fluke: when Thursday's time trials were done, the DeBlasio 5 was on the pole, clocked over four-tenths of a second quicker than Brett Hearn's 20, the defending race winner.

No one came close to matching that 32.021 run on Friday's icy speedway surface, so Billy became the golden boy of the moment, with all the flashbulb-popping and question-asking that follows any odds-on favorite.

Raised old-school, Pauch wasn't the kind of guy who took to that sort of hoopla, so he hid out in his trailer as much as he could.

"I hate it," he spat out, after a photographer unleashed a roll of film in his direction. "It's all a show. I'm just up here to race."

And he certainly did more than his share of that. On Thursday night, he jumped in Becker's small-block and gave it quite a whirl at New Venture (aka Utica-Rome) before driveline problems forced him to call it quits. Then, the next night, he was going for the lead (and the $4,000 to win) with two to go in Rolling Wheels' SBM satellite show, when he and Windsor/Flemington nemesis Doug Hoffman came together off turn four.

Now, if 50 witnesses to the incident swore that the rim-riding Hoffman came down on Pauch, there were an equal number of onlookers who testified that Pauch drifted high and crowded Hoffman. (Some 35 years after the fact, Davey Hoffman matter-of-factly remembered that "they were coming off of four, Billy was starting to get under Doug, and Doug chopped him pretty good, and Billy spun out.")

But regardless of who did what to whom, Billy was credited with giving Dougie a blatant shot under the yellow, almost sending Hoffman's Olsen Eagle into the pace car.

For that, he was fined $275 on Saturday morning by DIRT officials.

"The driver's attitude, when we meet with him, dictates how we handle each situation like this," DIRT's Robin Manus informed. "Billy had a very good attitude at the meeting. He made the wrong decision at Rolling Wheels, and he paid for it."

The bad blood between Hoffman and Pauch already ran deep: less than a month earlier, they'd both been booted out of East Windsor for the remainder of the season for fighting on the track. The Rolling Wheels run-in further inflamed the hostilities—heightened by the fact that Hoffman survived the skirmish to sail unscathed into victory lane.

High drama all week between Billy (41a) and arch rival Doug Hoffman, here battling on the mile in the 320 race.

DAVE PRATT

Hell was nothing compared to this kind of heated hatred.

The unfounded gossip in the Syracuse pits circulated like wildfire, from trailer to trailer, fueled additionally by Pauch's appearance at Fulton, a show deemed a definite no-no for any DIRT racer who wanted to make Glenn Donnelly's Good Boy list. Billy's fine was $1,000… $2,000…$3,500…He'd been suspended from DIRT activities and couldn't start Sunday's 200… The tales were incredible.

While the stories weren't true, they were unnerving. "I don't want to talk about it anymore," Pauch muttered. "I'm sick of it. It's over and done. I just want to go racing."

And he climbed into the Harraka 112 Sprint Car, his fourth ride of the week, and went out and won the first semi for the Supernationals. That machine overheated mere laps into the Sprint feature; then Billy cinched back into the 41a and clicked off a third-fast lap in 320 time trials, ending Saturday on an up note.

Becker's small-block didn't last through Sunday's 30-mile test (the engine went and the rear locked up with five laps left in the National Auto 320 event), but that was the last bit of bad news during the week that never ended.

In only his fourth Modified start at Syracuse The Kid proceeded to show the DIRT regulars how it's done, parlaying his polesitter status into a sizeable lead right from the gitgo. A smooth pitstop on lap 43, and Pauch—in clearly one of the fastest cars on the track—moved back up front. He got as far as third, behind Bob McCreadie and Danny Johnson, before his tires gave up and he could go no further. When Danny

As the laps wind down, Nick Lombardi is on the radio with Pauch while McCreadie crewman Tim Hatt signals his driver.

lost a wheel four laps from the end, the runner-up spot was all his.

"We had the runners extended on the intake manifold and one of the pieces broke off. It didn't go down the motor but it went into one of the ports going down to the cylinder and blocked off a lot of the air. So we lost power—didn't have the motor to run up there with Bob at the end," Billy rehashed. "It was probably for the better anyway, because our tires were bald and we probably would've burnt a tire and went through it."

KEN DIPPEL

The DeBlasio team couldn't have been happier if they'd won. "It's the first race we've ever finished here—that's like a victory, to us! And finishing second to a guy like Bob McCreadie is no shame," crewman Chuck Snyder crowed.

It was still second-place to Pauch. "That makes the second time I finished second in a big race," he remarked, referring to his $12,000 runner-up finish to $50K winner Kenny Brightbill at Nazareth National in 1983. And of this race: "Not bad for a car that's been sitting up in the top of the barn until last month, heh?"

Not bad at all: $18,335 is what Billy earned at Syracuse in the DeBlasio Modified. Add to that the $13,000 Fulton Victoria 200 win, and the couple grand he picked up there-and-about in Becker's small-block and the Harraka Sprinter, and the week's take totaled up to around $33,000—even after Friday's fine was deducted.

Said Pauch, summing up his long week in New York: "It had its moments."

Enjoy Coke.

WELCOME RACE FANS

CHAMPION trailers

MEL STETTLER

9.

Pretzelmania

If you're into analogies, you could liken the 1987 teaming of Pennsy car owner Glenn Hyneman and driver Billy Pauch to the arranged marriages which commonly took place in elite European social circles some 300 years ago: wealthy landowner (bourgeois but beaucoup bucks) weds penniless princess (big crown, little capital) and all benefit from the union—he, gaining a title and an accepted place in society; and she, acquiring a financial statement worthy of her royal station.

Hyneman was the boy-wonder of the Pennsylvania business world, responsible for turning the Keystone Pretzel Bakery—a small corner shop behind the stockyards in Lancaster—into a state-of-the-art snack plant doing $20 million in annual sales. In addition, he'd been a stop-at-nothing kind of car owner on the Pennsy Mod circuit since the early '80s, supplying drivers like Barry and Craig Von Dohren with enough equipment to sink the Queen Mary. A squad of Olsen Eagles? No problem. A fully appointed rig? But of course. Engines by the score? They got 'em and more. It had to be the most well-armed Sportsman-Modified operation the Keystone State had ever spawned, courtesy of Hyneman's appetite for competition and a seemingly unbounded budget.

And Glenn did see a return on his dollars. Barry Von Dohren delivered the Bridgeport Sportsman title in 1983; from '83-86, Craig toted up 48 wins in the Pretzelmania cars at all three tracks on the Pennsy small-block scene, as well as at Bridgeport, East Windsor and Georgetown. Although he claimed no championship honors anywhere, the younger Von Dohren brother did add a handful of big-block Modified wins and a lucrative Grandview Freedom 76 victory to the team coffers.

But Hyneman wanted more.

Following an up-and-down '86 campaign, Craig received his walking papers, and Glenn pondered his next step. Everyone in possession of a valid Pennsylvania driver's license was calling to inquire about the ride, but Hyneman vowed he wasn't making any hasty decisions. Brett Hearn, available for a one-shot deal, climbed in one of Glenn's 126 racers at Bridgeport in November of that year, to compete in a Four-Dozen special. Hearn won the second event and, unwittingly, altered Glenn's game plan.

"Until then, I had been considering a few of the local guys who run at Big Diamond, Grandview and Penn National. But after Brett ran the car, I knew I had to go with a top caliber driver, no matter what," was Hyneman's conclusion. "Not to knock the guys who run small-blocks—on the contrary, many of 'em are real good. But you just can't beat a top-notch driver with years of solid Modified experience."

Enter Billy Pauch, who happened, quite coincidentally, to be looking to cut a deal just about the time that Hyneman was reviewing driver résumés.

If Glenn was the affluent commoner, then Pauch was the impoverished aristocrat. Although he was regarded as one of the region's leading Modified talents, Billy had managed to carve out his reputation with less than high-tech tools. In 1986, he drove for four different owners on a regular or semi-regular basis—the DeBlasio brothers, George and Marilyn Van Varick, Jerry Becker and Sonny McCurdy. All had the will but none had the actual wherewithal to win consistently against better-equipped teams. Each, separately, was capable of keeping Pauch on-track a single night a week (McCurdy, less often than that) but none could afford to foot the bills for his full-time effort.

So Billy drove for four owners, and won for three of them, and collected 23 victories, a second-place finish in the big one at Syracuse in October, and his fourth Flemington Modified championship, utilizing five cars that were certainly serviceable but hardly

The team's first win: March 1987 at Port Royal.

PORT ROYAL WINNER

19 Miller

MADE THE AMERICAN WAY

ART RUPPERT

hot-ticket technology. The last steady season he spent with a single owner was in 1980, when he ran Joe Scamardella's cars, wrenched by Tommy Cimpko.

"There aren't many really good deals out there," Pauch noted at the time. "You've got the Blue Hens, Statewide…"

And the Keystone Pretzel ride, which opened

up at the very moment that Al and Dave DeBlasio decided to sell out and end their car-owning career.

"Billy called me, said, 'Hey, can we get together and sit down and talk about the possibility of me driving the car next year?'" said Glenn, who was floored when he received the call. "I was like—jeez, *Billy Pauch* is calling *me??!*"

They met at the Kirbyville Inn on Route 222, on the other side of Reading. Hyneman remembered the conversation. *Exactly.*

"We sat there and talked about things that he wanted to do and I wanted to accomplish. Then somewhere in the conversation Billy goes, 'I get 40 percent to drive the car. And if I keep it at my shop, I get 50 percent.' And I'm like—*Whoa! Wait a minute here!* I'm not paying that kind of money for you to drive the race car! This is an expensive sport!"

With absolute authority, Pauch laid out what the car owner would gain with such a winnings split.

"'Let me explain it to you: when I drive your race car, you will make more money getting less,'" Hyneman recapped Billy's claim. *Huh?* "He goes, 'Glenn, I will win races for you that you have never won before. I will win *big* races. I will win *lots* of races.' And he said, 'The difference that you'll be paying me will seem like a bargain.'"

Said Hyneman, on hiring Pauch: "I feel like an NFL team owner who just got his top draft choice."

What the hell is this guy talking about?? Glenn had never paid any driver more than 20 percent of the take. This was double that! "I told Billy I have to digest this. And I went home, my wife Bonita and I talked about it." Glenn considered what he wanted to do. "Billy would be the next step for me. He was already a well-known entity at Flemington and Penn National. I thought, y'know what? I'm just going to take a flyer and see how this works out."

If Hyneman was hoping that Pauch would take him to the next level, the feeling was mutual. "This is the kind of ride that anybody would die for," Billy said, after the deal was sealed. "I may have had the nickel-and-dime stuff in the past, but I never had the under-the-hood stuff. There are very few deals in racing like this. It's like heaven, for me."

Hyneman's friend and crewman, Donnie Miller, astutely sized up the stakes. "There was pressure on both Glenn and Billy, I think. Both of them were stepping their game up. Glenn had money and was spending money, and was wore out with the Big Diamond/Grandview scene. It was a big step for him to come to Jersey," Miller affirmed. "And I'm gonna guess that for Billy, it was his first professional team. Not that he hadn't done well before. But Glenn didn't stint on *anything*."

Not to worry: the partnership between Pauch and the Pretzel King was productive, to put it mildly.

In the time they were together—1987 and '88 exclusively, and then part-time the next two seasons—the team took down 44 wins in the big-block Mods, 42 in small-blocks, and six Sprint Car victories for a total of 92 scores at 14 tracks in five states. Included in those wins were "the big ones" that Billy had promised Glenn: the '87 320 Nationals at the Syracuse Fairgrounds; three consecutive Victoria 200s at Fulton (1987, '88, '89); Ransomville's Summer Nationals, Grandview's Freedom 76 and Hagerstown's Octoberfest in '88; 100-lappers at Flemington and Penn National; DIRT's Florida opener in '88; back-to-back Modified championships at both Flemington and Bridgeport, in 1987 and '88; and another pair of titles at Penn National ('88, '89).

The Pretzel crew went out of their way to fire up the crowd at Penn National. Check out their "Take the Money and Run!" shirts.

DONNIE MILLER COLLECTION

Roy, Glenn and Billy oversee the crew at Volusia in February of 1987.

MEL STETTLER

Other assorted goodies: the Eastern Motorsports Press Association voted Pauch its Driver of the Year in 1987; during his entire stint with Hyneman, Pauch was acclaimed by *Area Auto Racing News* as the winningest driver in the Northeast—in any division.

"We were winning in excess of 30-40 races a year. I was like—*whew!* I haven't even come close to that since then," Glenn exulted. "One of those years, I think it was '88, we won 60 percent of the races we entered at Penn National. Sixty percent!"

For the Keystone State team, Penn National was home base and the highlight of each week.

"It was game on there every Sunday," crewman Donnie Miller acknowledged. "The competition was very, very good at Penn National. But ultimately it came down to the Tobiases. Young Richie used to drive into the wall, trying to catch Billy. Richie probably would've won 50 percent more of the features if he'd just slowed down a little bit!

"And probably 50 percent of the features Billy won at Penn National, he was the second or third fastest car, if that makes any sense. He would get on that bottom groove and he'd be steady and consistent. And the guys with faster cars would be blowing 'em in on the outside, getting up over the cushion and into the wall. He would frustrate the shit out of 'em: the slower he'd go, the faster they'd go, and the further he'd pull away. He'd save the tires and be there at the end."

Dominating and devilish, the Pretzel crew didn't miss an opportunity to rub it in.

Miller remembered a summer night in 1988 when they almost instigated a riot.

"Billy won the rained-out feature from the previous week. Then he came out for the heat, started last, won that race, which put him in the cash dash. By that time, the fans were already in a lather—*this can't happen!* Then he wins the dash.

"By about five to go in the second feature, he was running only about fourth or fifth. Coming out of two, he got two or three cars. Now we're thinking maybe this is going to happen!" Donnie said of the possible shutout.

"Sure enough, with a couple to go, he muscled his way to the lead and we swept the night. Had a burlap bag stuffed with rags in the race car trailer, and me—just being a young pain-in-the-ass and wanting to stir things up—I took a big, fat black marker and put a huge dollar sign on this bag, and I held it up in victory lane.

"Well, I thought they were gonna rip the lights off the place! They booed and booed, and carried on. And we just loved it!"

The money bag. The broom. Donnie would diabolically parade these props in front of the grandstands, taunting the wild-eyed crowd, whipping them into an outright frenzy.

"After a lot of Billy's wins, as a crew we'd go out on the homestretch and stand in a straight line and he'd come down, put it in neutral and just rev the shit out of the motor—*rev, rev, rev*—and give us all hand smacks. You couldn't even hear the motor, the boos were so loud! The thunder probably reached down to Harrisburg. The place went crazy! We just ate that shit up! And we couldn't wait to come back and do it again."

The Keystone Pretzel team in action, changing a right-rear flat on the big-block car at Syracuse in 1987.

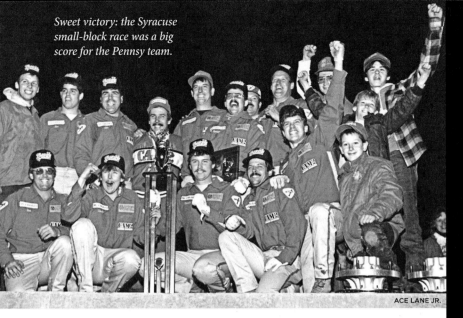

Sweet victory: the Syracuse small-block race was a big score for the Pennsy team.

ACE LANE JR.

It might have been fun and games in Pennsylvania, but it was cold-sober business up in New York. Back in those days, if you wanted your ticket punched into the major leagues, you had to show well at Syracuse. And the Keystone Pretzel team did, despite the fact that they weren't baptized DIRT apostles and the track was most certainly the epicenter of the DIRT universe.

According to Hyneman, Billy's mastery of Flemington gave them a leg up on the Fairgrounds mile. "Our success at Flemington translated into success at Syracuse, and Penn National always translated into Fulton. I think that's why," he reasoned. "We would go to Syracuse with our Flemington setup—and we were always good there."

Pauch's longtime crewman Chuck Snyder expanded on that same view. "Flemington was not a stop-and-go track, like all the New York tracks. Flemington was more of a momentum track. So he was used to the speed," Snyder observed. "Billy used to drive it right down in there at Syracuse—right to the max. Got all he could out of it."

So unlike many others, Pauch was not intimidated by that wickedly wide-open mile. In 1986, he'd set quick time for the big-block classic against 149 other entries,

VIEW FROM THE CREW

Crewman Donnie Miller remembered the team's big win in the National Auto Supply 320/358 Nationals during Super DIRT Week 1987:

"We had a Mike Ceganick 320 motor in there—one we ran at Penn National that might've been freshened up a little bit. Nothing special for the small-block race. Maybe a new body on it but it was the same program we ran at Penn National. That was that.

"Jeff Heotzler was leading that race, late. And Billy was second. At Syracuse, from pit road you only got to see maybe 200 yards of the race. There were no cell phones to watch it in those days; there were no jumbotrons. You got to see coming down the homestretch a little bit and into one—that's all you got to see.

"They were running pretty tight together, first and second, and with a couple or so to go, you could hear the crowd gasp a little bit or groan— probably groan because Jeff was very well liked up there—and all of a sudden, coming out of four, the 126 is leading. There's no Heotzler. *What's going on here?* Then the yellow came out—there couldn't have been two laps left, at the most.

"Two laps: that's a long time to hold your breath when you're leading a race at the mile!"

driving the DeBlasio brothers' 5. In Glenn's Olsen, he was second fast in '87, and grabbed the pole again in '88, which Hyneman counts as one of his proudest moments.

"To start that race from the pole…to stand out on the frontstretch at Syracuse with all my guys during driver introductions—that was a big deal for me," Glenn acknowledged. "I still have the pole award sitting on display in my race shop."

The year prior, in '87, Pauch triumphed to the tune of $21,000 (cash, contingencies and a Z24 Chevy Cavalier) in the 320 Nationals during Super DIRT Week on the mile, a victory that Hyneman described as "just huge, for me. We went into their stomping grounds and beat them at their own game," he rejoiced.

But that was the small-block race. Glenn wanted the headlining big-block W.

With a front-row starting spot, riding last year's wave, Hyneman felt he had the car to beat in the 1988 Miller 300. The team was in contention until lap 57, when Billy made a move inside Danny Johnson and—*crash, boom, bang*. Their day ended with a double-hook.

Billy leads the field around for the start of the 1988 Miller 300.

MEL STETTLER

MEL STETTLER

"If I have a regret, it's not winning that big-block race—because we could have," Hyneman mourned. "I remember it very well. That was my opportunity to win the biggest race of my life, right there."

Looking back on their run together, there is no question that Hyneman is happy he decided to hire Pauch.

"I probably couldn't have won all those races with any other driver. *Period*," Glenn maintains. "Billy is not only the ultimate racing *talent*—he's also the ultimate racing *mind*. That's what made Billy stand out from everybody else. He lived, ate and slept racing. He would analyze and dismantle and put back together a whole race in his head.

"He would call me and say, 'I think if we do this to the car, or that to the car, I think it'll be an edge.' I'm busy making pretzels, and he's racing! He's figuring out everything about the race car and how to get an edge," Glenn noted.

"Look, I've had other guys who are smart, and other guys who are talented. But not the whole package," he ascertained.

A savvy business broker, Glenn Hyneman is one person who knows about wanting it all. And getting it.

"I've gotta tell ya: it was the best move I ever made in my life, hiring Billy Pauch," he finalized. "He's the most versatile, talented driver that I have ever had in my race car. And if he isn't one of the top three ever to strap in—well, I don't know who is."

Pauch, car owner Pete Chesson and crew chief John Sine convene on the top of the trailer to set strategy.

10.
Take the Bus

Billy was coming off the best two years of his life when car owner Glenn Hyneman suddenly decided, at the close of '88, to change course. Hyneman was in the midst of selling the Keystone Pretzel Bakery, cutting back his racing schedule, sniffing around the Sprint Car scene. He and Pauch had connected in 1987 and did it all. Now, Glenn wanted to do something else.

In the wake of a 40-win season with Hyneman—Ransomville's Summer Nationals, Grandview's '6er, the Vic at Fulton, Hagerstown's Octoberfest, championships at Flemington, Bridgeport and Penn National, the Northeast's winningest driver—Billy appeared to have nowhere to go but down. How in blue blazes could anyone hit that '88 high-water mark?

But Hyneman didn't leave Pauch stranded: he stuck around to supply a once-a-week small-block ride. And he handed Billy off to Mod car owner Peter Chesson.

"Hyneman wanted to kick back a little bit," Pauch recollected. "So he called Pete and said, 'Why don't you take Billy on Friday and Saturday and I'll take him Sunday?'"

Chesson confirmed that it was Glenn who set them up. "I had a deal with Brett Hearn. We were going to do Middletown," Pete disclosed. He had put Hearn in the seat of his small-block car a handful of times in 1988, winning races at Orange County, Rolling Wheels and Fonda. It seemed like a good match. But, apparently, all the puzzle pieces didn't fit Pete's big picture.

"The long and the short of it was Flemington was much closer than Middletown. So we ended up taking the deal with Billy. And I certainly don't regret it."

Pete Chesson, owner of the Barker Bus school transportation company, from the upscale enclave of Pluckemin, NJ, had been a successful drag racer with a headful of ideas about how to make the wheels turn faster.

"I came out of drag racing, which—don't take it the wrong way—they're light years ahead of dirt track guys. We had a national record in 1967 with a '67 Mustang," Pete outlined.

"Things changed for us then. I went to Flemington, looked at the cars. And they were not really sophisticated—they were pretty...*basic*," he concluded, settling on a tactful word. "So I got involved with Geoff Bodine and he designed a suspension. Took a Scout

MEL STETTLER

chassis and made it a Modified. The car really performed well. I felt we were ahead of our time."

Chesson's creation, featuring independent front suspension, won the season-end Flemington 200 with track champ Stan Ploski at the wheel.

But Pete was still searching for more speed. "I always wanted to create different suspensions and be ahead of the curve. Something different than the average Modified guy."

His '74 Pinto, "The Sting"—built in the Dauernheim machine shop and featured in *Hot Rod* magazine—not only sported independent front suspension but also independent rear suspension. No one was doing that. It turned out not to be an advantage: "That car was junk," Pete laughed.

The failure didn't deter him. Chesson continued to incorporate any unconventional brainstorm into cars driven by everyone from NASCAR's Kenny Schrader to Late Model stalwart Freddy Smith and many of the region's Modified stars, including Billy Osmun, Frank Cozze and Fritz Epright.

And then came Billy Pauch. To someone making a living on race results, tried-and-true sounds a lot better than hit-or-miss.

"All I remember is we were dominating with Olsen cars. Pete comes in and says, 'We need Tobias cars! Everyone's winning in Tobias cars!' And I told him, 'Pete, we'd have to change all our spare axles, all our bumpers and rub rails. We'd have to carry all these spare parts with us. *Are you crazy?*'" Pauch fretted. "Then we got one and started winning with that, too."

Chesson wasn't fazed by Pauch's anxiety. "I think Billy had his mind made up on

certain things. And I think I would stretch his mind," he put it out there. "Everybody's happy to do what they normally do—and I'm not like that, as a person. That probably is why we succeeded. Billy's a great driver, and I always liked to think outside the box."

And although Pete always stressed, "I'm not a guy who spends money just to spend money," that wasn't the impression almost everyone else had.

As Roy Pauch pointedly put it, "He had the spending sickness."

"One time, Pete wheeled in the driveway with a brand-new trailer. And he comes in the shop and says to Bill, 'I need to use your phone. I gotta order another trailer. This thing's a piece of shit! I don't like it.' And he got on the phone and ordered a truck and a trailer," crew chief John Sine recalled. "Within two weeks, we had a tractor and a trailer. It held 40-plus tires. Back then, we had GF0s, GF1s, GF2s, 3s, D1Bs, Hoosiers for Pennsylvania—we had 'em all mounted with us. Plus stagger tires. An all-aluminum trailer. I'd never seen nothing like that."

Billy's long-time tire man Chuck Snyder thought he'd died and gone to heaven. "It was a 45-foot Gold Rush trailer, the biggest rig at Flemington—with 42 tires all mounted on racks, at all times. Windsor tires, Penn National tires, Flemington tires, all organized on racks. Never had to unload anything," Snyder warranted. "With Pete, money was no object. And it was the best of everything."

And Chesson's checkbook was certainly open to the motor builders. *All of them.*

"One year, he bought seven brand new motors: we had the Shaver 430, the two 339s, a 430 Prototype, a 358 Prototype, a 358 Precision, and one Feil big-block that we called 'The Dominator'—it dominated on the short-tracks but it really didn't run at Syracuse,"

Chuck listed the inventory.

"I remember one time Pete called me on the phone, said, 'Look, don't spend a lot of money this week on the cars,'" Sine said. He responded by ticking off items like heim ends and radius rods, minor maintenance parts that the team needed.

"Well, just don't spend a lot of money," Pete told him. "That was weird, coming from him," John thought. "Two days later, a truck shows up and two motors get dropped off from Prototype. One was a 430 and the other was a small-block, and it was all for Syracuse."

Chesson was full-bore in. "We had small-block 430s, big-blocks. It was about winning. It was about satisfying Billy…which you could never do. He always wanted more power, more of this, more of that," he inserted the not-so-subtle dig. "But that's what made, I think, the success we had. I enjoyed it more than you could imagine. I think we were totally on top of our game."

JACK KROMER

From a driver's standpoint, that no-limit level of largesse was an aberration. "Pete was the only guy I drove for that I hadda hold him down, to keep him from spending money. Everybody else, you had to pick them up, to make 'em step up to the plate. Pete, you didn't have to step him up—he was *there*," Pauch pronounced. "He had the parts ready, he had the motors ready, the cars ready. Everything we needed. That's why we went out and won 45, 48 features a year. Because he stepped up to the plate."

And the results—and the winnings—stacked up. Coming off his blockbuster 1988 season, with 40 wins for Glenn Hyneman and a pair for URC owner Joe Fiore, Pauch exceeded even that barely-attainable benchmark.

In 1989, Billy rolled to 45 wins in Chesson's big-block and Hyneman's small-block ride. He topped that in '90, driving Pete's Modifieds and

JACK KROMER

Glenn's Sprinter to an eye-popping 48 victories. In the course of two seasons, Pauch chalked up 93 wins at 11 tracks in five states, back-to-back Flemington Modified titles (six in a row, going back to the DeBlasio 5), a Penn National championship and four big scores on the Super DIRT Series (which he never even followed). That's more than the vast majority of drivers achieve in a lifetime.

Strings and stretches of note: five wins in a week in August of '89, including two of the four SDS triumphs, at Grandview and Williams Grove; five in four days in September 1990, including his fifth Victoria 200; southern sweeps at Hagerstown in April and Delaware in November '89; a pair of 100-lappers over Labor Day weekend 1990 at Flemington and Penn National (with an East Windsor 20 sandwiched in between); and two in one day at Delaware (SBM) and Georgetown (Mod) in November of '90.

"In 48 years of racing, I think I had the most fun with Pete," Pauch claimed. "We'd go to Hagerstown and qualify on Saturday afternoon and Pete would get us a plane to fly back to run Flemington Saturday night. Then we'd drive back to Hagerstown to run the features on Sunday.

"Pete would drive us. We'd always be scared shit!" Billy said of the white-knuckle trip. "He'd get to a stop sign, he'd turn all the way to the right and pass everybody—*right through it!* It was a four-hour ride to Hagerstown. He'd make it a two-hour ride. We all thought we were gonna die on the way! But he got us there."

The personal high point for Pauch during the Chesson years was a record-breaker that many believed would never be beaten: Al Tasnady's 96 career feature wins at Flemington. On July 15, 1989, Billy brought the Barker Bus 76 in for #96 and #97 at the square, winning the first and last races in a triple 20 program, knocking Tas off the top of the all-time standings.

"Had to pass Hoffman three times—the yellow kept coming out and they kept going back to the last lap," Billy said of the suspenseful struggle to achieve that stat-busting win.

"I never got to race with Al Tasnady," he remarked. "The only way I got to race with him is in the record books. It's a pleasure to even come close to what he's done."

"That was a wild night," Chuck Snyder remembered. "We did a lot of partying that night! I grew up at Flemington, saw a little bit of Tas when I was a kid. He was good. But he knew Billy was going to break his record. He told Billy, 'If anyone's gonna beat my record, it's going to be you.'"

In those years, Pauch was setting a bunch of records. *Area Auto Racing News* keeps a weekly running tally of drivers with the most wins in the Northeast, breaking them down by division and then—at year's end—announcing an overall winner for that season. That "best of the best" badge of honor was something to strive for—and for six straight years, from 1987-92, Billy held the title: two for Hyneman, two for Chesson, two with Ray Carroll.

It had been a cakewalk of sorts until 1990, when rival Brett Hearn started putting up big numbers. The year prior, Hearn had invaded Flemington and won the season-end 200, poking Pauch and Chesson during his victory lane comments. "MC Hammer was playing as we were driving to the track, and we started singing 'bus to move' instead of

Pete, Roy, John and crew never took a breath on race night.

JACK KROMER

HE-DID-IT!
THE RECORD: ALL TIME MODIFIED FEATURE WINNER
THE TRACK: FLEMINGTON FAIR SPEEDWAY
THE DRIVER: BILLY "THE KID" PAUCH
THE CARS: PAUCH "15 - DONNEBERGER "99"
NOVELIA "81 - SCAMARDELLA "121 - ARNOLD "57
LEIH "2 - SESELY "15 - DeBLASIO "5
HYNEMAN "126 - CHESSON "76"
CONGRATULATIONS BILLY PAUCH

Pauch accomplished what many thought was impossible: beating Al Tasnady's win record at Flemington.

MEL STETTLER

'bust a move,'" was the crack aimed at the track champion.

When Hearn threw down that gauntlet, Pauch was quick to pick it up, taking a pointed jab at Pete's almost-driver with a clever (and wildly popular) T-shirt designed by artist Dave Garboski. "Forget the Jet, Take the Bus," it said, referencing Brett's nickname and Chesson's Barker Bus 76. They took the game so far as to have a body built for their Windsor car that resembled a school bus.

"A picture of that car was on the T-shirt," said John Sine, who acknowledged the cold war of competition between Brett and Billy. "It was a thing: it always seemed Brett was winning all the races up there and Bill was winning all the races down here. And anytime we raced where Brett was—Billy had to win. Because if he didn't win, then this guy was better than him. That's how Billy was everywhere he went: he hadda be the best."

With Chesson, Pauch was the best. But it wasn't just Pete's pocketbook that put him there.

"For a couple years there, we won a ton of features," Billy noted. "That just showed the commitment Pete had for us and we had for him. Chuckie worked hard doing the tires. John Sine was full-time, working on the cars. We had alotta help. It was a helluva team."

BP3 models the controversial T.

DAVE PRATT

Tire specialist Chuck Snyder.

JACK KROMER

Teamwork was key. Based out of Pauch's shop, Sine would work on the cars, all day, every day. Nights, Snyder would work on tires. Keith Nonnemacher and his father and brother, Ronnie Totten and his son, Scott and Emilio Coraci, Carl Bleeker and others would arrive to do whatever needed doing. "You would teach them how to maintain the front end on one car, and when they got done with that car, you'd put them on another car," John explained. "So we had a really good system. A good crew, with Leroy taking care of the motors and Bill telling us what to do with the setups. All of us maintaining the cars—it was a well-oiled machine, for the time.

"We had enough guys and we would just constantly go through the cars," Sine got down to the nitty-gritty. "We weren't smart about it—didn't have charts or a board with how many laps were on each piece. We just rebuilt everything every chance we could. We repacked wheel bearings more than anyone probably did, or needed to do. But that's how we kept up with not breaking down: just constantly going through it, making sure it's good. Take the rods off, clean 'em, put 'em back on. That was part of our maintenance system. Repack the wheel bearings, check and change the brake pads. We just did that every week."

While John, Roy and a full crew of volunteers were handling maintenance and repairs, Billy and Pete did all the planning, setting the schedule and the strategy.

"He worked on winning races," Sine said of Pauch. "Like I said, during the day, I'd be in the garage working on the cars. And he'd be working the telephone, trying to find out what he could learn from other people, where he could get better parts, if we had a failure with a part where we could get a better deal or a part that wouldn't fail the next time. He was determined. He wanted to win the most races of anybody, every year."

Winning the most meant racing the most: Sine figured they ran 133 events one season.

"I remember once with Chesson, we ran Windsor on Friday night, Flemington Saturday night, Flemington Sunday afternoon. Drove out to Penn National, had the Penn National car meet us out there. We raced the 100-lapper, won that. Left there, drove all the way to Syracuse, got there 5:30 in the morning. Got a room, slept 'til 10, went to Syracuse, raced, went to Rolling Wheels, raced, then came home," Chuckie recited. "All in one weekend."

Trying to crowbar as many events as he could into a typical week, Pauch would come up with some off-the-wall game plans.

Like the time they took a car to Flemington with no motor in it.

"Brand new car with no motor," Sine recalled. They were out of time so the intention was to have a small-block delivered to the track and put it in the just-completed car in the pits at Flemington—"Pre-scale the car with no motor in it. You know how long we need the lines and the wires and stuff," Billy told John—while they were racing the big-block car. "Then we'd leave from there, that night, and go to the next race—which was at Penn National or somewhere in New York. I forget where."

The plan might have been feasible except for one thing: "In warmups, we blew the motor in the big-block car," John groaned, "so we had to change that motor, too. Two motors in one night in the pits at Flemington. While we were racing."

Sine was both admiring and incredulous of Pauch's do-it-all ambition. "Bill would

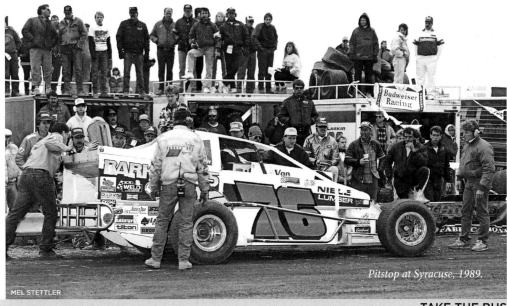

Pitstop at Syracuse, 1989.

MEL STETTLER

come up with these plans like this. I wasn't with him, but one time they went to Syracuse and the plan was to go there with a small-block in the car, pull the small-block out, put a big-block in and race, and then pull the big-block out and put the small-block back in and race again," he said, noting dryly, "Luckily, I wasn't part of that plan."

Of course, there were a lot of times things just plain went wrong; a lot of times when the team found themselves behind the eight-ball.

They were at Utica-Rome in September 1990, swapping out a Precision motor they'd raced the night before for a fresh Prototype piece that Chesson wanted to try. "And instead of changing this motor at the motel, they wait until they get to the track," Roy ominously set the stage.

They got the motor in but couldn't turn it over. "Pete put too long a bolt in the crank that holds the flywheel on and the drive flange. So when we went to start the motor, it went over and stopped because the bolt hit the block," said Sine. "It was a torque-tube car. In order to take the transmission out with a torque tube, it's a lot more work to get to that bolt. I forget why we couldn't take the bellhousing out—but we decided it was easier to pull the motor ahead and fix that bolt.

Pete and Roy thrash on the motor.

JACK KROMER

"So we took the fan off, got a wrecker, picked up the motor with the headers on, and just slid the motor ahead in the car so we could change that one bolt."

All of that took time. "Missed the heat, we got it together for the consi. Started last, got qualified," Roy recounted. "Then in the feature Billy started in the back and he just kept driving. And I remember he passed two cars for the lead—*boom, boom.* One was Ronnie Tobias and I forget who the other one was. And Billy won it."

That U-R win was right on the

heels of the $16,000+ victory he'd reeled off at Fulton the night before—his fifth Victoria 200. And that big-block motor change in the Flemington pits? Yep, he won the feature that night.

"Back then, I was winning one out of every three races I was in," Billy said of his Babe Ruth batting average.

At Flemington in 1990, he was running a car for Chesson that ranks at the top of his all-time favorite rides. "I could get in that thing, close my eyes, and just drive to the front," Pauch relived that heady experience. "It was an Olsen car, a 430 small-block. Man, that car was unbelievable! Won 14-15 times the last year of dirt there. That car just handled so good! Everybody would go in and slide up   and I'd just drive by. And it's funny because that was a high left-side weight car, just like an asphalt car. And it would only work at Flemington."

No doubt, they were the team to beat. "At that time I would say we had top-notch equipment. The finances were there, the tires were there, and the crew was there. We had volunteers who came in at night, and we could turn cars around fast," John considered.

And they had Billy. And Pete.

Until they didn't have Pete any more. At the end of their second year together, Chesson became embroiled in a dead-serious legal morass pertaining to his business dealings. And just like that—*poof!*—he was taken out of the game.

Sine still stuck with Pauch through 1991, as Flemington was black-topped and their world turned upside down.

Billy was determined to make a go of it. Initially, that was enough for John.

"I would have to say that Bill is very good at lining up his ducks. He's very good at organizing things. So when it comes to when you needed a part—it would be there. He knew what you needed and when you needed it. I always said he could line up ducks. And when he made a move and started knocking ducks down—they would go the way he wanted them to go," Sine reflected on the system of success.

"He planned his steps—nothing was ever done on a whim. He planned what he was going to do next year. Who he was gonna drive for. What they were gonna have. Who was gonna work for him."

As for the driving end of it, "he's like a natural," John pegged Billy's innate ability. "Back then, he was like what Friesen is now. Right? I go to the races now, to help someone— and what can I do to make the car be even somewhat competitive with Friesen?"

He thought about that problem. "When I was helping Billy, I thought, well, you just work hard and you make sure everything's right—and you win. You just do everything right—and you win. You got a guy in the seat who can drive. It just seemed like nothing could go that wrong. We'd have some problems here and there, but we could overcome 'em."

John took a long piercing look back at the Pete Chesson years—the years of 45, 48 wins a season. Anywhere. Everywhere.

"The biggest thing is: it just seemed like winning was easy. Y'know? With Bill, it just seemed easy," he grasped. "He's a natural, he's determined. When he gets in that car, his plan is to win.

"And as long as you're winning, you think it's easy. It's when you're not winning that you think, *this is hard*."

Since splitting with Pauch almost 30 years ago, Sine has worked for a succession of well-endowed race teams on the Modified circuit. In his role as car chief, he has mentored young drivers just entering the fray and supported aging veterans scrapping to stay on top.

"With a lot of other drivers and equipment I've worked with—it's hard to win these races." John finally settled on that stone-cold truth, repeating it.

"It's really hard."

JACK KROMER

A, B, C

"It was a pretty stacked field," Pauch remembered. "Like 80 cars there, alotta good guys. We set fast time."

"And then Billy goes out in one of the heats—and totals the freakin' car," Pete shuddered, thinking about it. "*Are you kidding me?* It was a new chassis we'd just got. Davey Brown did the motor. Bangs it all up, we're scrambling around, trying to put a front axle in it.

"There were so many cars there I think we had to go out in the C or D— whatever, it was way back. And he drives the thing from the back of the D to win, and the C to win, and just kept going..."

"It paid $10,000 to win," reminded Tommy Carl, who was well familiar with the fact that Pauch would put it into overdrive when that kind of cash was on the line. "When it's time to prove something or they add an extra digit to that purse—he's a different guy. I really believe that."

Carl succinctly recapped Pauch's "one-and-done" pickup ride for Pete at Susky. "He set fast time. Took the lead in the heat and flipped on his own. Then he came back and won the C and B and the A.

"That is a motivated Billy Pauch story," Tommy maintained. "It all goes back to that extra 0—it changes everything."

His legal troubles behind him, Pete Chesson was back on the scene in 1997.

"The kids, P.J. and James, were #1 in the country with Quads and AMA," he said—they were ready to step up. "So we bought a Sprint Car from Zemco, like the end of August."

Crew chief Tommy Carl was helping the boys get started. "The kids had been racing the Sprint Cars a little bit, wrecking 'em a little bit," Pete recalled their rookie season.

But when KARS announced a $10,000-to-win 358 Sprint special at Susquehanna in mid-October, the thought was to put Pauch in the seat.

He was racing 410s steady for Zemco. It was big money. It was right in his wheelhouse.

"So we decided we'd go there with Billy and see what happened," Chesson stated.

11.

Picking Up the Pieces

MEL STETTLER

Every bad omen would have to be lined up as precisely as dominoes under your astrological sign for the world to come apart like it did for Pauch in 1991.

In the space of less than three months, Billy lost his big-bucks car owner, his best-loved home track, and his tire, parts and driving school business.

In 1990, he had it all. In 1991, he had to start all over.

Pete Chesson was pretty much out of the picture. Flemington was paved over. After a career-best 48-win season, the party was over. Standing amid the aftermath of tattered confetti and empty champagne bottles, Pauch and crew chief John Sine were left to answer the biggest question of their lives…

What do we do now?

"Oh, yeah," Billy was acutely aware of how difficult it would be to keep the team going. "There were a lot of conversations between me and John, because we were left to either stay with the boat or sink with the boat. Either get out or stay with it and see if we could make it float.

"It was a challenge, after being with owners who could afford to do it for four or five years and then trying to do it on your own, with nothing going for you—no major sponsorship or anything," he allowed. "We had some cars and we sold what we could to

Ray Carroll (center) commiserates with motor builder Sam "Radar" Ceganick. That's Tommy Lynch entering the scene, with Billy busy in the trailer.

keep the whole thing together."

Enter Ray Carroll.

A cagey gamblin' man with flowing white hair and black cowboy boots, Carroll came out of the Penndel racing crowd. Partnered with George Moskat, they bought a Sprinter in 1975 and put 24-year-old up-and-comer Stevie Howard in the car; he was killed in a fiery wreck at Lincoln in August, one day after winning at Williams Grove. That shattering tragedy steered Carroll out of Sprint Cars and onto the stock car scene.

In '76, Carroll commissioned a Modified from Kenny Weld, got a Truppi/Kling big-block, had Jimmy Horton lined up for the seat. But when Weld delivered the finished piece, he told Ray, "I want to drive this car."

It lasted just three months before Kenny up and quit, careening off the track at 80 mph in the middle of a race at Reading to hand Ray his helmet.

The yellow Weld car became Gary Hieber's rookie ride. After Hieber, Carroll fielded equipment for Elvin Felty, then Chip Slocum—each car under the Tabloid Graphics banner, his brother-in-law Tommy Lynch's South Jersey printing business. Ray always aimed to stay under the radar, working all the angles well out of broad daylight.

Carroll sized up the opportunity to partner with Pauch in 1990, when car owner Pete Chesson's legal difficulties began. And then, Pete's problems and the consequences he was facing rapidly became more dire.

"We made a partnership deal because Pete Chesson still wanted to be quietly involved with the race team. Then, when the world collapsed and Pete was out, we hadda buy out the operation," Ray said.

So he and Pauch came up with a tall-order solution: the team would be self-funded. "We felt that Billy was capable of winning enough money to give him his percentage and run the race team."

The car, ostensibly, would pay for itself.

> *I will say this: that guy never, ever, never gives up on anything. He is the hardest driving sonuvabitch I ever met. Y'know what I mean? He will not surrender. That's just in him. That's just who Billy Pauch is. And that's why he wins so much.*
>
> **RAY CARROLL**

Ray and Billy sat down with a piece of paper and started drawing up a game plan. "We had a whole list of people, potential sponsors that I was going to call. So we put all these sponsors together," Carroll said. "They took care of a lot of the race car stuff—hubs and wheels and ignition systems, engines and brakes and calipers. So we were capable of building a team at that time with very little money."

Pauch's name recognition certainly played into that. "Look, Billy was a well-established, well-respected race car driver," Ray reminded. "I didn't have to fight my way into MSD and Lucas and Wilwood and Weld Wheels. I knew a lot of people and they knew Billy—they'd love to be on the car! And we had a couple of other good sponsors who put actual money into it. But pretty much, that's how we built the race team."

There was value, too, in keeping Billy's number 15. "I felt that if a driver had a number they were associated with, then we hadda use that number so the sponsors would get recognition," Ray reasoned, so he gave up his 86.

The fans also factored into the equation. Driver merch—shirts, hats, hoodies and the like—featured Billy's original number 15 and were sold by Barbara under the newly-formed K.I.D. Racing.

"K.I.D. Racing—you know what it stood for?" Pauch said of the acronym Carroll came up with. "Keep It Divided. This is yours, this is mine."

And every dime, every nickel earned was toted up and accounted for. "Oh, yeah, you got that right! He's very detailed about the money and the percentages. What Billy gets and what Billy doesn't get, and what he deserves, and blah, blah, blah." Ray rolled his eyes. "He knows every penny of it. You're not getting it over on him for a hundred dollars."

Run out of Pauch's race shop, the team paid rent for the space and utilities. Billy was paid his percentage of the winnings. "I think John Sine mighta been involved for a year or so. He got paid his percentage, too," Pauch noted.

"We tried to do it on a real business-like basis and keep it square," said Carroll.

"That's how we raced. All the money that came in—Billy got his percentage and all the rest of the money was reinvested into the race team. We tried to stay ahead—always building a new race car, getting ready for the next big set of races with engines and stuff. That's how you have to operate if you want to win."

But in 1991 they weren't faced with going back to the old Flemington clay, where Billy commanded His Majesty's throne. This was blacktop racing—a complete unknown.

"Look, I didn't care whether we went there or went elsewhere," Ray claimed. "But Billy—because of his huge connection to Flemington—he wanted to go there. And I'm sure there was a big connection with Paul Kuhl and he wanted Billy to come there and race."

So they went to Flemington. "Started out with the Olsen car with Tabloid Graphics and the car was terrible," Pauch said. He had already cut a deal to race Benny Scheer's Troyer in the track's Pepsi small-block mini-series. Admitting he was "out to lunch" in the Tabloid Mod, "we parked it and ran Benny's car. Benny took the small-block out and put a 430 in and we started running it with the Modifieds," he recalled.

Billy in the Flemington winner's circle with his son and Benny Scheer's 1a.

JACK KROMER

And even though he was able to put a half dozen scores in the win column in Scheer's 1a—even sweeping a twin 20 card on August 24th—Billy was never comfortable.

"He did bring Ray Evernham in, to give him some advice. But it's a tremendous transition from driving on dirt to driving on asphalt. Y'know? And he struggled with it. I mean, he was good. But he struggled and was always off a little bit," Carroll admitted.

Fear had never been a factor in the past, but there it was at Flemington, a pervasive, blood-numbing foreboding that menaced every move.

"It was a scary place," Pauch confessed.

"I crashed hard twice there," he told. In July of '91, "me and Hoffman got together, sent me into the outside wall and damn near killed me. The car was in two pieces—from the motor forward was a separate piece. It was pretty bad."

Benny Scheer got another frame, built another car—and Billy came back for more.

In early '92, he survived another brutal crash coming out of two. "What would happen there is guys would get sideways and when they'd come out of it, they'd turn right," Pauch described. "I was going around somebody, and when they turned right they just turned into my left-front, hit me and sent me straight into the fence.

Pauch's car was completely split in two in the frightening wreck at Flemington with Doug Hoffman in 1991.

MEL STETTLER

"I said, that's enough. I gotta get out of here before I get killed."

After that second big crash, "I didn't want to go there. Y'know what I mean?" Ray Carroll refused to live through anything like that ever again. "So we finally decided to get out of there and go to Grandview."

It made sense: amidst trying to acclimate to asphalt and holding down the fort at East Windsor on Friday nights, the team had won every big special that Grandview threw on the schedule in '91. Collected $5K+ in the Star Spangled Big-Block Blast on July 3rd. Took the $7,000 Forrest Rogers Memorial in August. The $15,000+ Freedom 76 on September 7th. And aced a $3,000 35-lapper—coming from

Billy shares the champagne with track owner Kenny Rogers.

21st after their heat-race win was invalidated when Billy forgot to go straight to the scale—a week after the '6er.

So at Carroll's insistence, the decision was made to abandon Flemington and sign up for Grandview on Saturday nights partway into the 1992 season. "Believe you me—he wasn't happy about it," Ray attested. "He had to give up on Flemington where he established his bones. He had alotta skin in that game—that place was his, *that was his house!* He outdid alotta great drivers there. Became the king there. And that's hard to give up, for anybody."

Still, they had made well over $30,000 in just four appearances at Grandview. Think of how lucrative a full commitment could be…

It was, with a caveat. While the Tabloid team won a dozen races at Grandview in '92-3—including two midweek specials, a second consecutive '6er, a 100-lapper, the '93 Forrest Rogers Memorial, and a twin-card shutout that was good for $12K with bonus—they also tore up a bunch of equipment.

"Grandview, that first year, we were—*whew!*—almost unbeatable there," Ray remembered. "And then the next year we came back and we couldn't stay out of a wreck! It was unbelievable—we got wrecked every week! I think there were five or six weeks in a row that we got wrecked. And I just said to Billy, 'I'm done going to Grandview.'

"And of course, that didn't play well. He wasn't happy about it because he doesn't like quitting once he commits to something. We had sponsors there," Carroll continued. "But I didn't care. I was done with it. Our cars were getting *destroyed*—they weren't just getting bent bumpers and stuff. After a while it gets really expensive."

"We started out at Grandview, got crashed every week, left and went to Bridgeport," summarized Pauch, who was starting to feel the strain of the whole self-funding team strategy. There was a lot of pressure to produce every dollar. It was honestly exhausting.

But what were Billy's options? He could go back to Flemington and chance getting killed on pavement. Or roll the dice on his odds of coming out alive in a Sprint Car.

It was the devil's dilemma. Pauch chose the latter option.

"It's funny: I left Glenn because he wanted to go Sprint Car racing and I wasn't really crazy about that. And then two years later, I wind up with Zemco, racing Sprint Cars because I really didn't have any other options," Billy reflected. "Whaddaya do? I gotta make a living, I had a family to feed. So I gotta go drive Sprints—it ain't my forté, or I'm crazy about 'em, but I gotta go do it."

Before switching to Sprints on Friday nights, East Windsor was Pauch's playground. He won 18 feature events in 1991 (including nine in a row), and 14 in '92.

DON MARKS

*Battling Kenny Brightbill
at Big Diamond, 1992.*

By '93, he was driving Sprints steady for Zemco, Fridays and special events. In '94, Billy knocked another night a week off his Modified schedule. Given Carroll's heavy history with Sprint Cars, he was not happy.

That was the beginning of the end.

"He wasn't concentrating that hard on the Modifieds. He was really into the Sprint Cars. We were pretty much running a lot of small-block shows. Very few big-block shows," Ray relayed. "And along came Bob Faust. While we were racing together, Bob Faust and Billy were talking, making some kind of big-block deal for the following year."

Faust, a Pennsy businessman who'd furnished quality equipment for Gary Grim, Craig Von Dohren and Frank Cozze, had his sights set on Billy. "With Von Dohren, we had 11 seconds at Windsor one year—and all of 'em were to Pauch," Bob muttered. That didn't sit well. "We were getting beat like that all the time. I wanted to be the one doing the beating, not getting beat."

When Billy told Ray about the deal with Faust—coupled with Pauch's decision to race the National Open for Zemco and not the 1994 Victoria 200 in the Modified—Carroll was fuming. "Then we went to Syracuse," he laid it down. "Let's just say there wasn't a lot of love there at that point."

And it all got worse pretty rapidly. On Friday night of Super DIRT Week, they were forced to change motors in the Modified: with the good Shaver presenting problems, Ray elected to replace it with a barely-complete T/K High Performance piece. "We stayed up all night to finish it. Got it fired at like one in the morning, getting yelled at by the State Police—*'Shut that thing off and get outta here!'*" Carroll recounted.

"So I go back to the hotel, I'm exhausted. Then I come back the next morning—and I can't find the race car! *What the $#@%?*" he snapped. "I'm walking around, I can't find it. So I go down to the Sprint Car pits, where Billy's with Zemco, and I say, 'Billy, where's the race car?' He said he didn't know. So I'm walking around and finally somebody tells me, 'Ray, your car's way out in the back.'

"I drive out there with Tommy from Tabloid Graphics. And they were taking the engine out that I put in the car. And putting in an engine from Bob Faust." Carroll was dumbfounded. "Nobody told me about it—so, of course, you know what happened then. I fired everybody.

"Then I went to see Billy and we had it out right there and then."

Ray hightailed it over to the Sprint Car pits, skidded to a stop, and proceeded to unleash his rightful wrath. The timing couldn't have been worse: mere hours before Billy was scheduled to start from the pole in the Supernationals, one of the biggest Sprint Car events of the year, with every out-for-blood Outlaw intent on trampling him into dust at the drop of the green.

"Him and I had this big argument—I mean, like a *really unfriendly* argument—right at the trailer. And John Zemaitis and his wife and all of them scattered. We were going at it! Right at the Sprint Car," Ray ranted.

"First, he started screaming at me, like I plotted it," Pauch recalled. "I said Ray, they told me they were going out there. I don't know! I have no idea. I mean, Saturday was

Ray and John put their heads together at Fulton.

Billy and the Tabloid Graphics team set overall fast time in the big-blocks at Syracuse in 1992— a new Modified track record that stood for another seven years.

MEL STETTLER

Sprint Car day—I'm there to race the Sprint Car! And he started screaming and hollering, mother-f'ing this and that. And I'm like: I don't need this now! I'm trying to keep my head into the Sprint Car race. Y'know?

"Finally he disappeared and he found 'em, down in one and two or something. And he started throwing everything out of the trailer."

The relationship had always been prickly between the two high-strung personalities, too much alike, and they'd banged heads before. "But that was a real firestorm," Carroll described. "If Billy really wanted that Faust engine in, he shoulda said it to me! But he told me that he didn't know what was going on. Since I didn't have bird's-eye-view facts—I can't really say whether he did or he didn't. But boy, did we have it out!

"That was the end. I was done—I was loading up and leaving. That was so bad that everything in the trailer that wasn't mine, I threw out onto the parking lot!" Glenn Hyneman, viewing the tirade, remembered a carburetor came flying past his head.

"And Tommy, of course, was the sane human being in the group. He would always say, 'Ray, calm down! Calm down! Don't be a maniac!' So I said, OK, we'll stay.

"I think behind the scenes, Billy and Tommy got together and settled that score. They came to me and said, 'Ray, would you run the team?' Because Billy needed someone to run the team if he was going to race," Carroll said.

"I wasn't really involved in the arguing. All I was involved in was trying to help Billy," justified Faust, who was and is a good friend of Ray's. "I really knew that I wanted to hire Billy. I knew they were struggling. I knew I had a spare motor, a good one. And I just felt it was the right thing to do."

"So we ended up putting the engine in and running it," Ray reported. In the middle of all the drama, one day after his stunning win in the Sprint Car race, Pauch reeled off a respectable ninth place finish in the Wheels Automotive 300 on the mile, driving the Tabloid team Modified with Faust's Feil big-block under the hood.

"We agreed to do that race and then end it. So that was that," Carroll concluded. "We were done. We did have some hookups after that, but it was pretty much over.

"It took quite a while to get back on friendly terms again. It's pretty much been on and off ever since," he said.

For Billy's part, "I understand the whole deal at Syracuse, him getting mad. But I had nothing to do with it! It had nothing to do with me! They all made a decision they were gonna work on the car in the pits in the morning. And then Fandel and somebody else decided they were gonna take it out to the backstretch somewhere."

Crewman Bobby Fandel had built motors for Pauch's asphalt owner Benny Scheer, knew his stuff. It's a certainty he was familiar with Pauch's opinion of T/K power plants: "Grenades," Billy called them.

"I'm driving the Sprint Car and Ray comes in. 'Where's the car?' I don't know. Then he goes out and finds them and starts throwing everything out of the trailer. The trailer was his and he was gonna leave! Then Tommy Tabloid, his brother-in-law, calmed him down and they put it all back together," Billy recapped. "I had nothing to do with it. It was crazy! He goes nuts, y'know?

"But I was fine, I understood the whole thing, why he would be mad. And I guess after that he went with Brightbill."

As Ray pointed out, following the Syracuse fallout, there was a long, icy silence between conversations.

But it wasn't the final word between the two. "He brought me back there years after that. Randy Strickler was involved—he hauled all the stuff up there, motors and the car. And I ran again for Ray," Billy disclosed, before dispatching one last definitive jab.

"I guess he believed I could still win a race."

BOB FAUST REMEMBERS...

Car builder Doug Olsen, Bob Faust and Billy at Bridgeport.

MEL STETTLER

"In 1995, when the DIRT cars came in from New York, Billy was racing for me and we were running Bridgeport, the big five-eighths. It was a real hot summer—dry as dry can be. And Billy called me and said, 'I think we should take the small-block, the Grandview car, to Bridgeport. You know how dry it is and everything.'

I said, 'Good idea.'

So he switches cars and they drive to Bridgeport. And into a major, major-league downpour.

MEL STETTLER

So there we are—with a small-block against all these big-block guys. Ended up we didn't qualify in the heat...we didn't qualify in the consi. Ed Kelly—who was a very good friend of mine, he owned Bridgeport at the time—he put us in as a promoter's choice. Billy started dead last.

I'm sitting in the pit grandstands and Brett Hearn's crew guy, Jay Castimore, was sitting right in front of me. And I want to say around lap 85 or 86, Jay said to Brett on the headset, 'Brett, you need to get outside.'

Brett said, 'I'm outside as far as I can go.'

And I'll never forget this as long as I live—Jay looked directly at me as he said to Brett, 'You're gonna see where the outside is here in about two laps.'

Well, Billy passed him for the lead with about six or seven laps to go. And on the last lap, we blew a left-rear tire. Running away from everybody! Billy came from dead last in a 358 small-block against all those big-blocks. And he destroyed the field!

It's a race that we lost. But it's probably one of the most memorable races I've ever been at."

ACE LANE JR.

12.
Sense & Sensibility

To this day, when Billy Pauch tells the story of the night he met Kenny Weld, his voice is still edged in awe.

"In '75, I was racing this Mustang at East Windsor and Flemington, and we weren't having such a great time at Windsor so my dad brought us down to Bridgeport," he remembered. "That was when Kenny Weld was in the Weikert Modified—and, man, he was so totally dominant at Bridgeport that he could've stopped on the backstretch during the feature, wiped off his goggles, and still beaten everybody by a straightaway. He was that dominant."

At the end of that night, "Weld walked up to me—*to me!*—and he knew me. Kenny Weld knew who I was." More than 45 years later, Pauch continues to shake his head in disbelief at the thought. "That just about blew me away. Really. And in '76, I built my car to look just like his—red, white and blue."

What Billy often omits when he brings up this incident are a few vital facts about himself: in that spring of '75 he was an 18-year-old novice racer who'd already won every Rookie division event at Flemington. The night described was his first-ever visit to Bridgeport; and when Weld approached Pauch post-race, it was to congratulate the Sportsman winner. The following year, carrying Kenny's colors, the sophomore grabbed 28 victories and every Sportsman Modified title the state of New Jersey had to offer.

Kenny Weld was no fool. He knew true talent when he saw it.

However, in the telling of this story—and similar others—Billy reveals his blind spot: even in the present tense, he really has no sense of himself. He's not playing coy and modest; truly, in the full scope of short-track racing, he can't imagine that a simple Jersey farmer's son with a knack for giving a race car a full-tilt tussle might occupy a place of worth.

And he certainly can't put himself on the pedestal where he places his own heroes. Jack Hewitt, for instance, "is somebody I always wanted to meet," Billy once told a group of local racers, gathered around his trailer between events at Penn National in late summer of 1993, his first night back in Modified competition after completing a Midwestern Sprint swing.

"I'd heard a lot about him, and here I was walking past him when we were leaving Eldora. And I wanted to say something but I was a little intimidated to just go right up to him. I'd heard Hewitt's pretty feisty. And what was I going to say to him—'Hi, I'm Billy Pauch'? *Jeez...*

"I couldn't believe it when he hollered to me, and came over and told me he wanted to meet me. Jack Hewitt wanted to meet *me!*" Pauch marveled. "Man, I was impressed."

That was the highlight the Penn National gang heard about. Not the fact that Pauch notched a fourth in Eldora's '93 Big One, his first time there in a winged Sprint, in his first full year of concentrating on Sprint Car rather than Modified racing. Not the fact that he'd easily made the A-main at Knoxville—a tougher battlefield than Gettysburg—and finished a not-too-shabby 14th in his second-ever try at the Nationals. No, Billy's big thrill on that road trip came from a tip of Jack Hewitt's cap.

Yet, it was a pretty good bet that somebody as well-traveled as Hewitt would have stumbled over some of Pauch's exploits. By that summer of '93, The Kid already had a résumé sporting just shy of 450 victories, taken down at 21 speedways in six states. That year alone, he'd won races in dirt small-block Modifieds, dirt big-block Modifieds, Sprint Cars with wings and Sprint Cars without wings, collecting $12,000 along the way in

BOB ARMBRUSTER

Billy kids around with Tony Stewart at New Egypt in 2003.

"I don't know if I was driving Scamardella's car or the 3n1 Champ car, but I was out at the Indy Fairgrounds. We were all lined up along the apron on the frontstretch, and they're time trialing. A.J. Foyt was there, driving. So we're standing there just BS-ing, and one guy who was with me says, 'Why don't you go see if you can get your picture taken with A.J.?' I was a big A.J. Foyt fan—he was number one! So I go up to A.J. and ask him if I can take a picture with him. 'Yeah, no problem.' It's in the trophy room— a picture of me and A.J. Foyt shaking hands. He's one of my heroes. Him and Tony Stewart."

bonuses, over and above his winnings. Ricocheting from ride to ride, division to division, Billy had bested the Sportsman Mod squad, won on the fierce Central PA Sprint grid, and beaten the CRA boys flat-cold when they came to town. It was a record that a guy like Jack Hewitt could well appreciate.

And the best was still to come. In the fall of 1993, Pauch racked up $50,000 in major scores at five raceways in New York, New Jersey, Pennsylvania and Maryland. Included in those was the still-talked-about Race of Champions shocker— Billy picking up a last-minute ride as a replacement pilot in an utterly alien asphalt Modified and outdriving every authentic NASCAR pavement hustler to post a huge win in a distance race as steeped in tradition as the flying red, white and blue.

It's the stuff of legends—if you believe in legends. And Pauch can't seem to place himself in that league.

Just back from the Chili Bowl in 1995, Pauch was amazed that a well-respected owner from out that way was offering him a full schedule for the USAC Silver Crown series

BOB ARMBRUSTER

Pauch, Bill Elliott and crew coach driver Ray Evernham as he takes Billy's driving school Sprint Car for a whirl during a "play date" at New Egypt Speedway in 2002.

in a top-flight Champ Car.

"The guy told me I'd come 'highly recommended' by John Bickford, Jeff Gordon's step-father," Billy wondered at the reference. "That John Bickford even knows who I am just about blows me away."

In reality, there is a connection. Gordon's former NASCAR Hall of Fame crew chief Ray Evernham, another Jersey boy, has been fast friends with Pauch for years. And Evernham had been telling everyone who'd listen that his good buddy had all the stuff that Jeff Gordon had. Maybe more.

In Daytona Beach in 2005, a special Short Track Racing Summit "Gathering of Champions" assembled all living Daytona 500 race winners—from Mario Andretti to Cale Yarborough and every history-shaping great in between. Ray Evernham, as keynote speaker, addressed that star-heavy crowd, then took questions. One attendee brought up a "play date" on dirt that Pauch had arranged a few years before at New Egypt Speedway, for Ray and drivers Bill Elliott, Jeremy Mayfield and Casey Atwood to mess around with Modifieds, Sprint Cars, even a top-notch Late Model supplied by Rick Eckert. So the question was raised in the room: *Just who is Billy Pauch?*

In front of all those racing luminaries, from every constellation in the country, Evernham made the pronouncement…

"Billy Pauch is the greatest race car driver that you've never heard of."

Two old friends: Frank and Billy.

MEL STETTLER

WHEELING & DEALING

"I don't know why we didn't race Hagerstown," Billy struggled to recall the 1992 Octoberfest finale.

But his good buddy, Frank Cozze, was there. "I went to Hagerstown, got qualified and they rained out," Frank said. "So they rescheduled the race for the next week."

Which presented a problem for Frank: on the rain date, he was already committed to compete in Orange County's Eastern States 200.

So with the track's consent, Cozze sold his Hagerstown starting spot to Pauch.

"He said, 'Well, we really don't want to do that but OK, go ahead,'" Cozze recapped his conversation with track rep Frank Sagi. "So I called Billy. I said if you want to go to Hagerstown and run that race, I'm already qualified. All you gotta do is put a number 44 on your car.

"And whatever you make, I get 20 percent."

Pauch's crewman Chuck Snyder remembered the race. "Billy bought Frank's spot. Started dead last. By halfway, we were third."

During the fuel stop in the 100-lapper, "Billy says to me, 'What are we running for air pressure?' Same as we were running at Syracuse. Had those bleeders in there, you could pop 'em out. He says, 'Eh, let's just drop 'em down to 4 and 8.'

"Then he just drove right to the front and won."

Ten thousand dollars.

"The next week, we're down in Delaware to run the end of the year races at U.S. 13," Cozze established. "And we stopped at some restaurant to eat breakfast the next morning. I happened to see Billy out of the corner of my eye — they were at another table, across the room."

Billy searched for the memory. "It was a long time ago! Little Frankie was still in a highchair."

Pauch came up behind Frank while he was eating, playfully grabbed him by the shoulders. "I guess I owe you some money."

Frank nodded.

"I do remember him saying to me when he handed me the check, 'Y'know, they probably would've put me in anyway because there wasn't a full field of cars,'" said Frank. "I just looked at him."

"But you make a deal, you make a deal. Here it is," said Billy, as he squared up.

"I made him a good deal: 20 percent," Frank acknowledged, grinning. "It was the easiest $2,000 I ever made racing!"

13.

The Vic

Ten thousand dollars. Back in 1986, that was a ton of money—an almost unheard-of amount—to win a Modified race on a dirt short track.

But Millard "Bub" Benway—owner/operator of a sleepy little riverside half-mile by the name of Fulton in way-upstate New York—was looking to make a big splash, so he plunked that $10K down and made sure every racer in the region knew it was on the table.

What was also noteworthy was the fact that this was no major-league big-block Modified program, packaged and promoted for the circuit's professionals in the Weedsport offices of the DIRT organization. It was, in fact, an unsanctioned event at an upstart outlaw track, located smack in the middle of DIRT-controlled territory, headlining the 320/358 small-block Mods—long considered a "second banana" class to the big boys, and certainly not privy to this kind of payoff.

But Bub Benway didn't care. Earlier that year his wife Vickie had died, and he'd decided, in part, to mount this race in her memory—the Victoria 200, the biggest and baddest small-blockers' blowout he and his staff could conceive. Two days. Two hundred laps. A head-turning ten grand cash on top.

Pauch takes the high line around Ronnie Tobias to win the inaugural Victoria 200.

KEN DIPPEL

Two for two in 1987.

DON EDDS

All the way down in New Jersey, Billy Pauch could smell the money. Now this was right up his alley: a big payday untainted by DIRT politics; an outlier show run by outlaws—just like he was.

Yet, despite his success in Pennsylvania and New Jersey, Pauch couldn't exactly be called a favorite for that first Vic. He had only raced Fulton once before in his life. And he wasn't the only one to pick up the scent of Benway's crisp dollar bills: 88 other drivers were equally anxious to count that cash.

And, despite his reputation, it wasn't like Pauch was showing up with a state-of-the-art entry.

To call the team "underfunded" was a generous description. Pennsylvania policeman Jerry Becker's 41a was a 10-year-old car originally built by Sprint Car driver Bobby Weaver for Gary Gollub.

"We had an open trailer pulled by a plumber's truck. We only had one car and one motor. No spare rear," said team manager Gene "Speedy" Franckowiak. "When we got to the race track, we only had about $60 between the four of us. Eric Kingsley, the promoter at the time, allowed us to go in and pay for our pit passes after the race."

Pauch won his heat and was leading at the 100-lap fuel break—which, for this small-potatoes team, was a pivotal moment.

KEN DIPPEL

The Fulton pits were always packed for the Vic.

"They had a deal going where whoever was leading at the halfway point would win $1,000," Franckowiak recounted. "I had to run across the track during the break and get Eric to give me the $1,000 so I could go buy tires to run the second 100 laps."

Billy stayed out front most of the race, and won it convincingly. "It was a phenomenal weekend," Speedy said. "We got $10,000 cash and a king can of Miller Light for every lap we led. I think we left with about 100 cans of beer."

No one could have imagined at the time that this race would turn into the annual Billy Pauch benefit party.

In 1987, Pauch was determined to take every dime up for grabs—qualifying at Fulton on Saturday afternoon, flying the 250 miles back to Jersey to race a 100-lapper at Flemington on Saturday night, then returning to New York the next morning to drive his big-block in the Rolling Wheels 200, prior to racing—and winning—his second Victoria 200 at Fulton on Sunday night. Talk about ambitious...

And harrowing: "Davey Adams' brother flew me from Fulton to Flemington one time—you hadda fly back because in four hours driving you could never make the heat races at Flemington. I forget where we flew out near Fulton, but it was a little plane and when we took off and left the ground, there was such a strong wind we were actually going up sideways!" Billy recalled. "It was pretty wild."

At this point, he had a steady ride with the well-heeled Keystone Racing team—which did make things easier.

In the '87 race, Pauch won his heat; a lottery draw placed him 18th at the start. What is car owner Glenn Hyneman's memory of that race? "Lots of beer!" he evoked that visual. "I think we won a six-pack or a case of beer for every lap we led. We must've taken the lead pretty early because of all the beer we got! I'm not exaggerating: we had a pickup truck just loaded with beer when we left there. So much beer that we needed a second pickup truck to haul it all out."

In '88, the agenda was much the same: a show in Bridgeport, NJ, on Friday night, then qualifying races on Saturday at Fulton (where Billy's car spun a drive flange leading the heat), then rocket back to Jersey for a subsequently weather-washed 100 at Flemington, before spending Sunday in New York—Fulton's 200 only that year, because trying to persevere through a pair of 200-lap events at two different tracks in a single day was "too exhausting," Pauch understated.

As he failed to qualify, Billy had to fall back on his guaranteed starter status for his

The champagne flies as Billy makes it five in a row in 1990.

KEN DIPPEL

third Vic attempt: he lined up 30th on the grid.

"I do remember starting way back. It was a long way to go," Hyneman said. Not to worry: "I guess all the action was in the first half, because we dominated the second half."

Bam! Billy had the hat trick.

Pauch had the place figured out, all right. But after a while the odds and the gods turn against you. Three in a row is a *tour de force*; four consecutive—never before accomplished in any major event in this neck of the woods—was a near impossibility.

"Just look at the luck factor, alone," Fulton publicity director Marcia Wetmore pointed out prior to the 1989 race. "It would mean running 800 laps without having a bolt break or a tire go flat or a squirrel spin out in front of you. In this sport," she shook her head, "it just doesn't happen that way."

Roy and Billy don't leave anything to chance in 1990, making sure the car will last through the second half.

Billy was all too aware of his diminishing odds. "I figured sooner or later that the car would break, or something else would happen to knock me out of the race," he conceded.

Glenn Hyneman concurred. "The thought was always in our minds: is it even possible to win four in a row?"

Against all logic, it was.

Starting 16th on the grid, Pauch propelled the Keystone Racing entry to the point by the halfway refueling break, despite battling all day with brake issues and a balky throttle.

And the crew well knew that the top of the track—Billy's preferred groove—could disappear into the parking lot by the end of the second segment. With rain causing Saturday's preliminaries to cram into Sunday afternoon, the low line was slicker than just-waxed linoleum. Time to sweat.

Their fears were well-founded. In the second half, the high groove had all but evaporated; former Fulton champ Bob Podolak and invader Rich Ricci Jr. were making time down low. In fourth and getting desperate with 55 to go, Pauch finally figured he'd have to venture into the slippery stuff.

"I had nothing to lose," Billy reasoned. "I came here to win. I wasn't about to finish fourth, so I dropped down to the bottom."

Not even a last-minute burst by tough

Pauch made a critical error in tire selection during the halfway break in the 1991 Vic.

KEN DIPPEL

Pennsy opponent Rich Tobias Jr. could alter the outcome: Billy took the 1989 Victoria 200, making him four for four at Fulton, the recipient of almost $51,000 in a quartet of appearances at a speedway he saw a single time a year.

That whole cynical theory of diminishing odds? It's a gambler's fallacy.

The incredible streak stayed unbroken in 1990. Five for five. Pauch pocketed a winner's share increased by a hefty $5K to $15,000, with bonuses bringing his take-home pay to $16,095.

"It's gotten so that you come to this race each year to find out who's going to finish second," one press-box observer sighed. "If Pauch wasn't out front, it wouldn't be the Victoria 200."

Yet, for most of the distance, Billy's Barker Bus 76 did not appear to be the car to beat. For one thing, Pauch's patented outside groove never came in, forcing him downtrack to find traction. And secondly, two Johnsons—Danny and Jack—were solidly in control.

But then, Danny's motor expired in a puff of white smoke on lap 140. That handed the lead to Jack Johnson.

"Y'know, it's 200 laps: you just wait, wait, wait, wait, wait—you wait for somebody to slip," Billy reflected. "And Jack finally slipped. He just hit the glaze in two and slid up a little bit. All I needed was an inch, and I was by him."

The storybook string finally snapped in 1991, when Pauch's buddy Frank Cozze became the second man to win the Vic in the event's six-year history. Billy finished fourth.

Make no mistake: when Cozze came to Fulton, for the first time ever in September '91, he was armed to the teeth. He was a DIRT series veteran, an expert in these long-distance grinds. The Kneisel car he brought to the Fulton fight had won the last two Eastern States 200s at Orange County. And if that wasn't enough: Frank had the inside scoop from Billy Pauch himself.

"I called Billy up, to see what tires I needed. I told him, 'I want one of these…one of these…one of these…' And he goes, 'Frank, listen to me. This is all you're gonna need. You don't have to buy all these drag tires.'"

Announcer Fred Osmun interviews the winner.

KEN DIPPEL

The two friends talked a little about setups for the race. Said Cozze: "Whatever you say, Billy. You oughta know—you're the one who won the race five times."

Both Billy and Frank started the event buried back in the 10th row. "I figured I'd follow him because he knew where to go," Cozze related. "I don't know if his car was no good, but my car was really good and I just took off…

"Anyone who's been to Fulton knows, especially in those days, you either rolled in the corner right on the bottom or all the way at the top. It was real wide," Frank explained. "I could drive right through the dead-slick part of the race track—had a whole lane to myself because nobody else could run there.

"Billy's the guy who got me on the right tires—and I wound up winning the race. Which I thought was pretty ironic."

Pauch ruefully admitted he'd outsmarted himself. "I always went with the same tire combination. They were GF2s and we'd run 100 laps and pit. Come in, change tires, change gears, make adjustments. We'd always change the tires—they could look real good but we'd always put new ones on for the second half and go back out and win," he said.

"The sixth year, I decided we were gonna go softer. Frank was on the GF2s I sold him. And that was the first year that I lost it, and Frank won," he submitted. "I was stupid. Why would you change something you won five straight years with?"

Once a winning streak is severed, all that potent magic is rendered powerless. After the loss to Cozze, Pauch came back in '92 to cruise in the first 100 laps, collect the $3,500 halfway bonus and lead most of the second segment, before track regular Tommy Kinsella and others created a lawless line—"*...running way low, off the racing surface...getting that left-rear tire down into that wet stuff and finding some bite that they're not getting out of the racing groove,*" was the call by track announcer Roy Sova—and left Pauch hung out to dry.

"I shoulda won it in '92," Billy believes. "Had the race won, I'm driving away, rolling around the top like I normally did, and with less than 50 to go, I look down and they're

Three-wide at Fulton: Doug Hoffman low, Bobby Holland in the middle, Billy in his preferred outside groove.

KEN DIPPEL

running off the track, through the infield! Four guys passed me. At the time I was running on seven cylinders because a plug wire came off, and when I dropped down to the infield where they were running, I wasn't that good. I didn't have the power to run down there where there was more bite.

"There was a berm around the inside of the track—and they were actually running on the *inside* of that berm. I couldn't believe they let 'em get away with it, but they did," Pauch griped. "I got back by Pete Bicknell for third."

A broken axle early on sidelined Pauch in the 1993 running of the Vic. And then, for the most part, he was gone—off running Sprints in Pennsylvania for the Zemco team.

Then came an interesting turn of events: during the 1995-96 winter season, Fulton Speedway, along with Utica-Rome, were sold to a partnership formed by über-promoter Alex Friesen and Pauch's Sprint Car owner John Zemaitis. After Friesen's tragic death in a snowmobile accident in December, Zemaitis stuck through the '97 season—which is when Pauch returned to Vic action.

It was his most dominant Fulton performance ever, sharpened to a point by his open-wheel experience. When Pauch pulled into the winner's circle for his sixth Vic victory, he'd lapped all but two cars.

"Drove that one like it was a Sprint Car," said Billy, who was added to the rear of the field as a provisional after forgoing Saturday qualifying to race the 410 at Williams Grove's National Open, where he finished fourth to winner Sammy Swindell.

"John wanted me to run both Fulton and the Grove. It was the first Victoria 200 after Alex was killed, so it was almost like a memorial race," he remembered. "And then there was a big wreck on lap 68—Alex's number. I was able to avoid it but it took out half the field."

Racing historian and former Fulton PR man Doug Zupan vividly remembered Pauch's $20,000 1997 rout. "He came from dead last to the lead in 68 laps. And from there, he absolutely obliterated the field," Zupan said. "Billy was running his own line—no one else could run there, right up against the wall in the turns; so close that every lap he'd brush the wall with his nerf bars. Anyone watching from over in turn three said he was throwing sparks! He was on his own planet. No one was even close."

Yet, the race wasn't without controversy. "When I went through tech afterwards, Danny Johnson's father was there, bitching and moaning that my wind sails were too high.

After a three-year absence, Billy returned in 1997 to claim his sixth Vic.

I hadda get back in the car, and when I got in the car it made it legal," Pauch said, shrugging off the confrontation. "Danny finished second, so they hadda scream about something to try to win."

Over the years, Fulton continued to change hands. Once the biggest bohemian outlaw show in the region, the Vic got swallowed by the DIRT establishment. In 2008, the race was moved to Utica-Rome—although purists insist it was never the same after it left Fulton. At the end, it was incongruously watered down to a 40-lap minor event under the now-defunct KOD banner. In 2018, the Victoria 200 disappeared from the schedule.

Through all those 30-something seasons…and all the iterations of the event…and the hundreds of drivers who competed and took their shot at it…Billy Pauch still is, and always will be, the all-time winner of the Vic.

How does Pauch explain his incredible success at Fulton, a track that's four-and-a-half hours from home; a track he only visited once a year?

He thought about that. "To be honest with you, when we went up to Fulton for the 200 every year, it would be like Flemington's 200—it would always be a different track. It'd be slicker or different than what we ran all year," he analyzed. "That would always throw me off at Flemington. And it would throw off all the regulars up there.

"And I think the biggest thing was I'd run around the top, get a momentum going up there. Just keep my momentum up. The track was so slippery, the other guys couldn't get a hold of it, they'd all be slow on the bottom. I'd be like *WHIRRR!*—keep rolling around out there," Billy considered. "Won with three or four different cars up there. Different teams and stuff. Different chassis. I don't know, it just seemed to work. A big part of it was luck."

But his friend Frank Cozze knows better than to chalk it up to any caprice of chance. "You know how Billy was when he'd get on a roll," he resolved. "When he'd get on a roll—how could you stop him?"

ART RUPPERT

DAVID

14.

RoC

Make no mistake about it: dirt or asphalt, the old Flemington Fair Speedway was a supreme challenge, to say the least.

As a dirt track, it was all hang-on-for-dear-life momentum.

"The most challenging track I've ever been on," asserted Stan Ploski, "The Polish Prince" of Flemington in the 1970s, before The Kid came along and knocked him off the perch. The speedway's unique square shape dictated a very different driving strategy, as Ploski explained.

It was all about trying to turn the square track into a more traditional circle.

"Kind of like a diamond," Ploski described the line you needed to run. "Most of the guys back then hung on the bottom. The only way to get around them was on the outside. So I'd follow 'em in the corner and just hang back about half a car length, so when they went into the turn and braked a little bit, I was already up alongside 'em. I had the car already turned so I could diamond off the corner. At that point," he said, "nine times out of ten, I had them already passed."

The technique required driver control and a considerable amount of daredevil confidence as the car would be hanging sideways, up against the outside rail, at least halfway around the track.

"Brakes?" Stan scoffed. "I didn't use any brakes at all!"

After the track was paved in late 1990, it became even more demanding to drive.

"It's so different. It's unorthodox," Ray Evernham warned top paved-track talent Tony Siscone, prior to a Goodyear tire test in preparation for the speedway's asphalt debut.

"We were used to going down in the corner—you'd lift, you'd brake and you'd dump the throttle again," Siscone described the driving approach at most paved ovals. "At Flemington, you would roll out of the throttle until about half-pedal—no brake going into the corner! The *slowest* you were going there was probably 100 miles an hour. Down the straightaways, I know we were going 138-140 miles an hour. You really had to be on your game, it was so fast."

All that speed took a real physical toll on a driver. "On dirt, when you go down in the corner and throw the car in there—your body's going with the car, the car's sliding," Tony detailed. "On blacktop, you go in and the car has grip, there's total traction. You're not sliding. So the lateral G-forces against your body—*oh, man...*"

The Flemington square: dirt or asphalt, it was a handful.

ACE LANE JR.

Billy Pauch was the undisputed King of the Hill on the Flemington clay—but this was a very different deal.

"I didn't take too well to it at first," Billy acerbically admitted. "When Flemington paved, I tried it for a year and almost killed myself."

Looking back, it was an upheaval that rated around 8.5 on the Richter scale. Until 1991, Pauch was *the man* at Flemington: all-time winningest driver, eight-time Modified champion, a winner in Sprints, big- and small-block Mods, Sportsman, Late Models, Modified Sprints and Micro Stocks. He'd started Pit Stop Tire Service, a speed shop business that serviced the track. He ran driving schools on the dirt.

Then, Flemington was paved—and everything Billy had built up over the years went bust overnight.

That first year on pavement, "the Troyer cars were hot; we were in Olsens. The Hoosier tires were hot; we were on McCrearys. What had worked on dirt wasn't the combination on asphalt—and that left me out in the cold," Pauch bitterly abided.

"I guess if it wasn't a track I'd won 100-plus races on as dirt, it wouldn't have bothered me as much. But it was a track I was so accustomed to. I loved it when it was dirt. There was nothing like running Flemington—a flat-out, all-around track; so many grooves and crossovers you could use on a guy to beat him! It wasn't there on blacktop."

The crashes were harder. The toll on equipment was greater. The fun was wrung out of it. "It wasn't my kind of driving, and I had no more business going there. The tire business was shot out the window, the driving schools, everything kinda went down the drain," Billy brooded.

"As far as making money, I wasn't. And I do it to make money," he reminded. "We won seven races there on the blacktop, so it wasn't like I left a loser. But I wasn't happy with that style of racing, so I just left."

Fast forward to Friday, October 22, 1993, qualifying day for the 43rd running of the Race of Champions at Flemington—an event circled in red on every NASCAR Mod team's schedule.

"I was in the shower that morning and my wife hollers up the stairs—'Flemington Speedway's on the phone, and they want to know if you want to drive,'" Billy remembered. He yelled back: "What car?" A pause. "Mario Fiore's 44."

He was dressed and out the door in a flash.

Fiore, owner of one of the top teams on the tour, was in a bind. His primary driver,

The 44 crew scrambles to make adjustments.

Mike Stefanik, was committed to appear at an off-track promotion for the sponsor of his Busch North ride. So the previous weekend at Thompson, Mario had tapped his former driver Doug Heveron for Flemington's RoC show. Only Heveron got his signals mixed: he thought the event kicked off on Saturday. When he was a no-show for Friday's qualifying, panic set in.

Pauch was on the way, but the Fiore team wasn't all that happy about it.

"Oh, great," Mario groaned. "I'm gonna have someone drive my race car that I don't even know—and he's a *dirt driver* on top of it! Just wonderful!"

Pauch, also, had his misgivings. "I didn't know those guys. I hadn't run asphalt all year," he worried. "But I knew that was a really good car. I knew that car could win races."

It began with a bang. "So I go up there and warm it up. Got up to speed pretty quick. I think it was in the heat race—remember that dip getting into three? Well, I hit it and the car spun and I crashed it," Billy recounted.

"Him being a dirt guy, Mario thought we should free the car up. Unfortunately for Billy, it was way too free and we got in that big wreck in the heat with I think it was Brian Scisco," crew member Rich "Haskell" Lavalette remembered.

"It was really tore up. We were worried we hurt the motor because we broke a valve cover and ripped the header off." Once the team got into it, they realized the damage wasn't

Said Tony Siscone, of the late pit stop that won the race: "Mario made an unbelievable call. He knew the game."

MARIO FIORE COLLECTION

as bad as they'd thought. "So we're getting the thing back together," Haskell said.

And they asked Pauch, "Whaddaya need?"

"I know I need you to tighten this thing up!" he promptly answered.

Mario's guys were contrite. "We thought you were a dirt guy and you'd want it freed up."

Billy gave them all a long look. "Buddy," he addressed Haskell, "there ain't no cushion on asphalt!"

They finished up repairs at Pauch's shop. Qualified through the last chance race the next day. The car would line up 43rd—next to last—in Sunday's main event.

Billy was well aware just how tough it would be. The race was 250 laps, far longer than any distance he'd run before, on a backbreaker of a track.

"Flemington was like a big circle—it would really wear your ass out," Pauch allowed. To push back against the punishing G-forces, he kept his helmet pressed upright against a side headrest, and strapped his left leg to the roll cage with a seat belt, so it couldn't be shoved onto his throttle foot during the race.

"So we're out there running the race, and I get up to about the 200-lap mark, and I told 'em I just couldn't get no more out of it—the car's too tight, I'm pushing. I just can't get it to turn," Billy recalled.

Mario and crew told him to pit during the next caution, which was on lap 211. They put new right-side tires on the car, made a chassis adjustment, and stood back to watch the final laps play out.

Tony Siscone had a front-row seat for all of it. "Mike Ewanitsko was leading, and I'm battling with him and Reggie Ruggiero. And the three of us were out of tires," Tony said. "So we're slipping and sliding—all waiting for one or the other to make a mistake so we could gain position. I was thinking, *maybe I could win this thing!*"

Siscone was at war with Ruggiero in the waning laps. "I'm trying to get by Reggie, and he's getting really loose, and I'm trying to make a move and get under him. And then I look in the mirror and see this red car coming. And I'm thinking, *who the hell is this?*"

The flash of color Siscone spotted down the backstretch was Mario's 44. And Pauch, on fresh rubber, was making his move.

"We go down into the next corner, and I go outside of Reggie because he was

Pauch was as surprised as anyone when he pulled into victory lane.

ACE LANE JR.

protecting the bottom. And all of a sudden, it was like—*whoosh!*" Siscone outlined the ambush. "It actually scared the hell out of me. I just couldn't believe he was that fast. I'm like—*where the hell did he come from?*"

"I think it was 5 to go, I was fifth. Reggie Ruggiero, one of the Fuller brothers and Tony Siscone—they were second, third and fourth. I came rolling into three, and I rolled right by all of 'em but Reggie—he started to come back down and we bumped a little bit, which he wasn't too happy about—but I got by him," Pauch proclaimed.

At that point, "Ewanitsko had about 10 car lengths on us; he was in a good place," Siscone said of the race leader. "Hell, Billy just tracked him down in like a lap and a half. I've seen the video. He just swooped in—could go anywhere he wanted. We were all white-knuckled, hanging on."

Especially Ewanitsko, who was nursing a broken coil-over. "I caught him coming around for the white flag and passed him," Pauch remembered. "I didn't know who was leading or what. I came around and took the checkered flag and they're telling me, 'You won!' And I'm like—*really?*"

The grandstands erupted like Krakatoa: their hometown dirt-track hero, pinch-hitting in a car he'd never even seen before, had just beaten every big name, all the stars in the NASCAR Modified firmament. Until the day he died, in 2016, Mario Fiore would

Car owner Mario Fiore (second from right) hangs on to the coveted RoC owner's cup as the crew and driver cut loose in victory lane.

maintain that the RoC win with Pauch was the most thrilling achievement of his career as a car owner.

Pleased as he was, Billy took it in stride. "They're all asphalt people—they don't know me," the driver snickered. "They're all like, 'Billy Pauch? Who's he?'"

Tony Siscone, who finished third in that race in Dick Barney's iconic "Big Red," a car that Billy would later drive after Tony's retirement, has said he became a Pauch fan that day.

Twenty years later, Siscone was invited to make an appearance and sign posters at a "Legends of the Track" event at New Egypt Speedway, where he was the 1983 Modified champion on the asphalt.

Following the autograph session, Tony tried to coax his wife Margi into staying to watch the race.

"My wife was always supportive, but after I quit racing, she could care less," Siscone stated. "She was like, 'Do we have to?'"

Tony convinced her to stay, and told Margi to keep an eye on Billy Pauch.

"I think it was a 50-lapper. And there was a rut developing in the third turn. It gets down to 15 to go, they're all running single-file through three and four. So I guess Billy decides to hell with it, he's going to go to the outside and run through that rut," he framed the story from that night.

"Billy goes in there, he gets up on two wheels for a moment, comes back down, and passes two guys going through three and four. So now every lap, Billy's going through this big rut. Margi's got her fingernails in my thigh and she's screaming—*'My God, he's going to flip over!'*

"I think he either won it or finished second. But in any event, it was exciting as all hell. So as we're walking out, I said to Margi, 'That wasn't so bad, was it?'"

Mrs. Siscone didn't hesitate. "I'd come back and watch that again!"

GRACIE RYAN

15.

Winging It

That Billy had equal success in Modifieds and Sprints, beating the best of both worlds, is contrary to the laws of nature.

Car owner Glenn Hyneman tried to explain the conundrum. "Sprint Cars run off their left-rear wheel—the wing *makes* 'em run off the left-rear wheel. Modifieds run off the right-rear wheel. When you jump back and forth between those two, that's a huge difference," he said. In chassis set-up. In driving style. *In everything.*

Pauch remembered when he first ran Hyneman's 410 Sprint in 1990, "I was running out there rolled up on the right-rear, and the Sprint Car guys are looking at that like I'm *crazy!* They're telling me, 'You better do something with that or you're gonna get hurt!'" he said of the learning curve. "Until they got the car set up to where it would lay left, I didn't know any better. I was out there rolled right and driving my ass off, trying to beat those guys."

It's like a right-handed batter trying to hit lefty—the stance, the approach is completely different, at odds with every instinct ingrained since birth. Those who can bat from both sides of the plate are a rare breed. In professional baseball, less than 10 percent of players can productively switch-hit.

"But Billy could do it—at the same track on the same day!" Hyneman attested.

Actually, it was the prospect of two paychecks—at the same track on the same day, always a plus—

Billy started out in the winged ranks pulling double-duty at Flemington in Joe Fiore Jr.'s URC Sprinter.

MEL STETTLER

that first put Pauch into a Sprint Car. Starting in 1987, on nights when the traveling URC club would visit Flemington, Billy would climb in Joe Fiore Jr.'s Trostle Sprinter and pull double-duty. For a part-timer like Fiore, it just made sense to tap Pauch. Who better knew the lay of the land?

"When you do it like I do, on a limited basis, you know you're gonna have to come from the back. So you go with someone who can start in the rear, get to the front, and take care of the equipment at the same time," reasoned Fiore, whose past driver roster includes names like Buckley, Balough, Tobias and Fitzcharles. "Not everyone has that gift."

A 410 Sprint win at Flemington in October 1990 with Glenn Hyneman.

Pauch picked up three wins and a half-dozen top five finishes for Fiore in 18 starts at Flemington in '88 and '89, and made a few random appearances in Bill Brian's 16 on the Pennsy side of the border.

And then, his Modified car owner, Glenn Hyneman, had an earth-altering epiphany.

After partnering with Pauch to score 73 wins and five championships in just two seasons, including Mod biggies in six states and all manner of media honors—Hyneman decided to go Sprint Car racing.

"I grew up with all these Sprint Car tracks around me—Port Royal and Susquehanna, Lincoln and Williams Grove," the Pennsy-based owner offered as explanation. Hyneman had dabbled in URC with Craig Von Dohren, determined he didn't care for club racing. He wanted the full-blown, fire-breathing 410 experience.

So in 1989, he hired Dave Kelly and committed to Williams Grove on Friday nights. "At that time, Billy really wasn't into the Sprint Cars as much, which is probably why I didn't go further with him with that," said Glenn, who put Pauch into good hands with Modified owner Peter Chesson.

Even as Billy was setting the Modified world afire in Chesson's Barker Bus 76, the relationship continued: Glenn still fielded a small-block for Pauch in '89, and in 1990 he had him in a Sprint Car—part-time only, of course, as the guns-blazing Mod effort took precedence. Billy's first win in a 410 Sprinter came in Glenn's 126 that summer at Susky.

"I don't remember why we got away from the Sprint Car with Glenn," said Pauch, who admitted, "I don't know if I was really all that crazy about Sprint Cars."

Nonetheless, when car owner John Zemaitis called in late August of '92, asking him to run a second Sprinter to team driver Bobby Weaver in a Thunder on the Hill special at Grandview, Billy accepted. And promptly went out and won the race. *Bam.*

"In a Sprint Car, at that time anyway, nobody got around Grandview better than Billy," Zemaitis noticed. "So that's how it started—as a one-race deal."

Pauch ran a few more TOTH shows for the Zemco team that year, and made a couple of promising season-end starts in big events at Delaware and Hagerstown, where he walked away with the Modified portion of the programs.

"On the way back from Hagerstown, we stopped at a Bob Evans and ironed everything out for the following year," crew chief Tommy Carl recalled.

Wingless for a USAC race at Big Diamond.

MEL STETTLER

Zemco was looking for a primary driver. But that was a big commitment for Pauch.

"John flew down and picked me up in his airplane. We flew up to Tower City to go look at the cars and the whole operation. It was pretty impressive," Billy conceded. "So I'm like—maybe I need a new challenge. *Let's do this.* I took it on and starting running for them in '93."

Back up a bit, two years or so, to better understand all that transpired to influence Pauch's decision. From 1987 through 1990, he had driven exclusively for two of the most well-appointed teams in Modified racing. Then, Glenn Hyneman segued into

Billy and John hash it out on top of the trailer.

JACK KROMER

Sprint Car racing on a much more limited basis; and Pete Chesson's Modified team crumbled in a controversial cauldron of legal troubles. And to cap it off, Billy's home track, Flemington, was black-topped. So in 1991, he was literally starting over, piecing together a full-time Modified effort with remnants of Chesson's operation and help from owner Ray Carroll, Tabloid Graphics and some minor sponsors.

"It was a challenge, after being with owners who could afford to do it for four or five years, and then trying to do it mostly on your own, with nothing going for you," Billy considered. "I was getting by, doing good... But well, maybe I needed to try something different, y'know?"

Signing on with the Sprints, though, meant sacrificing one of his bread-and-butter Modified tracks—East Windsor, where he won 14 feature races in '92 and a career-high 18 in '91, including nine in a row. He certainly wouldn't be able to stack up those kind of stats at Williams Grove on Friday nights.

"It's hard when you're a winner to be a loser. But I'm gonna do it. I may get my ass kicked, but I'm gonna try," Pauch resolved at the time.

"I'd probably be the top driver if I won a handful at the Grove. And I'm not crazy about Sprint Cars, but then again, I think I can drive them as good as anybody," he allowed. Billy went on to outline his rationale. "Maybe it was security: I was waiting for

BOB YURKO

A big CRA win at Grandview in 1993, the first full year the team was together.

MEL STETTLER

the right deal to come along, with somebody who could afford to race. I wanted to knock one night a weekend off where I was a bag man—I could carry a bag in, the car would be ready, it would be good equipment and I could just drive it. That was one of the decisions.

"The other decision was dollars and cents. I'd get more shows in. If I didn't take the ride, somebody else would have it. I wouldn't have a ride for the Thunder on the Hill series, I wouldn't be going to Florida for a week, I wouldn't be running a month earlier with the Sprints until the Modifieds opened up. And all the special shows," he calculated, toting up the extra cash on the line.

"The purses were far better in the Sprint Cars," John Zemaitis pointed out. "He knew he could make a lot more money in a Sprint Car—and during that time period, he did.

"Because the more it paid—the harder he drove," Zemaitis astutely zeroed in on Billy's trip-trigger. "At any of the big money shows, you just knew that when you got to the track. He'd be more conscious of everything, up on the trailer, watching what everybody else was doing. *Really* paying attention. And then he'd go out and drive his ass off."

Fred Rahmer, who raced Mods against Billy before he quit stock cars dead-cold and crafted a world-class Hall of Fame Sprint Car career, gave Pauch props. "If Billy Pauch finished second to you—you had a good night," Rahmer affirmed his respect. "He's probably one of the best, if not the best, racers I ever drove against on a weekly deal. One of the fiercest competitors.

"And if it was for more money? He was another notch up. You could actually *see* him run harder for more money—which I never understood because he ran hard before." Fred shook his head. "I can say this for a fact: whether it was in a Modified or a Sprint Car, if Billy was there, you'd better be looking over your shoulder. That's the way it was."

Straddling the divide between Mod and Sprint Car terrain, it didn't take Pauch long to acclimate in '93, his first full season with the Zemco team. By June, he was in the winner's circle at Williams Grove—impossible for a first-time regular at that mercilessly-held PA Posse command post. By season's end, he'd won four more times, including an upset against the CRA non-winged warriors at Grandview in May.

"We had never run wingless before. Billy was probably a little more accustomed to that, racing the Modified all those years," Zemco's Tommy Carl deliberated. "But it was still a different animal."

Ferocious rivals: Freddy Rahmer and Billy go toe-to-toe at Path Valley.

ART RUPPERT

Billy backed it in the wall at Syracuse in 1993. He redeemed himself—in spades—the following year.

MEL STETTLER

To get dialed in, they brought the car to one of Pauch's early season driving schools at Grandview, kept making adjustments in between student runs in Billy's class cars.

"We'd try something, talk about how the car acted, discuss what to do, and he gradually got to where he liked the feel of the car," said Zemaitis. "But as we kept making changes to make it easier for him to drive and more comfortable—the lap times got slower! So we tried other things, went in different directions. The car got a lot harder to drive but it got faster and faster."

Pauch didn't hesitate. "Make the car the fastest you can," he told John. "I'll learn to drive it that way."

"And he did," Zemaitis bottom-lined. "Of course, Billy adjusts very, very quickly. A few laps and he knows what he's gotta do to run in a fast groove."

1994 started off on a high note, with an All Star win in Florida at East Bay. Back home, Billy dropped another night a week from his Modified schedule, committing to the Zemco team on Fridays at the Grove and Saturdays at Selinsgrove. The early season went great guns: three wins at Williams Grove and four at his new Saturday night stop, to add to the February Florida score.

Ted Johnson might've shaken Billy's hand but he was not happy.

BOB YURKO

And then came the World of Outlaws Sprint Supernationals at the Syracuse mile, where the team did it all. Fast time—so quick, in fact, that the 144.590 lap blitzed the existing world record speed on a closed dirt course. Best appearing car and crew. And a gauntlet-down win that put the Sprint Car world—promoter Ted Johnson's universe—into a state of shock.

"I always contributed running Selinsgrove to helping me win Syracuse—you ran flat-out at Syracuse, you ran flat-out at Selinsgrove," was Pauch's takeaway.

The upset didn't sit well with the Outlaws: Ted

Johnson came unglued, demanding the Zemco 1 be torn apart. *"That car's gotta be checked! It must be illegal!"* It was, after all, the only time all year that an outsider managed to steal an Outlaw paycheck.

"We were planning to go to the race at Rolling Wheels after that, but with the tech they did on our car—tearing everything apart—there was no way we could get it back together in time," Zemaitis said. "They really must've thought we were cheating, the way they tore everything apart—we had to take a head off and everything! Nobody does that; they just pump it."

While Pauch and team were the focus of Ted's wrath, DIRT promoter Glenn Donnelly was crowing, taking credit that one of "his boys" beat the Outlaws. "I almost think Donnelly stood up for me," was Billy's sardonic remark, "which is the first time *that* ever happened!"

During the next four years, Pauch and the Zemco team continued to click, despite downtime for two serious injuries—a badly broken arm at Knoxville in 1995 and a shattered kneecap suffered at the Grove in '98—that forced Billy to the sidelines.

Master mechanic Davey Brown discusses setups with John and Billy.

CHAZ TORNETTA

Returning after the knee injury at the end of '98, "he came back with a passion," Zemaitis testified. "Billy was going to prove that he didn't lose anything. And he didn't. His ability was probably even *better* than it was prior to that. He *hadda* prove he's not afraid of those Sprint Cars."

From late August on, Pauch pretty much won everything there was to win. Won Williams Grove his first night back in the Sprint Car. Won an All Star TOTH show at Grandview. Won Grandview's Freedom 76 in the Modified for the fifth time. Won Hagerstown's $10,000 Octoberfest in the Sprinter.

Billy and the Zemco team dominated the Grove's National Open in 1998.

And he won the Holy Grail of the Pennsy 410 Sprint circuit: the National Open.

It's a race so soaked in history it's just dripping prestige, with Indianapolis 500 winner Gordon Johncock, USAC standout Larry Dickson, Weld, Wolfgang, the Kinsers, Swindell all among the weighty index of winners. Every principal Posse power-player wants his name on that list. Heck, National Sprint Car Hall of Famer Fred Rahmer flat-out called it a career right in victory lane when he finally won the elusive thing in 2013, after 28 years of trying.

For sure, it was a big deal for the Zemco team to win the Open the way they did in '98—setting fast time, leading from lap 3 to the finish. Yet, all of them—Billy, John, Tommy—suppose that there's an asterisk next to the victory: the original date was rained out and the WoO travelers couldn't return for the rescheduled event.

"I guess it never meant as much to any of us because it was a rain date and it didn't have as full a field as it normally had," Zemaitis acknowledged. "There were still a lot of outsiders there, guys from Ohio and other places, a lot more competition than there was on a regular week at Williams Grove. But not those few cars that were always on the top of the Outlaw roster."

Pauch agreed. "It's a big one. But I didn't have to run the Outlaws so it wasn't as tough as it could have been, to be honest."

"I don't think anything touches Syracuse," Tommy Carl put it in perspective. "All the Outlaws were there—they *owned* that place. And Syracuse paid over $25,000. It's still Billy's biggest win, financially."

Lots of success stories. But there was a stream of unrest seething beneath the surface.

"When I got hurt in '98, John was going to park the car. And I said, nah, put somebody else in there—we always seemed to fall off during the summer months, see if somebody else can tell us where we're lacking, y'know?" Billy recounted.

So the team tapped Kevin Gobrecht as seat-filler. "He did pretty good, and when I came back in the fall, instead of getting rid of him, they had two cars. And they kept Gobrecht into '99."

Teammates Pauch and Gobrecht.

Two Type A personalities in the driver's seat is one too many. There was tension during the Florida swing, where Billy won at East Bay and they both scored at Volusia, before Kevin destroyed a car in a fiery flip. When the team returned north, it only got worse.

"I'm not really observant about this stuff, but after we came back from Florida and went to Williams Grove, my kid told me the motor that was in my car was now in Gobrecht's car. So that wasn't real good," grumbled Pauch, who had motor problems at the Grove, losing oil pressure that week—and the next.

"They never fixed it. So they're changing the motor at the track, and I'm sitting in the truck. I was livid."

It kept escalating from there, every perceived slight being scrutinized for intent.

"That was Billy being a competitive person," Carl honestly assessed. "No driver wants a teammate."

Pee Wee, John and crew sweat out the end of a race.

MEL STETTLER

Pauch figured it was time to make a move. "So I called John that week and told him I'm done," he said. "At the time, Gobrecht was leaving to go with Blaney's deal, the 93. He was leaving, so I would have been the number one driver again—the *only* driver. But I was just mad. And maybe it was just time for me to get out of Sprint Cars."

Zemaitis hadn't seen it coming. "Right before the split, we had Kevin Gobrecht in another car. And I don't think Billy was happy with that, even though Kevin never got the good stuff and he didn't have Davey Brown helping him, at all. It surprised me, when he quit," John granted. "But he didn't leave to get in another Sprint Car. He said he was going to concentrate on the Modifieds again."

It was an opportune time to switch back: in '98, the Grosso family had salvaged New Egypt Speedway from the scrap heap, transforming the old asphalt quarter-miler into a postcard-pretty dirt track, paying good money. A lot of the old Flemington crowd—Pauch's people—started calling it home.

"That was the first year I started running New Egypt, in '99. I was doing good there,

Not a fun night at Volusia in 1998.

MEL STETTLER

winning races," Billy said. "I figured I'd been riding all the way up to Pennsylvania every week. I busted my knee, I busted my arm. It's like—maybe it's time to get out of Sprint Cars. I told John, 'I'm done with Sprints. I'm not gonna go out and look for another Sprint Car ride or nothin'.'"

But he kept getting sucked back in.

In June of that year, Fred Rahmer took his first poke at promoting, partnering with New Egypt to present a big 410 special—all Sprints, no heavies. Of course, it was in Rahmer's best interest to make sure the track's resident Mod kingpins, Billy Pauch and Kenny Brightbill, were in the field.

His first time in the J&M car at New Egypt in 1999.

JACK KROMER

Pauch was going to be there anyway: New Jersey Governor Christie Todd Whitman was scheduled to appear; Billy was taking the Gov for a spin in the two-seater Late Model he'd built for his driving school.

Although part-timers on the Pennsy Sprint scene, the J&M 55 team owned by Gene Jenkins and Scott Mertz had success with pickup drivers like Bobby Allen, Tim Shaffer, Daryn Pittman and other notables.

"They called me. I didn't know who the hell they were. But they wanted me to run their car in that Sprint Car race at New Egypt. When I walked into the pits, walked into their trailer that night, that's the first time I ever met those guys. First time I ever drove for them," Billy said. "And I won."

The understatement of the century: against the heaviest hitters in the PA Sprint lineup—guys like Hodnett and Dewease, Kreitz and Kauffman, as well as event promoter

Billy and Dave Blaney discuss the differences in Sprints and Modifieds.

MEL STETTLER

Rahmer, the Keystone State's winningest driver in 1999—Pauch just about swept the night. Flew from seventh to win his heat. Took the $300 dash. Came out on top in the $1,000 pole shuffle. And had a stunning straightaway lead when he aced the $3G main event. In a car he'd never seen before.

The second time he drove the 55, at Hagerstown's season-end Octoberfest, he won again. That was a big day, even by Billy's standards.

"I won the Sprint Car race, the small-block race and finished fourth in the big-block race. *In one day.* There weren't many guys who used to do that stuff—run three divisions in one day," noted Pauch, who banked $21,120 in total winnings. "The only thing I didn't run was the Late Models. They offered me a Late Model ride, but I said, nah, my plate's about full with 250 laps. I don't have to run *350* laps!"

Billy continued to run the 55 Sprinter sporadically, posting wins at Grandview in Thunder on the Hill winged and wingless events, and taking the TOTH title for J&M in 2001, his fifth crown in the series.

It was at Grandview that Pauch made his final triumphant score in a Sprint Car—and it was a doozy. On August 22, 2006, he climbed in Al Hamilton's legendary 77, sight unseen, a one-shot, last-minute deal. And he blew them all away. Hamilton was so impressed, he handed Billy the whole purse.

At the time, Pauch was pushing 50 years old.

In a moment of retrospect, Zemco team manager Tommy Carl took measure of Billy's career. "He raced Modifieds for a long time—I forget how old he was when he started racing for us. But unfortunately, he missed a lot of years with Sprint Cars that would've been his prime years," Tommy observed. "I always felt that maybe we got Billy a little late in his career.

"If Billy had started off in Sprint Cars? You'd be talking about him and Steve Kinser together. I think that Billy was that kind of talent," he determined. "That's my personal opinion."

It's not only Carl's viewpoint.

In Pennsylvania, where Sprint Car racing ranks above religion and politics in people's closely-held beliefs, news venues like Harrisburg's *The Patriot-News* have been reporting on the sport since the first wheel turned. To that end, journalist Jeremy Elliott compiled a list of Central PA's best Sprint Car drivers in the past 30 years, first published in 2013 and updated six years later.

Pauch called Al Hamilton's 77 "one of the best cars I've ever driven."

MEL STETTLER

In the latest ranking, Elliott still rates Billy Pauch 12th on the list, pointing to his 59 Sprint Car victories, including big scores in the 1994 Syracuse Nationals and the '98 National Open, and commenting: "Pauch had wins at Williams Grove, Selinsgrove, Port Royal and Susquehanna Speedway, despite his part-time status. It's hard to imagine what his numbers would have been if he had dedicated all of his efforts to the class."

Zemco's Tommy Carl—who's worked with drivers like Danny Lasoski and Kasey Kahne over the years—also gave thought to where Pauch stands in the big scheme of things.

"Billy could drive anything. But he never fully dedicated himself to Sprints, so I can't say that he was the best Sprint Car driver I've ever had. He's certainly right there," Tommy analyzed, naming Stevie Smith as his top talent. "But Stevie did nothing but drive Sprint Cars his whole life," he underscored that point. "Stevie Smith is the best *Sprint Car* driver we've ever had.

"But I always felt that Billy is the best *race car* driver we ever had in the car."

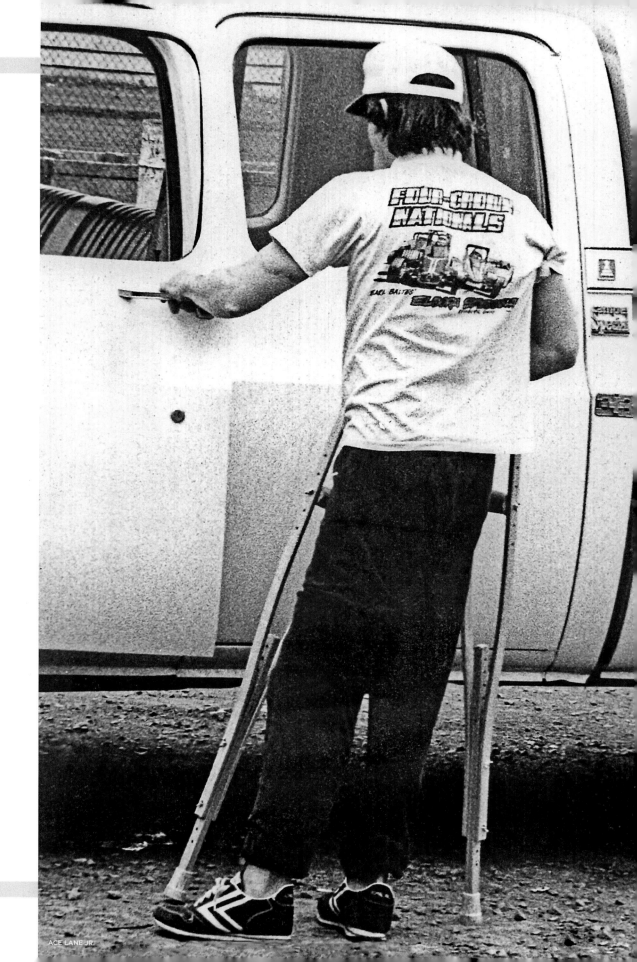

ACE LANE JR.

16.

Playing Hurt

"Billy is the most tenacious driver you will ever meet," a long-time friend observed. "He has this burning desire to win because, when all is said and done, he doesn't want to disappoint *himself*."

That intractable "refuse to lose" mindset has taken its toll on Pauch—not just mentally, but physically as well.

In 1985, a hot streak he'd started in Florida came to a drop-dead stop in late April at Penn National, compliments of a brutal crash that destroyed the D.A. Hanson Mod Pauch was piloting—a hit so violent the impact all but knocked off his kneecap.

Unconscious at the scene, Billy was cut out of the car and brought to Hershey Medical Center, where he withstood two-and-a-half hours of surgery to wire his kneecap back into position. He was released from the hospital some five days later, still in a lot of pain, with a hard cast from his foot to his groin.

Doctors called for physical therapy once the cast came off and a lengthy convalescence, predicting Billy would be sidelined for months, at a minimum.

Even crippling around on crutches, Pauch would have none of it.

"There wasn't much going on because Billy wasn't racing. I was up at the shop one night, doing something in the back room," said Dave DeBlasio, who owned the 5 Modified with his brother Al. "Billy comes in, he puts his crutches down and gets in the car. He's sticking halfway out! He says to me, 'If we put a hole here and move the brake pedal out, I think I can drive this.'"

They secretly worked all week to modify the car: cut a hole in the firewall to accommodate the driver's unbendable wired-up leg, moved and adjusted the brake pedal and hooked up a hand clutch assembly. A scant four weeks following the horrific accident, Pauch crammed himself back in the cockpit.

"He knew he was going to do this since Tuesday, but he didn't tell me until today," Billy's wife Barbara sighed that Saturday at Flemington. "I guess he thought I'd try to talk him out of it. But he was bound and determined. I can't hold him back; I just have to encourage him. I can't let him go out there, thinking he's gonna get hurt."

Racing injured didn't seem to impede the momentum: On June 1, Pauch was back in victory lane. By year's end, he had added another 20 wins to the four he'd picked up in the early season, and rebounded to claim the '85 Flemington Modified title—despite missing four shows.

He's gotten more than his share of hurt in his career.

In '83, Pauch suffered serious burns, racing Tony Sesely's Modified in the Delaware State Championships. "I was running up front in the feature, maybe third, and the car was running hot." Billy tried to signal Tony that it was overheating, "but he's motioning me to keep going." A few more laps and the top radiator hose blew off and came back through the throttle opening. "It blew and then I turned in the infield, spun the car and jumped out," Pauch winced. "The hot water scalded my left leg, from my knee to my ankle. They took me to the hospital. Had to put that white cream on and rewrap it every day. It was pretty nasty."

He was injured in Glenn Hyneman's 410 Sprint at Lincoln in 1990. "Billy flipped onto the first turn wall pretty hard and his knee hit the steering box," Hyneman recollected. "He hurt his knee pretty bad."

Sticker in the cockpit of the Zemco Sprinter.

"Coming down the frontstretch, I was gonna go around Donnie Kreitz. And I went to the outside of him, and he went to go to the outside of somebody else— when he moved up, it caught me and flipped me," Billy distinctly remembered that one. "You ball up in the fetal position and hope for the best. I was sitting on my head, cage first into oncoming traffic."

Pauch was warming up the Zemco Sprinter at Knoxville in '95 when something—track debris, a clump of mud, maybe a quick-change gear—shot into the cockpit. "I was coming down the backstretch, it was late in the day and the sun was in my eyes. And I just seen the side panel flare up. When it did, my arm started hurting and when I looked over, it was broke," he narrated. "I knew it right away: my arm was going downhill and back up where the bones were broke. It hurt like hell, too.

"I got out of the groove, rode around to three and four, stopped at the crossover gate. They came out with the ambulance—an old Dodge ambulance with no air

Billy was limping after he smacked the wall at Syracuse in 1979, in one of his first outings in Joe Scamardella's 121.

ACE LANE JR.

conditioning and it was hot as hell. *Jesus*," Billy described. "They didn't even have a hospital—they took me to like a first aid or a doctor's office or something. I don't know what you'd call it. Took me there and they wrapped me up and got another ambulance to take me to a hospital in Des Moines. That's where they operated on it."

The surgeon on call told him he'd broken both bones between his wrist and his elbow. "Snapped 'em both," Pauch confirmed. "They put in plates and screws to hold 'em together."

All that hardware remains in his right arm, a little reminder of the Knoxville ordeal. "I never had 'em taken out. I don't like to volunteer for stuff, y'know?" Billy regarded. "They really don't bother me. Figure you take 'em out, the arm'll be a little more sensitive 'cause it would be like Swiss cheese with all the screw holes in it."

In early 1998, he flipped the Zemco Sprint Car in the third turn at Williams Grove: another bad break.

"Busted my kneecap. They sent me to Harrisburg, told me it was busted, this, this and that. Asked me what I wanted to do," Pauch recalled. "With my first knee injury at Penn National, I went to Hershey Medical and I thought they did a good job, so I said I wanted to go there. I forget who I was with, but they drove me down to Hershey and they operated.

"That one was pretty bad: they were almost gonna take my kneecap out because it was shattered." Billy shivered. "They managed to wire it and screw it and pin it all back together. I sat out for a couple months or something. Came back at the end of the year and won everything—won Grandview, won the National Open, won Hagerstown. Just like after the time I got hurt at Penn National—I came back pretty good."

The Comeback Kid: nothing could keep him down, put him out of commission for very long. He was never afraid to go fast, never worried about the consequences. But Pauch definitely gave pause to the Flemington pavement.

Up and over: the 1998 crash at Williams Grove landed Billy back at Hershey Medical Center with a shattered kneecap.

AARN ARCHIVES

"I think the hardest I ever crashed was at Flemington on asphalt," Billy said. "Me and Doug Hoffman got together coming through three and four. Turned my car, went straight out into the wall. Between the time we hit and I hit the wall, I thought I was dead...

"I hit so hard, it pulled the seat ahead, the crotch belt got me, I got stitches in my chin from hitting the cowling," he cringed, reliving the point-blank impact that put him in the ER. "When you crashed at Flemington, you crashed hard. You were *flying* around there—doing 120 on dirt; on asphalt, it was unbelievable.

"I've flipped in Sprint Cars,

One of the hardest crashes Billy ever survived was on the Flemington pavement in July 1991. The car was split in two.

flipped in Modifieds, but man, I hit the wall hard there that night."

What Billy always felt was his big shot was derailed at Flemington on Saturday, August 3, 1996, when he got caught up in a crash that jammed his right hand into the steering wheel of Dick Barney's asphalt Modified—breaking, as Pauch's son described, "the bone that makes my dad's hand close."

ER ADVICE:

"They bring you in the hospital, they push on you, they ask you where it hurts. After the first time, I learned: the interns asked me where it hurt. I told 'em, here, here and here. And don't touch it or I'll punch you!"

Initially, Billy refused to accept the setback. He had worked hard to secure a ride in a NASCAR Craftsman Truck and was scheduled to make his division debut at Flemington the next week. Come hell or high water, he was not going to miss that opportunity. Trying to convince himself that it was only a sprain, Pauch stubbornly trekked to Maryland the day after the wreck, to drive the Zemco Sprinter in a World of Outlaws event at Hagerstown. He toughed it through qualifying, but was forced out of the feature when the hand became too swollen to continue.

On Monday, doctors confirmed what Billy already knew. Reluctantly, he gave the Truck team his anguished regrets, then sat out a scheduled WoO race at Grandview. Tuesday, Pauch saw the same orthopedic specialist who'd treated the arm he'd badly broken at Knoxville a year earlier. The physician was blunt: the hand was broken; if Billy didn't want to risk further damage to it, he'd have to sit out the next couple of months. If he didn't, there was a possibility of permanent disability that would eventually require major surgery to correct: a piece of hipbone would have to be removed to replace the bone in his hand.

At that point, Pauch threw in the towel. All the television coverage, all the national exposure, all the chances were gone, all gone. It was early August. The big-paying shows were still to come. Knoxville, in fact, was the week after the Truck race. As a guy who butters his bread with race-track winnings, it was almost too much to bear. Pauch wanted desperately to compete but he couldn't. So he tuned out the entire world and settled into a deep blue depression.

He was in that state—optionless, beaten down and bitterly disappointed—when David Quier called on Thursday.

Pauch walked away unscathed from this vicious flip in Bill Brian's car at Grandview. Said Billy: "I'm tough."

"He was a fan we'd met once at a truck stop," Barbara remembered. "He read about Billy getting hurt in the racing papers, and he told me he thought he could help him. Billy was so down at that point, I figured anything was worth a try."

Talk about divine intervention… Turned out Quier was a neuromuscular therapist who regularly administered to a diverse group of athletes and was, in addition, a world-class wrestler and weightlifter himself. On Thursday night, he drove from Hellertown, PA, to Billy's Frenchtown, NJ, home where he'd holed up. Quier examined the hand, pressed and prodded, while Pauch provided a detailed explanation of how the accident occurred and what he felt when it happened.

With an understanding of the injury, Quier quietly offered a solution: he would apply a homeopathic pain-relieving cream, then tape the hand and wrist in a way that would immobilize the broken bone and surrounding ligaments while allowing enough freedom of movement to drive. According to Quier, Billy could race—without risk of long-term damage if he was careful and followed instructions.

"All I did was give him hope," David later downplayed the meeting. In any case, "Billy was a new person, had all his confidence back, after Dave saw him," Barbara maintained. "He came out of the bedroom and immediately said, 'I'm going to race Williams Grove.'"

Call it new age medicine, call it alternative therapy, holistic massage, call it faith healing if you want. Whatever it was, it worked better than a heaven-hung miracle. On Friday night—less than a week after the accident—Quier met Pauch at Williams Grove, where he strategically taped the hand, left directions to ice it completely post-race, and proceeded to watch from the grandstands.

Now, the Grove is an absolute armful for any two-fisted man to tackle, let alone one with a busted paw. And hauling a full-throated Sprinter around that dirt half-mile ain't no picnic in the park. But Quier had given Pauch the hope to be in the hunt; coupled with the driver's

#1 RICHARD RUTLEDGE; #2-6 R. PHILLIPS

own dead-eyed determination, it was enough.

Not only did Pauch lap such notables as Lance Dewease and Todd Shaffer during the course of the 25-lap event, he managed to toss that baby right over the cushion coming around for the last lap, to pass Mark Richard and win for the Zemco team.

On Saturday, Pauch was a wistful spectator at Flemington's Craftsman Truck Series 200, watching someone else strap into the ride he'd been slated to steer. That was before he suited up, taped up (with help from Quier) and climbed into the NASCAR pavement Modified he'd been injured in a week earlier.

On that night, however, there were no hospital visits and no heartache. In front of

Doctor's orders: Billy ices his broken hand after winning the asphalt Modified race at Flemington.

MEL STETTLER

an overflow crowd estimated at 15,000, Pauch quickly brought the car to the lead from deep in the pack, and held off a hell-bent bid by his teammate and eight-time '96 winner John Blewett III, to score an emotional and popular second Flemington win of the season.

In victory lane ceremonies on both nights, Pauch publicly credited Quier. When traditional medicine had failed him, a fan out of the grandstands had read about Billy's plight and stepped forward to lay hands on him, easing his suffering. At Flemington, he hoisted his four-foot winner's trophy and handed it to Quier. "This is yours," Pauch told him. "You earned it."

When the hubbub subsided, David hesitantly explained that he didn't see it that way.

The safety crew helps Billy from the car after a wreck in Flemington's October 1996 Challenge of Champions.

ACE LANE JR.

"I owed him one," the therapist stated firmly, and then related a pretty amazing prequel to the story.

"My dad had race cars, so I was always involved when I was younger. Then I was away for about 10 years; and when I came back, all the drivers I had known and followed—Al Tasnady and the rest—were gone. And this kid, Billy Pauch, was winning everything in sight. I watched him win three features in one night at Flemington. When I went to Penn National, I saw him start on the pole and just walk away with it…

"In sports," Quier continued, "when one person dominates like that, it's usually an indication that the competition is lacking. And that lack of competition spoils the sport.

"As far as I was concerned, Billy Pauch made for bad racing and a boring show. And when my dad and I left Penn National that night, after he smoked everyone from the 'favorite' position on the pole, we just ran him down on the ride home, saying all kinds of awful things about him."

It was a long ride, as Quier recalled, because an accident on the PA Interstate had brought traffic to a standstill. Seems a van had crashed and caught fire up ahead. "When we finally got close enough to see what was going on, we saw that Billy and his crew had pulled their rig off the road. They were right in there, trying to get the man out of that burning van."

David flinched at the memory. "After all the things we'd just said and thought about Billy, I felt terrible…just terrible. That was when we started following him, as fans. And when I read that he'd gotten hurt and doctors told him he couldn't race—well, I knew that was my chance to make it up to him."

MIKE FELTENBERGER

D.A. HANSON REMEMBERS...

"In the mid '80s, I was racing down at Volusia with Bobby Gerhart Jr. and Billy was racing big-block. I heard he had nothing going on at Penn National. And you know me—I'm brazen, talk to everybody. Some people are shy and don't ask. But I ask!

I didn't know him at all! But I walked up to Billy and said, 'Hey, you wanta drive my car at Penn National?' He said, 'Yeah, I think you got some good stuff.'

That's how it started...

They always ran Easter Sunday at Penn National. Brand new Olsen, an orange car. We were running good—top five, seven, eight. We were in the mix. And you know how Penn National was—he got into a fracas, got turned around. And Randy Fortna and Mike Follweiler drove right through the cage.

That's how Billy got hurt. Took the top of the carburetor and the magneto right off the motor! Only raced the car the one time. Billy broke it in half!

Back then, I didn't know Billy from shit or Shinola—I mighta spoke 50 words to him in my life. He was never even at my shop! So I go in the hospital to see him—his leg's up in the air, he's hurt, his knee is all f'ed up. And he looks at me and says, 'D.A., we had a good car. We mighta won tonight.'

And I'll never forget this: laying in the hospital bed, all messed up, Billy says, 'Do you have the whereabouts to get another car?'

Years and years later, we were taking two cars to race Bridgeport. My wife Patty was just smitten with Billy—you know how wives are smitten by race car drivers? Y'know what I'm saying? So I'm taking one car and she's riding in the truck with Billy, hauling the other car.

Billy was wearing shorts and Patty looked over and said, 'Omigod, your knees are all tore up!'

And Billy laughed.

'Yeah, that's from D.A.'s car.'

Patty had no clue that it was my car that Billy got hurt in back in 1985!"

DAVE PRATT

17.
The Hill

Steely-spined Sprint Car ace Joey Saldana once likened racing at Grandview Speedway to "flying a jet fighter plane in a high school gymnasium."

He wasn't far off.

"I grew up there so I'm used to it," Craig Von Dohren considered. Over the past 40-some years, Von Dohren has done it all at Grandview: 12-time track champ, nine-time winner of the Forrest Rogers Memorial, five-time winner of the Freedom 76 biggie, all-time winningest driver in the Mod division. If anyone has a bead on the high-banked bullring on the hill, it's CVD. "But I still get butterflies going into that place," Craig confessed. "Other tracks, I don't. At Grandview, I always get butterflies. Nerve-racking. I don't know what it is about it…"

Everything about the track is extreme: the roller-coaster banking, the claustrophobic confines, the no-regard actions of wild-eyed competitors uncontrolled by any pretense of playing nice.

"Aggressive," sums up the attitude needed to survive there, as per Jeff Strunk, a 10-time Grandview champion and all-time winner of the '6er. "If you go there with a chip on

There were plenty of nights Billy got to pop the champagne—especially in the big-money shows.

MEL STETTLER

Three-wide at Grandview in 1993, with Pauch down low, Duane Howard in the middle and Jeff Strunk on the outside. You could only run so long like that before all hell would break loose.

your shoulder, you'll leave with a boulder on your shoulder! The Pennsylvania drivers in general are just rougher; the guys don't have the respect they should. It's just a tough place to race.

"I always called it hockey on wheels," said Strunk, before quickly amending that thought. "*Playoff* hockey!"

"Yeah, it's a contact place, that's for sure," Billy Pauch agreed. "They're not shy. The better guys you can race with. I didn't mind racing there at a DIRT show or something like that because they're running for points; they have to finish.

"But man, on a Saturday night it's a free-for-all!" he contended. "Like the coliseum with the gladiators, y'know? Beat on each other until the last guy's standing. And he's the winner."

In 25 or 30 laps, "you've gotta get with the program and go. You're not out there to make friends," Pauch dryly determined. "Frank Cozze ran Grandview for a few years. He said it best: 'Before you go there ya gotta eat a raw steak, just to get into the mood of the place.'"

In 1991, "we went to Grandview—only went there for the special shows, we weren't regulars there—and we won all the big races. The Forrest Rogers, the '6er, all the special shows. Won like 30 grand or something at Grandview that year. In the pits, they all knew they were running for second," said Pauch crewman Chuck Snyder.

"The year after we won all those big races at Grandview, we tried to run there steady," Snyder continued, "and it was like we had a big X on the car! Got tore up every week."

Abandoning the Flemington asphalt after "I damn near killed myself a couple times,"

Billy and partner Ray Carroll took the team across the Delaware River in early 1992 to join Grandview's weekly roster.

They lasted less than a year.

"I just couldn't take it. It's a tough place," Billy yielded. "It's hard to leave there without something being bent or getting aggravated because it's such tight racing. Wasn't my forté. Too rough."

Grandview's weekly shoving match might not have suited Pauch, but he still pulled a lot of money out of the place. In the course of his career, he won the '6er a half-dozen times, the Forrest Rogers twice, and is tied for 11th on the list of all-time Mod winners, with 23. In his sole abbreviated season as a regular in '92, he finished third in points. And he didn't even start running there until late May.

"All in all, I never ran Grandview all that much. But I had a lot of success there. The Rogers family has always been good to me. Grandview's been good to me," he offered.

But Billy admitted that racing Grandview is not like racing anywhere else.

"Every track takes 100 percent of your concentration. But that place takes way more than that. Things happen so quick because it's so small and so tight!" he said. "Just getting in a rhythm there…trying to figure out how to get through guys, get around guys. The banking makes it different. Until Bridgeport changed the track, there was nothing banked like Grandview around here."

Pauch is out of the car and disgusted, after a brutal wreck in 2000.

MEL STETTLER

Pauch always had a knack for reading the place. "When to move up, when to move down, when the track would change and all that. I really had a good read on it for alotta years," he evaluated. "How to approach a 76-lap race and be there at the end, and have your car still in good shape to win it.

"It was just like going to Fulton for five straight years and running a thousand laps and winning five times. Just had a rhythm to it. How to do it, when to push, when not to push, how to read the track.

"Grandview would change a lot more than I think Fulton did," was Billy's appraisal of setting up for the big races. "Grandview you'd run the top, top, top. Then you hadda know when to go to the bottom, when the bottom would open up and be faster than the top, and get through and be in the right groove at the end. That was the main thing: if it does turn to one groove in the end, you need to be in the *right* groove. And you'd need to be in front."

But he hadn't only figured out how to get around in a Modified—Billy won in every division he ever ran at Grandview. "Small-blocks, big-blocks, Sprints with wings, Sprints without wings, SpeedSTRs…" he ticked off the list.

Grandview's Thunder on the Hill Series—a long-running schedule of midweek special events promoted jointly by Bob and Donna Miller and the Rogers family—provided plenty of opportunity. Although he hasn't raced Sprint Cars in the last 10 years, Pauch still holds the top spot in the TOTH Sprint standings, with 11 victories and five series championships.

"I think the first Sprint Car race I won there was with Glenn Hyneman, the very first Thunder on the Hill," Billy said of the inaugural event in 1990. "Then I won with Zemco, and then the J&M 55. Three different owners. Plus Al Hamilton."

If there was a dollar to be taken—Billy took it.

MEL STETTLER

Everybody who was anybody was dying to drive for Hall of Fame Sprint Car owner Al Hamilton. Jan Opperman, Mitch Smith, Lynn Paxton, Keith Kauffman, Stevie Smith, Fred Rahmer, Lance Dewease, Greg Hodnett—every 24K solid gold Sprint Car driver in the state of Pennsylvania had steered Hamilton's storied 77.

Hodnett had the ride in 2006 before a June crash broke two bones in his left leg. Almost as soon as he returned to competition on August 18th, Greg injured his arm at Williams Grove. So the sought-after Hamilton seat was open for the following Tuesday's TOTH show at Grandview.

"Bob Miller called me and says, 'I got you a ride if you want to come up and run a Sprint Car at my race.' I thought, yeah, yeah, whatever," Pauch brushed aside the offer. "Then he goes, 'It's Al Hamilton's car.'"

AARN ARCHIVES

"And I said, *I'm there! I'll be there!*"

For Pauch, it was a rewind of how the winning RoC ride landed in his lap. "Just like at Flemington: I'm in the shower and my wife hollers up, 'It's Flemington on the phone. Mario Fiore doesn't have a driver. They want to know if you'd be interested in running his car.' And I said, *I will be right there!*

Barbara and little Billy look on as Pauch is crowned King of the Hill.

"When you know it's a good team, you want to be driving that car. And Mario had a good team. I knew the car could win the race—*I'll be there!*

"It was the same thing with Al Hamilton."

When Pauch got to Grandview, helmet bag in hand, the car owner laid out the rules. "Al told me, 'Look kid, this ain't no box of eggs. Don't worry about breaking nothing.' I was like, *huh?*

"Then I get in the car and there's *no gauges*. I never been in a race car with no gauges! And I'm like, *where the hell are the gauges?*" Billy was baffled. "Y'know what he told me? 'You'll smell it or feel it.'

"So OK, he pretty much told me to go out there and run the wheels off it. If you crash it, break it or blow it up—don't worry about it. I don't think I've ever been in a deal like that!"

Apparently, both Pauch and Hamilton were unaware that it was a "features only" race format this night—and neither was happy about it. Hamilton gave promoter Bob Miller a good piece of his mind, even threatening to pull his car out of the event.

The whole deal was so last-minute. Billy hadn't run 410 Sprints in two years. There would be no track time. He didn't know this car from a bucket of beans. And the crew didn't know him.

But, ultimately, they stayed.

"I don't think I even got a warmup—our warmup was our timed dash. And I forget where I started—maybe ninth or something," Pauch said. The entire team was doubtful—including the driver. "You usually don't start that far back in a Sprint Car race and win, y'know?"

Defending race winner Alan Cole set the early pace with Doug Esh and Fred Rahmer chasing. But Pauch was on a crusade of pride and purpose, passing Lance Dewease to take fifth on lap 6, then dispatching Blaine Heimbach for fourth, and quickly closing the gap on Rahmer.

"Man, I took off and went through 'em like Grant took Richmond. The car was so good!" Billy raved.

The two sticks were extended when Pauch made a thrilling dive to the inside of Cole and pulled alongside the leader, just as the red flag waved for a flipping car in turn three.

The red became a fuel stop, with the crew coming onto the track. "And the crew chief, Timmy Elwell, goes, 'I talked to Al. He said if you win the race, you get the whole purse,'" Billy relayed.

That's all he needed to hear. Three to go at the green with Cole protecting the bottom going into one and Pauch putting his right-rear tire right up against Grandview's battered outside boilerplate. They were dead-even down the back. It was Pauch by a sliver at the flag stand, then all Pauch the next time by. Cole couldn't figure what the hell happened.

It was pandemonium in victory lane after Billy brought Hamilton's car in for the win.

MEL STETTLER

"There were two cars that I drove that were really, really good. Exceptional cars," Billy reminisced. "One was the Zemco car that I drove in the National Open; and Al Hamilton's car that night at Grandview.

"That was probably the best handling car I ever

Billy scored his final Sprint win for car owner Al Hamilton.

ran at Grandview, in all the races I won. It worked top, bottom—wherever I wanted to go, that car went. I think during that red they told Alan Cole that I'd be coming on the top. And I drove under him and just passed him. It didn't matter what they told him—wherever he went, I went the opposite way."

Certainly, those extra dollar signs sparked Pauch's belly-fire. "I was out there to win the race, no matter what. But it definitely gives you more incentive when the owner says you can have the whole purse! So I ended up winning the race, Al gave me the whole purse and I split it with the crew. They were part of it, too," Billy reasoned.

"Everybody thinks it's always just the driver. It's the whole team—the crew, the owner, the sponsors. There's more to it than just the driver."

When the checker fell, Pauch put on a rambunctious display—smoking the tires and kicking up clay, completing another lap around the track in the opposite direction while the stunned fans—both the lovers and the haters—were spilling out of the grandstands, their screams still echoing down the hill.

It was a sublime night. And Billy did enjoy many moments like that at the track. But not enough to ever call it home.

"I give Howard and Strunk and Von Dohren a lot of credit for hanging in there all them years. It's a tough place," is his assessment of Grandview.

"It gives true meaning to the saying: It's a nice place to visit—but I wouldn't want to live there."

JEFF STRUNK REMEMBERS...

MEL STETTLER

"The first time I remember seeing Billy was probably '77 at Reading. The Daniel Boone 200. I was a big Kenny Brightbill fan so I wasn't paying a lot of attention to him—I was nine, maybe—but I remember he was a *banzai-er* and that's how he got in the race.

The first interaction I had with Billy, person to person, was at Fulton my rookie year. We went up for the 200 and we didn't qualify. So at the 100-lap break, his team was thrashing and I kinda jumped right in and got involved. Ended up siping and grooving tires for him. He wound up winning the thing, and I think after, when we were all loading up beer in a pickup truck, he came over and started talking to me, thanking me for helping him.

Billy and Barb actually sponsored me the third year that I raced, in '90. Pit Stop Tire Service was on the back of my car. Glenn Hyneman kinda connected us: everybody was switching to Hoosiers here then, but I liked the McCrearys and Billy was selling 'em so we stayed with 'em, got 'em from him. Then he hooked me up with Koni shocks, got me in the door with them, and I wound up getting a good product sponsorship. It was a good deal. I was proud to have his name on the car.

That was right before he started building the Pauch-Olsens—when you either had one or you had to get one, y'know what I mean? They were the dominant car at that point in time. He was really on top of his game then—not that he wasn't all the time, but especially then. That was when John Sine was working with him and they were doing over 100 shows a year.

The Pauch-Olsen was quite a bit different than Doug Olsen's standard deal. Something that you might not have thought woulda happened, but it definitely worked out good for both of them. For everybody, really, because it made everybody better. Definitely something we bought and started using—and I was a true Olsen golden boy! People picked 'em up at Billy's shop and he or John scaled it with 'em, right there, and did everything the right way. Those cars were kinda like the Teos when they first came out—everyone who bought a new one was instantly fast. What he had going on during a four, five, six-year period back then—it was quite an empire, if you want to call it that.

The first year Billy sponsored me, I picked up a ride at Penn National in the Fach car, one of Bill's old cars with Glenn. So I ended up driving this car in July, two weeks before the four 20s, and we got it going pretty good. In the four 20s I got a good starting spot in the first one and ended up winning it. I think Kenny won the second one. I sandbagged in the second one so I could start up front in the third one, and I won the third one over Billy, beat him by less than a tire. He goes into the last one, wins it ultimately—overall, I think he had three seconds and a win.

And Bill was so mad in tech, I'll never forget that night! 'You sandbagging young punk!' he goes to me. 'What the hell! You were up to *sixth* and you finished *ninth!* That's a sandbagger! You should make it look better than that!'

I was really intimidated so I didn't say anything back. He was hot because I sandbagged and I wouldn't admit it to him. I kinda backed away when I realized he wasn't joking. *He was pissed!* We were OK the next day, but in the heat of the moment, when the helmets were coming off, he wasn't happy with me. But at that point, that was the highlight of my career. The headlines read: 'Strunk 2, Brightbill, Pauch in Four 20s.'

I never thought I'd pass Billy's record of six wins in the '6er. I thought he'd sit on that record forever, maybe win another one or two. Just to say that I've won two more than him is awesome. I never thought I'd win one, no less eight! Me: the Go-Kart kid from down the road."

ACE LANE JR.

SYRACUSE AT SPEED:

"It ain't that bad if you're going in the right direction. But if you're going in the wrong direction, the car starts hovering over the ground—it gets your attention pretty quick."

18.

Syracuse

It wasn't like Pauch was afraid to go fast at Syracuse: he'd already set pole time twice in a Modified, in 1986 and again in 1988, and was the first to break 30 seconds, a new track record in '92—despite the fact that he never approached that be-all and end-all DIRT race with anywhere near the dedicated effort or fine-tuned focus of the series regulars.

But taking on that treacherous Fairgrounds mile in a 1400-pound Sprint Car, putting out 900+ horses, was a whole 'nother definition of danger.

"The top speed I ever ran in an Indy Car was 250 at the end of the backstretch in turn three at Indy. I've run 212 at Michigan going into turn one," Tony Stewart has affirmed. "But I want nothing to do with running a winged Sprint Car on a mile dirt track."

Billy underscored the risk involved. "They're really not meant to run on a mile," experience had taught him. "I've had the wing blow up; I've had the wing blow down. I was going down the backstretch there, 100-something miles an hour, and all of a sudden the front wing mount broke. The wing stood straight up, put me in a wheelie going 100-plus miles an hour. *You crap your pants!* Lucas Wolfe was behind me, later said to me, 'I don't know if that scared you—but it sure scared me, watching it.'"

As driver Fred Rahmer, one of Pennsy's finest, sardonically stated about the Syracuse mile, "If you don't get killed, you missed a good chance."

The first time Pauch drove the Zemco Sprinter at Syracuse, in 1993, "I started on the front row, went down into one—everyone told me, 'Ya gotta beat 'em into one'—and it was slick and the car winged down so hard the right-rear was off the

MEL STETTLER

Billy and Jac Haudenschild discuss the dangers.

ground, the right-front was off the ground, and it turned like *THIS*," Billy tilted his arms at a radically acute angle. "I turned to the left and looked down the frontstretch, saw all those cars behind me coming, and I thought, *This is it. I'm gonna die right here…*

"Somehow I got it turned and straightened out. Made a few more laps until I finally spun it out and backed it in the wall," he said. "But it was one of those 'I'm-gonna-die' moments."

The Zemco team learned from the car's performance, came back in '94 with a slicker, more purpose-built piece for the mile.

A lot of it was aerodynamics. "The first year, Billy had trouble with his helmet trying to blow off his head down the straightaway," Zemco team manager Tommy Carl recalled. So they trekked over to the Troyer tent, where Billy Colton fabricated a piece of cowling to divert air from the cockpit. "That solved that problem."

For the '94 effort, the team borrowed more tinwork tricks from their previous Modified experience—tucking in and enclosing the headers, covering up the front shocks, raising the belly pan, gluing teardrop-shaped extensions to the back side of the roll cage tubing. "The first year I think we were running a little hot, so we had to change the openings a little bit. We paid more attention to the ram air we'd built into the car," Carl detailed. "Some things the officials made us cut apart after we got there. They weren't happy with some of the things we did, but we tried to take it as far as we could," to gain an aero edge.

Davey, John and Billy pow-wow pre-race.

MEL STETTLER

MEL STETTLER

Most importantly, the motor in the car was built by National Sprint Car Hall of Fame master mechanic Davey Brown. Though John and Pee Wee Zemaitis' Zemco team had been running Brown power for a few seasons, this was the first time Davey would be on site with them at Syracuse. "That made a difference," Tommy said of the legendary motor wizard's presence in their pit. "He probably gave Billy a little more confidence. And of course, tuning the motor. That's what Davey's best at."

All the pieces for success were there. Pauch knew what he had to do—and did it. *All of it.*

The 24.898 lap Billy reeled off in time trials not only put him on the pole: it set a new world speed record on a closed dirt course—144.590 mph—that would stand for four more years, until Sammy Swindell eclipsed it at Springfield in 1998. With the demolition of the track in 2016, Pauch's one-lap record will forever stand in history as the fastest official time anyone ever turned on the Syracuse Fairgrounds mile.

Initially, though, Billy had no idea what he'd done. "I can actually remember him coming off the track, and someone tried to show him a two and a four—that he'd run 24 seconds—and Billy thought they were telling him he was second or fourth quick," Carl chuckled. "He wasn't happy when he came in with the car. He felt the motor was flat, it didn't feel fast. And we had to explain to him that he'd just set the world record."

It took a second for it to sink in. "I just held it to the floor for two laps," Billy was matter-of-fact. "The car was so glued, it felt like it was no effort. When you're all assholes and elbows, you feel like you're fast—but that's when you're not."

Tommy Carl agreed. "When a car's really good like that—you don't feel like you're hanging on."

That quick time put Pauch on the point for the start of the 35-mile main event—with every established, platinum-certified World of Outlaws professional right behind him.

Understand that every single Sprint Car event during Syracuse Super DIRT Week had been won by a card-carrying member of Ted Johnson's traveling World of Outlaws band since the organization sanctioned the speedway back in 1980. And no outsider all season had managed to steal a payday away from any of the WoO regulars. *Anywhere.*

Pauch wasn't even a full-time Sprint Car driver. He knew this wasn't going to be easy.

The adrenaline was flowing like a severed spigot. Officials called back the initial start as outside polesitter Andy Hillenburg got antsy and jumped too soon. Pauch was also anxious, causing another caution to bring the field back together. Both drivers were shown the blackboard chalked with the big, white words: *LAST CHANCE!*

When the race got going, Pauch charged out front. By lap 5, he was dealing with heavy traffic.

"At Syracuse, the more laps you run, the more the track rubbers up and gets bitier. That's usually right around the bottom, because not too many people want to run the top," Billy explained. "Early in the race, I came up on lapped traffic and I moved up a little bit

MIKE FELTENBERGER

to try to get around 'em. I got out of the rubber a little, and whoever was second passed me," he described the near-miss. "But then the caution came out, saved my butt. So it got me back in the lead. After that, I was really, really careful…"

Following a fuel stop at halfway, it was "The Wild Child" Jac Haudenschild who hounded the Zemco 1, racing shoulder-to-shoulder unrelentingly through the turns, with Billy pulling away down the chutes. Haud's only shot was a ballsy do-or-die move flying into the apex of the first turn.

"He hit the inside berm in traffic, and crashed out trying to pass me," Pauch said of Haud's Hail Mary attempt. "If I had a mirror in the car, he probably would have scared me to death."

On a subsequent restart, Billy had Dave Blaney and Steve Kinser to contend with. King Kinser, a four-time winner of this race, slammed under Blaney, trying to get a bead on Pauch. But the dramatic bid backfired: Kinser's car careened sideways, losing the line sliding into four.

Five laps remained, and no way was Blaney willing to settle for second. He kept pace with the race-long leader until the white flag lap, when he made his banzai pitch going into one.

Everyone standing atop the Zemco trailer held their breath.

Navigating through traffic, trying to hold back Blaney, Pauch had a milli-second to make a commitment: go to the outside or the inside.

"I decided the last time I went to the outside, I lost. So I stayed to the inside," was Billy's decision. "Blaney rolled up the outside of me. It looked like he was going to roll right by me, but he was in the ice. He couldn't get on the throttle coming out of two. I was in the rubber, drove right by him and we won the race. But it could've been the other way around if I went to the top.

"I'll tell ya, Dave's one of the best drivers I've ever run against and I gotta give him a lot of credit," a grateful Pauch said afterward. "He gave me room there. And thank God!"

Blaney knew it was a make-or-break moment. "I had a chance on that last lap and I missed it by two inches in the center of that corner, slipped in the dust a little bit and let him get back by me," Dave kicked himself afterwards. "It was the only chance I had."

The crazed crowd knew they had just witnessed a race they would remember the rest of their lives. A stock car driver from New Jersey, who only dabbled in Sprints, had blitzed the world speed record and beaten the best Sprint Car drivers in the country. *Dead-cold.*

"It was unbelievable to win it," Billy said of the $26,875 victory—still the biggest single payday of his career—then exhaled in relief as the crew celebrated on the Syracuse frontstretch. "The best part of this race is stepping out of the car in one piece when it's over. And I'm just happy to do that."

Bottom-lined a weary Steve Kinser, as he packed up his trailer, "We're lucky to be getting out of here alive."

19.
His Own Drummer

In a world where most racers rarely venture for long outside their chosen division, Billy Pauch is a maverick.

He is arguably one of the most versatile drivers of his generation, having won with NASCAR, WoO, DIRTcar, USAC, CRA, SCRA, All Star, KARS, URC, MODCAR and CVRA—just about the entire alphabet soup of sanctioning bodies.

As a reader once commented in *Speedway Illustrated*, "He wins in dirt Mods, pavement Mods and Sprint Cars, at times all in the same weekend."

"I'd be running a 410 Sprint at Williams Grove on Friday night, go to Flemington on Saturday and run a pancake car on asphalt for Dick Barney, then go to Penn National on Sunday and run a dirt Modified," Pauch said of his unconventional schedule in the mid '90s. "I just wanted to run anything. As long as it's fast and up front—I'm in."

Yet, he was always—at the beginning of his career and now at the end—a dirt Modified driver. And so: the elephant in the room Billy's entire adult life has been his refusal to follow the DIRT circuit.

By the late 1970s, DIRT Motorsports—the sanctioning body spearheaded by charismatic New York promoter Glenn Donnelly—had soundly solidified their status as the be-all and end-all of dirt Modified racing. DIRT standardized rules, signed up independent speedways, and formed a points-paying series that snaked through five states and Canada, culminating in Super DIRT Week at the Syracuse mile, the world's richest race for the division and a career-maker for any driver to ace. Donnelly attracted major corporate sponsors, mounted television coverage, brought the sport out of the hinterlands and into the headlines. If you were a professional dirt Modified driver, expecting to race for a living, you had to be DIRT. All capital letters.

Heck, even Jersey boys like Jimmy Horton and Brett Hearn—200-300 miles away from the nucleus of DIRT action in Central New York—had pledged allegiance to Glenn Donnelly. Pennsy stars Doug Hoffman and Frank Cozze were tour regulars. Even Kenny Brightbill was an off-and-on steady. All the big guns were aligned with DIRT.

Except for Billy Pauch.

For years, all the haters in the spectator seats accused Pauch of dodging the competition, avoiding having to put himself up against the region's heaviest hitters, who were all flush in the klieg lights of Donnelly's publicity machine.

Pauch wasn't in it for the glory. He was in it for the money.

"I'm not looking at the limelight. It doesn't impress me," Billy noted, back in the early '90s. "I don't know what's involved with DIRT's point money. It looks attractive, it looks impressive. But if you sit down and try to figure out all the towing and the gas money and motels and all that, I don't think it looks that impressive.

"It just costs so much to go run the road. And I never wanted to take advantage of any of the owners I drove for, to push them into something like that," he considered. "I like to run close to home. And I always figured if I can make as much running close to home, why should I go across three states and Canada to make money?"

Billy had a wary relationship, at best, with DIRT officials.

KEN DIPPEL

And it's always been Billy's belief that as an outlaw attempting a run against Donnelly's team players, he wasn't privy to any privileges.

"I got a bad taste of DIRT early in my career," Pauch admitted. "When I went up, there were certain ways that the field was lined up, and I wasn't on the right end of it. And it bothered me.

"Look, I didn't care what they did for their drivers—give them money to show up or motel rooms or whatever. But when I go to the race track, I want a fair shot. I want to know that when we reach in that hat, we're all reaching for the same numbers. That's all I care," he declared. "I didn't want to have to go there and start dead last because I'm not a regular. I wanted a fair shake. If they didn't want to do it that way—well then, fine, I didn't show up."

Always blunt, Billy didn't bother to temper his distaste for the DIRT way of doing things. Sitting atop his rig during a rare appearance at Rolling Wheels in the '90s, he was approached by DIRT VP Andy Fusco, who was

Billy's Super DIRT Series win at Grandview in 1989 was one of three that season, despite the fact he didn't follow the tour.

MEL STETTLER

promoting shows with partner Dave Lape.

"We really wish you would support our event at Can-Am," Fusco called up to Pauch.

Taking a long drag on his cigarette, without even glancing down at Fusco, Billy bit out, "People in hell wish for ice water, and they ain't getting that either."

It wasn't like Pauch couldn't compete. In fact, just the opposite.

In July of '89, on a roll driving for Pete Chesson, Billy won back-to-back events on the Super DIRT Series tour, which is a pretty neat feat. "Went to Williams Grove, beat Jack Johnson. Then we turned around and backed it up at Grandview the next night. We just had our act together that year," he said. "So everyone was like: 'Why don't you go run DIRT?'"

Billy had to bite his lip every time he was asked that question. "Nobody seen all the politics that were involved. I remember one time we were at Rolling Wheels, me and Pete, and we finished second or third or something. Pete was out in the infield, standing right next to the scales. Danny Johnson goes over, comes up light, and they're like, 'Go ahead, you're all right!'

"Pete was having a fit! I finished third, Pete's carrying on. *'Screw DIRT! Let's get out of here!'* And I'm like, whoa, let me pick up the payoff. We ain't screwing DIRT by not taking the payoff. He wanted to leave the payoff!" said Pauch, trying to simmer Pete down so he could collect his money. "I just ran 100 laps—I wanta get paid, even if it's for third.

"That's the kind of politics you put up with up there."

The Syracuse Fairgrounds was the DIRT battleground where the haves and have-nots were always sorted out, where loyalties were rewarded.

Pauch crewman Chuck Snyder recalled DIRT chief tech inspector Bob Dini going out of his way to target them.

"We'd be coming through tech under the grandstands and Dini would be in another row of cars. As soon as we'd get up there, he'd go, 'Whoa! I'll inspect this car personally.' And he'd jump from wherever he was right to us. Every year. He'd start looking the car over, and then he'd say, 'Billy, Billy, Billy—what were you thinking? Whaddaya call this??'" Chuck remembered. "We always gave him something to look at, so he'd maybe forget about the other stuff."

Pauch's good friend and crewman Nick Lombardi concurred. "At Syracuse, they would really nitpick us, and let other people get away with things. That's the way that DIRT thing always was—they never liked any outsider to come in there and beat Brett Hearn or the Johnsons or any of their other guys. They just never did."

Tech inspection at Syracuse was always stressful.

MEL STETTLER

"Those are the stories you always heard: *Why is Hearn starting up front all the time?* It was obvious," was Lombardi's opinion.

RUSS DODGE COLLECTION

Doug Olsen and Billy at Syracuse.

"With the guys that came from the southern regions of Modified racing—they always nitpicked everything, especially at Syracuse," reiterated car builder Doug Olsen, who divulged, "the officials did most of the cheating with the draw. There were always two cans to pick from: one had the good numbers, the other had the rest of the numbers. Most of the cheating came from the officials."

Pauch further identified the depth of the dishonesty in the system. "Is it cheating when you call up the track and say, 'You give me the pole and I'll show up'? *Is that cheating?* Yeah, it's cheating! It's the biggest cheating you can freakin' do!"

Billy was wound up. "It's always easier to start on the top of the shit pile and slide down than it is to start on the bottom of the shit pile and try to climb up. That's what you went through when you went to New York in Donnelly's world. You were at the bottom and everybody else was at the top. It just sucked. *Why don't you go up there and race?* they'd ask me. Well, why should I?"

Even on semi-neutral ground in Florida, Pauch still felt singled out. Following the 2016 Nationals at Volusia, DIRTcar fined and penalized two drivers—Pauch one of them—for chemically altering their tires.

To clean his DIRT-mandated Hoosiers before prepping, he had used the degreaser Castrol Super Clean, "and I guess that threw off the tire test," Billy surmised. "I've read and been told if you buff your tires without cleaning 'em, you'll buff the release agent the manufacturer uses into the tires and it will screw them up.

"That stuff cleans the tires and opens up the pores, but I didn't think it would affect a tire test. It isn't a tire softener, so I didn't think anything of it."

The hit was hard: Pauch was fined $2,000 plus any winnings he'd earned and a $150 lab fee for a total $3,050 rap. He was also put on probation and banned from DIRTcar competition until the penalty was paid.

"I think it's funny that Tyler Siri bought a race track and signed an American Racer tire deal, and I'm an American Racer dealer, and we're the only two that got caught," Billy cynically said, referencing DIRTcar's longtime alliance with rival Hoosier Tire.

"The older I get, the less patience I've got," he admitted. Pauch's list of pet peeves—politics, preferential treatment, personal agendas and unfair practices—is getting longer as the years click off.

That's why he's boycotting Brett Deyo's Short Track Super Series. When Deyo reverted to lining up the heat races by a blind draw at the gate, rather than setting the field by time, Billy decided he was done. He wasn't about to put in all the hard work to get the car ready and tow to hell's bells and back, only to randomly draw a high number and get buried in the bottom of the lineup.

"I don't agree with it. That's why I stopped running Deyo's series—because he went back to picking. And we know about picking back in the day up in New York: after all the DIRT guys got all the top spots, what was left? *In the back...*" Billy avowed.

"That whole DIRT deal up there: the only races I felt I stood a chance at were the ones where they time-trialed because then they couldn't screw you with the pick. You *earned* your spot. It's pretty hard to scam a time-trial deal."

So that's where he is now. "I ain't picking. I'm done picking. I work on talent and preparation. I don't work on luck. If I worked on luck I might as well go to Atlantic City and sit there and drink and play cards."

No DIRT. No Deyo. That puts him pretty much where he's been since his beloved Flemington closed 20 years ago: A man without a country. The last cowboy.

He knows who he is. And he's more philosophical as he gets older.

"There are politics in every kind of racing, I think," Billy finally conceded. "I don't have any grudge against DIRT or any of 'em. Every kind of racing has to have an organization whether it's DIRT, NASCAR, IndyCar or whatever.

"When you decide to go with them, you decide to run for the point money. At the end of the year, you're hoping that's gonna be your paycheck," he summarized.

"I was never running for points. I was running to win."

20.
Cheating

Cal Peters' junkyard in Pennsy is where Billy unearthed the motor for his first race car in 1974.

"Went over there and pulled the motor out of this big old dump truck, fighting bees and everything else," he remembered. "Got it back and the old man rebuilt it. Probably put a cam in it. It was a truck motor, with truck heads. At that point, I just wanted a motor that I could get some laps with."

The problem was: the junkyard motor was a 350; and the cubic inch limit for Sportsman at Nazareth was 318.

It was illegal.

But that's not to say a lot of guys weren't using them anyway. "The Chevy 350 was everywhere, in every car you picked the hood up on," said driver Roger Laureno, who came up through the ranks about the same time as Pauch. "A lot of guys ran 'em because

Not much got past tech inspector Chet Crane at Nazareth.

JACK KROMER

they had no money. The 302s, even the 327s weren't plentiful. But the 350s were readily available, and they made more power without putting any money in 'em. If you didn't think you were going to win anyway—well, that's what you ran."

The 350 salvaged from Peters' junkyard was in Billy's car when he and Roy towed into Nazareth for a big Sportsman show at the end of '74—and were faced with a thorough pre-race tech inspection.

As soon as Pauch saw they were puffing motors to calculate cubic inches, "we turned around and went back out the gate," he said. "Took it up in the woods, and put paper matchbooks under the valves to try to let off some compression so it wouldn't be big.

"The car was super-light, too—I don't know, that's the way I built it," Billy added. "And the tires were full of water to make weight."

Tech inspector Chet Crane was waiting for them when they rejoined the inspection line. "'Why'd you guys pull around and leave?" Crane asked, suspicious.

Billy told him they left to add weight to the car. Crane peered around the racer. "Well, where'd you put it?"

Pauch was caught. "We couldn't show him because we didn't have no weight that

> *East Windsor was right in his wheelhouse. He was very creative. They had no weight rule. When you give Billy Pauch a rulebook with no weight rule—you better be getting ready to get your ass kicked.*
>
> **CREWMAN DONNIE MILLER**

MIKE FELTENBERGER

we'd bolted on. So we told him it was in the tires—the tires are full of water," he admitted. "So Chet took a key and hit the valve stem—and water shot in his face!"

This was going downhill in a hurry. "He puffed the motor, and it didn't come out right. So he says, 'Pull the header off,' then left to tech some other guy." Roy and Billy were scrambling to pull the matchbooks out from under the valves when Crane walked up behind them. "You'll burn your valves doing that!" he cracked.

"So we got busted."

Although Pauch did not compete that day, and, in fact, never won a race with the truck motor, "it seems that always tagged him for life, being a cheater," Roy said of the incident, news of which was carried by the cackling hens through the pits. "Just that one time."

When Billy went on a tear the following year with a legal 302—and with all the motors and combinations that came after—that black mark followed him.

"He was too fast for them. And right away, they were all like, 'He's cheating! He's cheating!' Y'know?" Roy argued: "They weren't seeing that the way he was running, he had more throttle time. They were backing out of it. A lot of 'em were backing in their cars and when they got to turn left, they were sideways. If you can keep the wheels behind you, like a drag car—you go straight faster with your wheels behind you than if the wheels are coming around."

But no amount of logic or facts could completely repair the knock on Pauch's reputation.

"All the big technology and that 800hp? That don't mean shit. We went to Bridgeport and won the most races there with 690," Roy bristled. "Of course, when you're winning all the races—now you're cheating. *The bastard's cheating again! He's got the big motor in! We've gotta find out what he's got!*" Roy shook his head. "You ever see a shell game?"

Let's not be naïve: they call it an edge because it's razor thin. And every single racer who's worth his salt—from the Cup down to the Crate ranks—is perched precariously on that delicate point, trying to find an advantage without tipping over into illegal territory. In order to be competitive, you have to take chances, carefully threading the needle through the loopholes in the rulebook.

In the top NASCAR leagues, Junior Johnson, Andy Petree, Ray Evernham, Chad

Knaus, Todd Parrott—all of 'em, really—understood what the game is about. "If you ain't cheating, you ain't trying," was Johnson's favorite phrase.

Stated Petree for the record, during an interview on *The Dale Jr. Download* podcast: "If you built a car by the rulebook, you wouldn't even know where they went!" the former car chief for Harry Gant and Dale Earnhardt Sr. emphasized.

Do all the good guys push the boundaries? "Of course!" affirmed Doug Olsen, who, along with his famous father Budd, built some of the region's winningest Modifieds for many of the top talents. "But most guys accused of cheating aren't winning because they're cheating. They're just that much better than everybody else. As soon as you're really good, they all think you're cheating.

"Everyone thought Brett was cheating all the time, too," Olsen continued. "But really, how much cheating can you do with one of these cars? You could try a locker rear, try that for two races, throw that away. Try this. Try that. The next thing you know, you're back to basics again."

The reality? "You have a much better chance of winning with a talented driver than with a cheated-up race car," Olsen declared.

"The easiest thing for people to say when you beat 'em is, 'He's cheating.' Y'know? It's never, 'He's better than me…His car's handling…He's got his car running.' Nah. It's always, 'He's gotta be cheating. Because I'm better than him!'" Pauch grudgingly accepted. "It's just the way it is in life: nobody wants to give anybody credit."

And in many cases, racers trying to walk that fine line get tripped up by semantics and interpretation. But so do the tech officials.

"With me, it just came natural: when I would read a rulebook, something entirely different would come to my mind rather than what the person who wrote that rule was thinking," reflected Rich Tobias Jr., who's been on every side of the issue as a driver, builder and promoter. He gave the example of Canadian racer Joe Plazek, years ago at the Syracuse mile. "In the rulebook, the maximum was 22 gallons of fuel. Well, Plazek was carrying 22 *imperial* gallons that year—it was still a gallon! It was all in how the rulebook was written and how you're reading it.

"Really, the one who started a lot of that, a guy that I learned a lot from, was Kenny Weld. I sat down and talked to him only once or twice, and the things he told me were

Post-race tech at Penn National in 1993.

amazing—just outside-the-box thinking! And naturally, the epitome of that for him was the Batmobile," said Tobias, referencing the radical Weld design that busted right out of the envelope to scandalize the Syracuse crowd in 1980. "What is good, bad or ugly... cheating or not cheating?"

And although no one wants to admit it, personalities and loyalties undoubtedly come into play. "It may not be like that anymore, but years ago, when the guys from New Jersey would go up to race in New York State, the rules for the Jersey guys were definitely different than the New York guys. What they could get away with—we couldn't," maintained Olsen, who often traveled the circuit with house car drivers Brett Hearn and Doug Hoffman. "If you weren't one of the boys, you were not going to get the same deal.

"Most officials, I thought, are pretty good people," Doug concluded. "But then they become more like politicians—they have a little power in their hands and they try to wield that power over you all the time."

And if you're a big winner—and not in "the club"—inspectors tend to take a much more exhausting look.

Crewman Chuck Snyder remembered an engine teardown after a win at Grandview. "Took the intake off, took the heads off. Then they wanted to flip it over, took the oil pan off. Took the crank out. Some guy came in and looked at the crank to see if it was legal, because one track said you could cut it one way, the other track allowed you to cut it another way," Snyder reported. "Finally, they said it was legal."

But at that point, it was almost daylight. And Pauch and crew were still sitting in the pits, surrounded by a mess of motor parts that needed to be put back together. "We couldn't race the next day because we had no motor," Chuck fumed. "That's the way it went."

It was more of the same at Penn National. "Ceganick did our motors and Larry Lombardo used to throw a fit every week, because he did the stuff for some of the Tobiases and Craig Von Dohren," Keystone Pretzel crewman Donnie Miller distinctly recalled. "About every other week, they'd pull us into tech and pull the headers off, stick their fingers up there, stick a piece of wire up there, put a mirror up there with a flashlight…looking at stuff on the heads and the valve guides or something. Lombardo would be saying, '*What about this? What about that?*'

"We kicked their asses on a regular basis," Miller laid down the logic for such intense and ongoing examination. "Smokey Warren used to bitch and piss and moan about Billy every week! I think Smokey actually *was* cheating and he was still getting beat and he couldn't understand how. What they all didn't seem to realize—Billy wasn't always the fastest car. He was the smoothest and the straightest."

Making sure the motor's right at Syracuse.

ACE LANE JR.

Pauch fans made a statement with their entry in New Egypt's annual banner contest, weeks after the track took a win away from Billy for a minor infraction.

Cheating. Cheating. Like the swarming bees Billy fought off as he pulled that first truck motor out of the salvage yard, the buzz in the pits was a constant hum in the background.

"You hear it about everyone who wins races: 'He's got traction control…He's got this or that…'" Pauch submitted. "I never really say much about anyone else. Maybe I'm too trusting, but I pretty much believe that they're legal. I know I wasn't cheating for 700-some wins. So does everybody else have to cheat to win?"

He brought home the point, condensing it down to the most essential truth. "What it comes down to is this: *What pleasure is there in cheating to win races?* What's that accomplish? Does that make you feel good? It wouldn't make me feel good," Billy bottom-lined. "Sure, there's gray area, where you push the limit on a little weight, or an inch here or an inch there, or try something a little different. You have to size yourself up with the competition, too."

Rich Tobias agreed. "You don't want to leave anything on the table. You want to use every advantage you can find."

But balancing on the high-wire of that legal tightrope puts you in a tenuous position, at best. And partisan politics, in the end, can bring you plummeting down.

That was pretty much the case with Pauch's most recent tech skirmishes with the powers-that-be at New Egypt Speedway.

From 1999 through 2006, Billy was the man to beat at New Egypt when the Grosso family had the place, pocketing more than 60 victories and three Modified titles in that time.

Then, in 2007, the track was sold. And the new regime seemed intent on toppling every standard that had been established. Divisions. Rules. Affiliations. And Billy Pauch.

Right away, they adopted a DIRTcar sanction which included a Hoosier tire mandate. As the track's longtime distributor for American Racer tires, Billy was out. He picked up and went to Bridgeport, where he won five races and the championship.

New Egypt dropped DIRT in '08 and they were back on American Racers, so Pauch returned to competition to take up where he left off, reaching his 100-win NES milestone in 2011 and adding three more titles to his record.

But it was a rocky relationship, especially in the tech line. What followed was microscopic scrutiny of Pauch's every move—a witch-hunt, really—and major penalties. As a person close to the situation admitted, "What it amounted to is they brought a drunk out of the grandstands who hated Billy Pauch and made him the promoter."

He was targeted in that regime early and often. "You're not allowed to have ballast weight on the outside of the frame. I had 20 pounds on the outside of the rub rail, on the inside of the door or something. That was the first infraction," Billy ticked off. "What was funny about it, the night I was getting teched for that, the Sportsman winner, Brian Roemer, had his weight in the same place. His race was first, so he went through tech first. He told me later, 'Yeah, I had weight bolted there, too, but they didn't even look!' But they busted me," Pauch said.

"I guess you beat on the big dog, the rest of the dogs will stay in line."

He sighed. "Then there was the bullshit with the wind sails being two inches too high. It was actually a mistake when we built the car—and we ran like four weeks with it before we realized it. At that point, we just let it go, figured they weren't going to bother us," Billy conceded. "Two weeks later somebody ratted us out on that. Got busted for the wind sails being too high."

Undergoing a fuel check at Grandview in 2012.

How much of an edge does two extra inches of tin provide on a short track? "None at all," according to Doug Olsen. "I've seen Brett and Billy and Horton get their bodies ripped halfway off, go to the rear and still come back through and win the race!" he chuckled. "Actually, I thought Jimmy and Billy got better when their cars got torn up. Because then they'd feel like they *really* had something to prove—they'd go to the rear, get right back up front and win the race anyway."

Of course, enforcement is all subjective and there's some leeway with penalties—not every misdeed is or should be a hanging offense. Yet, NES considered that infraction, and any others Pauch got clipped for, egregious enough to warrant outright disqualification: he was stripped of those wins and any accompanying paychecks.

A second-place finish was taken away on a night when a fight broke out in the pits and, to circumvent the mayhem, Billy didn't drive directly to tech.

"I'd watch other guys do the same thing and they were fine. I watched Williams pull into his pit spot and then back out and go to tech. And he was all right—that's OK. That's not you. *We only want to screw you! We don't care about Williams. We only want to do it to you!*" Billy groused.

"The wind sails are high...The location of the weight...It's a rule, it's a rule. Whatever. I'm not complaining," he was resigned. "But they overreacted. They take your win, they take your points. They take your handicapping for three weeks, you gotta start in the back. It's pretty brutal for minor bullshit. Even NASCAR isn't that bad!

"But that fuel deal—that broke the camel's back," he blazed. "That wasn't true! I didn't have illegal fuel."

When track officials tested Pauch's fuel following a victory in June 2016, they determined his racing gasoline was contaminated—another win out the window.

"They checked the fuel, they said something was wrong with it. I talked to the two inspectors there and they were gonna send it out to a lab and have it rechecked," Billy said. Apparently, track owner Fred Vahlsing overruled that plan, and let the DQ stand.

"He wouldn't even listen to me! If he's not gonna give me the benefit of the doubt to prove I'm innocent, I don't need to race there," Pauch raged. To settle the point for himself, he drove the fuel sample to Sunoco's PA headquarters to be evaluated. The resulting analysis confirmed that the gas might have been dirty but did not contain any performance-enhancing additives.

"That was the last year I ran New Egypt. Haven't been back since," blasted Billy, who still stands as the winningest dirt Mod driver in the track's history. "Hey, look—I'm fine with it. If I'm wrong, I'm wrong. I'll get slapped on the wrist or whatever. But if I'm not wrong and you're blaming me? I'm done. I'm outta here.

"Nobody stood up for me at New Egypt. They're all dead to me. Screw 'em all."

Since the exodus from NES in '16, Pauch has added 16 victories and two Modified championships to the body of work he's compiled over the past 48 seasons. A win total of 743 and counting. And even in his 60s, he continues to hone his craft.

"On nights when I'm not working on the race car, I'm going through the rules, trying to make the car faster. You're not looking to cheat, but you're always looking for an edge," Billy informed. "Like I said, what kind of gratification is there in cheating and winning? I'm not desperate to make a living at it any more. At this point, I'm doing it for fun, to see if an old guy can still win. Just trying to prove myself, y'know? That's all I've done my whole career: try to prove myself."

He's done a damned good job of it. "He don't give up. That kid *don't give up!*" asserted Roy, who stood both proud and in awe of his son's determination, whether he told him so or not.

"You've seen all those guys—when something goes wrong with their car, they'll jump in someone else's car and go win with it. Look at Stewart Friesen: he's in a DKM car, a Bicknell car, it doesn't matter. Stewart is like Billy and Brett were back then—*he's that good.* Timmy McCreadie is like that, too. Amazing. He never gives up," Doug Olsen pointed out. "It's not the cheating end, it's the talent end of it."

All those top-tier drivers—Brett, Billy, Jimmy, Doug, Stewart, Timmy, every single one of them—have gotten nailed for drawing outside the lines at various points in their careers. They've all taken their punishment.

But that's not why they win.

"I hate when people want to take it away from Billy all the time. *This happened because of this, or that happened because of that...* Certainly, there are more Billy haters than likers! That's when you know you're *really* good—when you're hated that bad!" Rich Tobias observed.

"What I'm getting at is: he got in a blacktop Modified—and won! Y'know what I mean? It ain't like, *Oh, he cheated this or cheated that and that's why Billy won.* He got in this strange car and that other car he's never been in before and a Sprint Car—and he still won. So now what are you gonna say? It's just like Kyle Larson. *There is a difference in drivers.*

"There are ones that race hard. Every lap. Every minute," Tobias concluded. And he clearly puts Pauch in that category.

"And even though Billy pushed the envelope—that wasn't why Billy won. I don't think anything Billy did to the car made him win. Billy won because Billy's Billy."

21.
Anger & Attitude

We all live with the anger of our elders. And then, we inherit it.

"It comes from both sides of the family. My father had a temper…my oldest brother had a temper…" with Roy himself right in line, along with his wife. All hardscrabble farmers, hell-bent on trying to scratch a living out of the land. Fists to the heavens, cursing droughts and deluges, bugs and blight. Perennially pissed off at all that is out of their control.

That's the world Billy was born into.

"My grandmother had a hot temper and Leroy would antagonize her. And it was just…it wasn't good. It was a volatile environment," Billy Jr. allowed. "My dad got a little bit of both of them—sometimes you don't know what you're going to get from him, like Dr. Jekyll and Mr. Hyde. But it's the way my grandmother and grandfather raised him."

Every car owner, every crewman was aware of the toxic dynamic. "I believe Billy had a rough childhood," Leon Liedl said with certainty. "Roy was a son of a gun. Billy could win 500 races and Roy would say he shoulda won 510. *'He shoulda won the heat two laps earlier! It took him five laps, he shoulda won it in three!'* He never had anything positive to say. Roy was a tough, tough guy."

Having his father at his side was a double-edged sword for Billy: it put him at the receiving end of both Roy's mechanical talents and brutish temperament.

Ray Carroll acknowledged just that. "Yeah, he did have Leroy there every day. Oh my goodness, they would scream at each other! I think Leroy enjoyed doing that! He enjoyed irritating people, he liked the confrontation. It was really something.

"I'm not gonna say Billy *hated* him," Carroll clarified. "Billy *understood* him. But this was a guy who'd won 250-300 races at the time, and Leroy's telling him he's an idiot and he doesn't know how to drive and he couldn't win a race without him. And start lecturing him on how he's driving—omigod, it would be crazy!

"And then, after they got done screaming and yelling, he'd come into the race shop—he always chewed tobacco—and he'd spit the tobacco into one of Billy's coffee cups. Billy was a fanatic—very anal about his shop. And Leroy would do that just to irritate him. Billy would go crazy—*'Clean that up!'*"

The behind-the-scenes demeanor was always one tick away from detonating. "Where do you want to start with Roy?" Billy Jr. threw out. "I can remember when I was a kid he punched Chuckie out in the shop—had an argument one day and knocked Chuckie out cold... Pissed a couple owners off... He told one of my crew guys one time, 'Churches are for communism.' That guy never came back again...

"As far as Roy goes: he was the greatest asset for my dad for 30 years, in racing," Junior summed up. "But he also hurt him a lot. He was the one who'd always 'tell it how it is,' whether people around my dad wanted to hear it or not."

All that anger and attitude got packed up in the trailer and brought to the race track—a flaming red field force radiating from every fiber of Billy's being.

Stay out of his way.

"People would want to come up to him and talk to him during a race, and that's not a good thing," Nick Lombardi laid it down. "He is so focused and motivated to find out what's happening on that track—he's watching every move that every other driver is making. He just doesn't want to be bothered to talk to people then. I know it. He tries to be as nice as he can, but he's kinda short with people because of that. But that's why he's so successful—because of that intensity."

ACE LANE JR.

Chuck Snyder put it more bluntly. "To this day, everyone still avoids him when he first gets out of the car. When I'm helping him and he comes in, I walk the other way. I don't want to be around him. Ya gotta give him a chance to get his mind back to being focused, his mind set. Let him cool off. Y'know, he puts a lot of pressure on himself. He figures we're giving him 100 percent—so he needs to give us 120."

And if things didn't go as planned? The mood was a thousand times more tense, with flying steering wheels and helmets and tools punctuating Billy's frustration.

"Cliff Welton's truck had a cap on it, and we'd bring everything out to go racing," said Leon Liedl. "All of a sudden, you'd hear a *WHACK!* Billy would take his helmet and throw it up in the back of that truck—it's a wonder he didn't break the cap off! He'd be all pissed off because he didn't do real good in the heat race.

"Tommy kept him grounded. 'Calm down, I'll fix it, I'll make it better for the feature.' And he always did—you could see the wins," Leon spelled out.

But the crew steered clear. "He'd be walking by and we'd get out of his way. *Here comes Pauch!* You didn't want to piss him off. We very seldom talked to him during the night," Liedl let it be known. "But at the end of the night, we talked like you wouldn't believe."

Glenn Hyneman didn't put up with the tantrums. "I always said he would win the Olympic steering wheel toss! He came in the pits one time, I was three pits down and the steering wheel went flying by my head! *What the hell was that?*" Glenn told him, "The next time you throw the steering wheel, I'm gonna wrap it around your head!"

Car chief John Sine acknowledged that Billy wasn't always the easiest person to get along with—but he fully understood why. "If things didn't go right—well, yeah. That's how determined he was to win. If you made a mistake and it cost him—yeah, he'd be mad about it. Because it cost him: he didn't win that night because of something somebody else did. Out of his control. Or if he felt he was wronged on the race track by either another competitor or even an official, he'd be mad. Yeah, he'd be mad.

"Because he wanted to win—that's all that mattered," Sine underlined Billy's fanatical laser focus, which he shared. "I was doing the same thing: if he won more races, I made more money. When we had a bad night or a bad weekend, we didn't make any money. That's like going to work all week and not getting paid! You're there trying to earn money.

And you make the most money by winning."

Fred Rahmer, who started in Modifieds before storming the Sprint Car ranks, retiring with a Hall of Fame career, is cut from the same bolt of cloth. "I never really knew Billy personally until after I'd stopped racing," Rahmer revealed. "And I'd go to a SpeedSTR race, walk over to him and you can't even talk to him, because he's so focused on what he's doing. I guess I was the same way, when I was running Modifieds or Sprint Cars—you just do your deal.

"But if you see him afterward—that's a different Billy Pauch than at the race track. When I was able to stand back and look at that—if you didn't know this guy, you'd think he's a f-ing dick. But it's just that he's so focused. He's there to win and there's nothing else."

And if you've got that kind of compulsive passion—all bottled up, like a pressure cooker set to blow—it can be conducted into purposeful energy.

Rahmer offered his thoughts on that. "I think anger, directed properly, gets results. Anger, when you let emotions get involved, equals a crash. You know what I mean? I try to tell my boys that. You can't drive with emotion—but you can use that anger.

"Turn the anger into positive energy. Figure out a way to use it to work harder to get back at 'em. If somebody does something to you on the track, you've gotta be very careful not to retaliate in a way that'd be counterproductive to your cause. But you harness that energy and use it to get by 'em."

Rahmer gave an example from his own experience. "One night I got crashed on the first lap of a race at Susquehanna." Returning to the track after quick repairs, "Kenny Adams motioned that I hadda go last. And I could tell inside the car, he was *laughing*." That's all Fred needed to get fired up. "I restarted dead-last, went straight through, I passed him for the win and waved to him as I was going by.

"On the ride home that night, I was thinking there's *no way* my car was that good," he decided. "I just had that much extra motivation because he pissed me off. Therefore, I'm cheating myself every night that that don't happen!"

Just as in Rahmer's case, there are rival drivers who could trip Pauch's hair trigger.

"There are other competitors over the years who have pushed him to his best—and his worst. At the end of the day, I think that's what drives him," Billy Jr. said of his dad's antagonists.

"Doug and Billy were beating on each other the whole race, like they always did. At one point, Doug tried to slide in front of Billy and didn't clear him, and Billy wound up hitting the outside wall. Billy got out of the car and when Doug came back around, they exchanged words, and Doug jumped out of his car. The track guys broke it up before it became anything," was photographer Dave Pratt's recollection of the September 1986 incident at East Windsor. The altercation got them both thrown out for the remainder of the season.

DAVE PRATT PHOTOS

At the top of the list: Doug Hoffman.

"They never got along," Chuck Snyder swore. "They used to get into it at Windsor! One time, Hoffman drove him so hard in the left-rear, it blew the transmission right up in the car—it was in pieces! They got fighting there. They got thrown out. It was something about those two."

Billy Jr. agreed. "My dad and Doug Hoffman: that was as tough as it got. They were the fiercest rivals," was his description of their bitter, ongoing feud that played out like a sordid subplot each week, at East Windsor, at Flemington, at Penn National. "My dad did not have much good to say about Doug. Whereas guys like Kenny Brightbill and Jimmy Horton—my dad had a lot more respect for the way they drove and the way he felt about them, on and off the track, compared to Doug Hoffman.

"And I think that's what drove him to try to win more races than Doug. That was a major factor into his big win streaks at Windsor—trying to beat Doug. They didn't see eye to eye: I can remember them fighting on the frontstretch at East Windsor…you can go down the list of it."

Front row at SDW 1987: Hoffman over Pauch by .077 seconds.

Actually, there were a lot of similarities between Doug and Billy—both strung-tight personalities threatening to bust right out of the bandwidth on a mega-charged mission to be the best, to win no matter what.

But according to Billy Jr., there was a difference in how they got it done. "My dad is gonna figure out how to go around you, and he's gonna drive it harder than you, any which way he can to prove that he can beat you," he said. "While Doug was gonna nudge you just the right way to move you out of the way. Whether it's dirty or clean? It's just a different way of winning races."

Jimmy Horton raced with Doug and Billy, won and lost against both of them. Who would he trust to race him clean? "I would say Billy just because I knew where both of us were coming from—how we raced each other and what our rules were," was Jimmy's analysis. "Doug would *surprise* you. There were times you'd think you could race with him and couldn't, and then there were times when you could race with him all night long."

In Billy's mind, it's about talent and intent. "Look, there are always people who are idiots in racing. They do stupid shit, but you know they don't mean it. They don't know any better. But when a good guy scums you? That's different. *He knows better.* A guy like Doug Hoffman knows better," he stressed. "Y'know, there were a lot of people who didn't like Doug Hoffman. He almost killed me! Hoffman was rough."

Horton would agree that Doug's reputation was warranted. They were all professional racers, all hungry, all out there to accomplish the same thing. "But I'd say 75 percent of the time Doug went over the line to win, if you know what I mean. He would put another racer in the wrong situation," Jimmy assessed.

As for intent, Jimmy holds a different view than Billy. "That intentional deal—when a good driver does it, I don't think it's intentional. He wants to win and he's running hard and he probably went over the line and got too aggressive. But it wasn't *intentional.* He didn't drive it down in the corner and say, *I'm gonna take him out, I'm gonna win this one.* He drives it down there hard enough where he's gonna use you up. And if you don't give up? Then you're probably gonna have trouble.

"Me and Doug never found that fine line," Horton admitted. "Me and Billy did. We knew how much we could push each other, and how much the other one would give. Where Doug…there were times he would take it all, and not worry about the consequences until after."

The cold war of competition between Hoffman and Pauch only began to thaw after Doug quit driving in the mid 2000s, to take on the role of promoter, first at Mahoning Valley and finally at Bridgeport.

"The best part was—I won some big-money race at Bridgeport at the end of the year. Doug goes to me, 'Huh, you made more money than I did this weekend!'" Billy was gleeful in getting one over on his old enemy. "And I said, 'That's the way it's supposed to be!'"

Nick Lombardi laid bare the backstory. "The last year Doug had Bridgeport, he called Billy, left a message. 'Billy, I really need you at my track. I don't care what it takes, I need you here regularly.' Billy was shocked. And he never erased that message from his phone, even after Doug died.

"Doug knew that Billy would draw people."

WORKING FOR THE ENEMY...

Davey Hoffman—Doug's brother and former crew chief—is the last person you'd ever expect to be calling the shots in Billy Pauch's camp. But for a time, he did.

"I worked for Billy in '95-96, back when he drove the black M1 for Faustie and he broke his arm at Knoxville. Roy punched Chuck in the eye. And Chuck quit. And I was down in Delaware with Norman Short, we were supposed to put a speed shop together. And Billy called me, asked if I wanted to be crew chief for him. Things weren't gonna work out in Delaware the way they were supposed to so I said, *Sure. Why not?* I needed something to do.

"I told him then that Faustie'll fire me come wintertime because he didn't like to pay anyone through the winter. So Billy said I could work in the speed shop. Me and John Sine were there, we built a couple of cars.

"With Doug's reputation with Billy, I never expected a call like that ever in my life."

Crossing enemy lines, Davey had a wholly unique opportunity to compare and contrast the two relentless rivals.

"Billy was really quiet. Never had much to say. Y'know, Doug got the same way. When them guys win like that... In the beginning, like in '81, '82, it was fun. We had alotta fun! Later—in '85, '86 when Doug was driving for Conklin, winning and making money...

"I don't know if it's determination, that they want to win so bad. And if they don't win, they're not happy. It was the same with Billy.

"Y'know, when you're Frank Cozze and you have Deerfoot Auto Parts—racing is for fun. I mean, Frank was still competitive and wanted to be a winner. But he always knew, when he got home, he had a business to run that was gonna make money. It's different for guys like Danny Johnson, Alan Johnson, Billy Pauch, Doug Hoffman—all them guys that did it for a living. People don't realize how hard it is to do that."

Intense. Focused. Keyed up. Anxious. And yes, *angry.* On all those counts, Davey recognized the resemblance between Billy and his brother.

"I'd say they were identical. They really were! Doug was just more thickheaded than Billy was.

"The incident that got me the most was at Flemington when it was asphalt. We had the blue 60over, Billy was in Benny's car. We were on Hoosier tires, Billy was on McCrearys. And that was a big rivalry, too: the tires.

"Doug got underneath him in three and four and they bumped a little bit. And you know, there on that asphalt, it didn't take much. Broke our right-front spindle. I don't know if that made the car hard to control, but the impact sent Billy into the wall really, really hard. I mean—*really hard.*

"I think Doug ended up winning. And afterward we said to Doug, 'Maybe you oughta call Billy to see if he's OK.' Or something. *Anything.* That was a bad hit! But no. Doug was too thickheaded to call him up. Which I didn't like.

"I didn't have no problems with Billy: him and Doug were both hard racers."

22.

Chances

All good things happen for a reason. Or they don't.

Such are the big chances in life.

Billy Pauch was ready to step out of his comfort zone in 1981, try to set foot on the national racing scene.

So in the winter of '81-82, he began working with the Mataka brothers in nearby Lebanon, NJ, helping Bill and Ed build a new Champ Car in hopes of driving for them in the USAC Silver Crown series.

In the open cockpit ranks, in these parts, the Mataka moniker was solid gold: in 1963, none other than Mario Andretti won three Midget races in the same day for the brothers. From then on, the cars from their Raceweld shop carried the number 3n1.

The ride, his first outside of a Modified, was an opportunity for Pauch to step out and showcase himself to the USAC crowd. Yet it also made sense for the Matakas to put Pauch in the seat, as Flemington Speedway was on the '82 Silver Crown schedule.

Pit road at Nazareth National in 1983. Billy finished second to Gary Bettenhausen.

MEL STETTLER

But it didn't pan out as planned.

The main thing Billy remembers: "I got fired at the Indy Fairgrounds."

That would've been September 11, 1982. "I flew out there and my flight was late," Pauch said, then explained, "USAC gives you an hour practice— that's it, they give you an

At speed at Nazareth National in 1983.

JACK KROM

hour. When that's over, you're done. Then you go out and qualify, and they take so many out of qualifying—say, 15, and then they take another 10 out of a semi.

"Well, I missed half the practice, and I didn't make the top 15 in time, so I had to run the semi. And I'm sitting in the car and the two brothers, Bill and Ed, were arguing back and forth about what tires to put on for the semi. And the semi started without me."

But that wasn't the worst of it, as per Pauch. "With that, the one brother, Bill, walks over to me. I'm sitting in the car and he goes, 'Bill, you're a nice guy—but you're fired.' I was like, *are you serious?*"

With no money to be made in Indy, Billy's immediate thought was of the Modified race he was missing that night at Flemington, a Tri-Track 100. He had already arranged for Larry Kline to drive the L car in his absence. But then, Pauch was suddenly available.

"So we went back to the airport and we got a flight to LaGuardia, and the Liedls sent their uncle to pick me up. He got me back to Flemington in time to run a heat race," Billy recounted. "And I remember in the heat race, I was running neck and neck with Karl Freyer, and we went into the third turn. I swear he broke, because I heard his car rev up. And when he revved up, I slowed but I hit him, sent him into the wall and he crashed."

Despite Billy's insistent defense that Freyer's car broke, track official Al Tasnady set him down, forced him to requalify in the consi. "I wasn't very happy about it—I didn't have to run nobody in the wall to beat 'em," he grumbled. He finished fifth or sixth in the last-chance qualifier—barely making it.

"And then I started the feature in the back—*last*. And I drove through," stated Pauch, propelled by a righteous rage after all the events of the day. "And then I drove through a second time. I lapped everyone but Kenny Brenn. I pushed him across the start-finish line. And I won the race."

The Modified race winnings were a consolation prize, but didn't make up for the indignity of losing the Champ Car ride.

So Billy decided to give it a second shot.

"I got fired from the Mataka deal, and I figured I had to redeem myself." In '83, he talked Joe Scamardella into buying a Silver Crown car—a Nance formerly driven by Sammy Swindell. "And we bought a motor off of Freyer, because he had pretty good small-blocks at that time. We put it together, we went to Nazareth," which was the opening event for the USAC series.

"I was in contention for the win," Pauch recalled. "But I was up the wall, and in the wall, and everything else, and ended up finishing second to Bettenhausen. Won a fair amount of money for second—I think it was $2,000—and that carried me through the rest of the races in the season."

Towing the circuit in his own GMC van with an open trailer, during one of the hottest summers on record, Billy ran the 10-race Silver Crown series in 1983, credited with three top 10 finishes and 12th in the final point standings, behind guys like Gary Bettenhausen, Ken Schrader, Chuck Gurney, Sheldon Kinser and Larry Rice. "It was so hot! The van didn't have air conditioning, so we'd turn the wing windows in to get some air—and it felt like the heaters were blowing in on you!" he remembered.

"It was an experience and I did it. When you're trying to make a living at it, and you ain't making no money at it—it's like, well, I gotta try something different," Pauch said in retrospect. "But at the time, I thought it might be a stepping stone to better things, y'know? I did it for a year. That winter, I disbanded the whole program and Ronnie Dunstan bought the car. I kept the motor, ran it a little bit in the Modified."

It would be almost a decade before Billy made another serious stab at a national series.

"I really had no plans. Went and ran Silver Crown, enjoyed that. That was pretty neat. That coulda been a stepping stone, but I didn't keep pursuing it. It was a lot of traveling. And not a lot of money. And not a lot of shows, only 10 or 12," said Pauch, who depended on race winnings to set his family's table. "That was a national deal. Maybe I shoulda stayed pursuing it, I don't know."

Oh, he veered into Sprints (very successfully), flew out occasionally to pilot a pickup ride in the open cockpit classes. But for the most part, Billy wasn't aggressively pursuing any big chances on a national tour until 1996, when Flemington booked a NASCAR Craftsman Truck race and he angled a ride, driving for Missouri team owner Mike Mittler, who later provided a launching pad for such top-tier NASCAR stars as Jamie McMurray and Brad Keselowski.

But it wasn't meant to be: Pauch broke his hand in an asphalt Mod crash a week before the Truck race. And that ended that.

However, the seeds were sown. In the last half of the '90s, local Dodge dealer Dick Greenfield decided he wanted to get in the game. "He wanted to get into NASCAR, and he thought that Trucks were the way to go. A fan of mine talked to him about putting me in a Truck. I think I was the first guy to drive for him," said Billy. "So he bought a couple Trucks—one was actually a car and they cut it up, made a Truck out of it."

Billy with the Dick Greenfield Dodge Truck at Nazareth National in 1997.

MEL STETTLER

And they went racing.

"It was kind of a mess. My crew was the service department at Dick Greenfield Dodge—nobody knew nothing! And I didn't know nothing! It was like the blind leading the blind, trying to run the Truck series against teams like Childress and Hendrick," Pauch admitted.

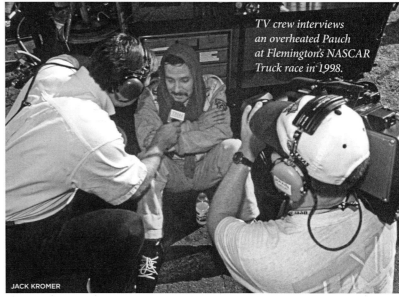

TV crew interviews an overheated Pauch at Flemington's NASCAR Truck race in 1998.

JACK KROMER

"He spent a ton of money, Dick did. But the biggest thing back then—in fact, it still is—they took advantage of the Northerners down there. Y'know? I guess they figured that was payback for the Civil War! Every time they could screw a Northerner, they'd screw 'em.

"Dick wound up with a bunch of junk. And I got involved with him."

Doug Olsen had a similar experience when he and driver Brett Hearn tried to break into NASCAR's Busch Grand National series in the late '80s. "If you weren't from North Carolina, you weren't getting any breaks or any good rides down there—unless you brought down a lot of money with you for them to steal," Olsen maintained. "Even today, down south they'll still charge more if you're from up here and not down there. And they charge for everything: if you need a piece of 6x6 inch screen to cover a headlight, they charge you for the whole roll! And they're pretty blatant about it."

In between 410 Sprint and Mod appearances on dirt and pavement, Billy ran the Dick Greenfield Dodge Truck in 1997 and '98. "Then finally, I just got to the point where I could see it wasn't going anywhere and stopped doing it," he said. "They sold the Trucks and Dick bought asphalt Modified cars," which Billy Jr. drove for a time on the NASCAR Modified tour.

Moving out of the Modifieds, into a national spotlight, was easier said than done.

Pauch believes his biggest chance and best opportunity to make it into the major

" *He can drive any damned thing! He gets in it and learns what he's gotta do to put it up front. There's not many drivers like that. In the old days, one of the drivers who could do that was A.J. Foyt—he could get in anything and do well, although it was probably easier back then. But you take Kyle Larson today: to me, I look at Pauch and Kyle Larson—they're the same person! Billy just never got a NASCAR deal.*

CAR OWNER JOHN ZEMAITIS

leagues came in 1988, when he was with Glenn Hyneman and his Keystone Pretzel team.

"That was one of my first big rides. I mean, *moneywise*. I drove for other people, we did it on a shoestring, won a lot of races. But Glenn had *money,*" Billy underscored. "I think we ran the first year and then he was selling the pretzel factory to Southland Corporation, which is 7-Eleven. They bought it and they were going to give us a Busch deal."

Glenn Hyneman detailed the business arrangement. "I sold the bakery to Southland at the peak of my racing with Billy. I got in with some of the higher management there and they were looking to do something with NASCAR. As it went, we were supposed to get a sponsorship to start a Busch team—it would've been Southland 7-Eleven on the car."

But it all fell apart.

"Two months after I sold the bakery—that's when the stock market went crazy, Southland had a leveraged buyout and everything came crashing down around them," Glenn reported. "They ended up selling the bakery, all the snack food companies were sold off, and there was a giant divestiture. Two months after they spent billions buying all this stuff, they divested themselves of everything. It was a huge shakeup."

Hyneman, as well as Pauch, lamented the lost opportunity.

"It would've been exciting. NASCAR was expanding! Other people were dabbling in it a little bit—remember, Donnie Kreitz had a little stint trying to do it; then Jimmy Horton had a little stint," said Glenn. "Back then, it was the next step for everybody—everyone wanted to get there."

If the company and the deal hadn't unraveled, Hyneman is convinced Billy's career could have taken a different trajectory. "I certainly think he had the talent to do it," he contended.

"That probably was the biggest chance I had. I did go down and talk to Richard Childress afterward about driving a Truck. They opted to go with Johnny Sauter over me. It was the closest I got," Pauch disclosed.

The motorsports media was certainly behind him. "The inside story in the Winston Cup garage is that Pauch is the most talented driver not regularly running in the big league," Dr. Dick Berggren wrote in *Stock Car Racing* magazine in late 1997. On air, TV commentators Dave Despain and Bob Jenkins made the same observation. "The book on Pauch is that he should be running every week with a top touring operation."

Billy and Glenn Hyneman at Pocono in 1988. A Big Chance Contest sponsored by Champion Spark Plugs put Pauch in an ARCA car for the day. He and Hyneman had plans to go further in the NASCAR ranks, but sponsorship fell through.

MEL STETTLER

But it just wasn't his time.

Billy's father, always the pragmatist, offered a somewhat more plain-spoken perspective: that many times, real life gets in the way of reckless ambition.

"There was a point in time he shoulda moved up. But what happened: he got his roots down here, he got married down here, then he got this big place, had kids…" Roy let the thought trail off. He started again, to explain.

"Maybe he never made it to the big time. But he did what he had to do in life. He kept his family together. The kids went to college. He straightened this place out here," the old man said of the ramshackle chicken barn sitting on acres of fallow farmland, that Billy bought and built into a state-of-the-art race shop in the late '80s.

Never bitter, Billy is philosophical about the way his career played out.

"When I was younger, they wanted an older guy. When I got older, they wanted a younger guy," Pauch contemplated, sizing up the truth.

"I never fit in."

23.

Respect

In his own funny way, Billy Pauch is a historian of the sport.

In the loft above his massive race car shop, he's curated a collection on par with most racing museums—hundreds and hundreds of trophies, plaques, photographs, program books, vintage signage, shirts, helmets, firesuits; in display cases, in cabinets, on shelves, mounted on the walls, even up the staircase. Each item documenting an indelible memory, a moment in time.

Pauch painstakingly preserves all that has happened before. He respects the past.

But it's not only the tangible treasures that Billy is bent on embracing. It's the valued relationships he's cultivated over his career.

That's the reason for the biennial "open house" events Pauch began in the late '90s, the summer he sat out recuperating from racing injuries.

"I busted up my knee pretty bad in '98, so I was out of racing for a while. At our first open house, I was laying with my cast on in a lounge chair all day, talking with everyone and signing autographs," he said. "It grew from there."

DAVE PRATT

Every other year since then, Pauch has opened his shop to the public so fans can tour the racing operation and the trophy room, meet him and the family and crew, try out the racing simulator, and spend an enjoyable afternoon "behind the scenes." The Pauch family provides snacks, snow cones and drinks, and also fun activities like face painting or bounce houses for the kids. All of this is free of charge.

What other racer does that?

"I got the idea from Richard Petty—he used to do something each year called Fan

ROBIN GILLESPIE

Appreciation Day, and I always liked that," Billy pinpointed the impetus for the event. "We do it to keep a connection with our fans—they support us, they buy our T-shirts, they come out to the races to watch us run and cheer for us. It's giving something back: like I tell my kids, 'Sometimes you've gotta bring water back to the well. Ya gotta give back.'"

The mutual respect was evident at the most recent Pauch open house, in July 2021, where close to 1,500 fans crammed the complex during the course of the day. Among those attending were seven of Billy's former or current car owners: the Liedl brothers, Tony Sesely, D.A. Hanson, Al and Dave DeBlasio, Glenn and Bonita Hyneman, John and Pee Wee Zemaitis, and Kevin Bifulco.

Which brings us to a whole other level of continued loyalty, in a game where what happened yesterday is frequently—and completely—forgotten.

"I know for a fact he still calls all of these car owners and touches base with them. Because he knows that they're the ones who put him into the lifestyle he has now, and made him as successful as he is. And he appreciates that," longtime friend and crewman Nick Lombardi pointed out. "He always used to visit Paul Kuhl, before he died. He does not forget the people who got him where he is."

A big part of that is his relationship with the fans, especially the kids in the crowd.

"He was always very good at being focused on the racing, but at the end of the night he

Fans check out the hundreds of pieces of memorabilia in the trophy room during the Pauch open house.

Billy greets young fans post-race at Flemington in 1989. He had a bad night—getting crashed out of the feature at the first green— but stuck around for the kids.

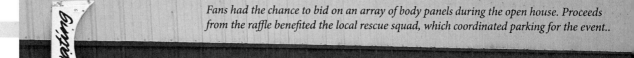

DAVE PRATT PHOTOS

(Below) Billy signs a door for a young fan, while attendees try out the racing simulator.

would make sure to take the time to say hello to everybody and sign for every kid," said Billy Jr. "I can remember sitting there for hours after each race while he did that. It's what made him, from a fan perspective."

Flemington fan Tim Weber recalled his own late-night encounter with Pauch, in the summer of 1991. "A week after he took his D/A Modified head-on into the wall, suffering serious injuries, my kids and I toured the pits post-race. Billy was sitting there with a line of kids waiting for autographs. So we decided to walk around the rest of the pits, then walked past Billy's pit again and saw him sitting by himself.

"I said to my kids, 'Billy looks tired, let's talk to him next week,' when he motioned us over. Sitting there looking like hell, with two black eyes, he wound up with both kids in his lap and a big smile for them," Weber appreciated. "He wound up with three fans for life."

And with Pauch, it's not just a regard

Scenes from the 2021 Pauch open house: (Above) A small portion of Billy's "big check" collection. (Right) Former crewman Artie Van Solkema debuted this gorgeous restoration of the original L car from 1981. (Below) Close to 1,500 fans attended the biennial event, some of which are gathered here for the raffle drawing.

DAVE PRATT PHOTOS

for his own followers. It's not all a "me" thing. He never made a big deal out of it, but he had—and continues to have—a genuine care for a lot of the drivers he raced against.

The crash house to the crash house: Hunterdon Medical Center was diagonally across the road from Flemington Speedway—and that's where an alarming number of drivers ended up on Saturday nights.

"You know how many times I visited Glenn Fitzcharles in the hospital after the races?" Billy laughed, then sobered. "I don't know, I just had a habit back then when somebody got hurt at the track, I always went over to the hospital after the races and checked on them. I remember going over there for Fitzcharles—two or three times! I went over there for Ploski. Went over there for Evernham. I don't know what it was. I just couldn't go home until I went over there to make sure they were all right."

The drivers Pauch most respected should not be buried by time and muddy memory, as far as he's concerned. That's where his self-appointed role as historian comes in. Their stories need to be told, and retold, to keep those racers larger than life, which is a stature that they have earned and deserve. Relevant, even in retirement. *Remembered.*

To that end, Billy works the phone, routinely checking in with drivers, car owners and others. Gerald Chamberlain…Ken Brenn… Bob Rossell… Sammy Beavers…Bob McCreadie…

"Y'know, we were never that close because we didn't live close. Only raced against each other maybe a couple times a year. But that sonuvabitch calls me two-three times every year, just to shoot the shit," said McCreadie, surprised by Billy's consideration. "He don't realize how good that makes me feel."

It's all about doing the right thing. "When I won Syracuse, Billy was the only driver who came in the press room after and congratulated me. *The only one*," Rich Tobias emphasized. "It gave me a lot of respect for him."

Bob McCreadie and Billy at Hagerstown in 1989.

LARRY KAVE

LEN SWIDER

FRIENDS & FOES

In May of '87, two-time Modified track champ Ken Brenn Jr. made an appearance at a Flemington drivers' meeting wearing some improbable apparel: a Billy Pauch T-shirt.

Why would he promote the image of one of his fiercest rivals?

"Anybody who goes that fast I'm a fan of," was Kenny's half-kidding comment.

The respect was mutual.

"In my era, which I would consider the '80s on, the one guy who was the toughest was Kenny Brenn," is Pauch's immediate response whenever he's asked to single out his stiffest competition. "He had good equipment, he was a smooth driver, we never really beat each other up—and we got along good. If you look at the records, me and him won the most races in our time. I'd have to say, week in and week out, he was the guy to beat at Flemington. I'd try to beat him and he'd try to beat me. And I don't think we ever really beat on each other."

It made for some great racing.

"I remember one night they battled each other through the whole feature, side by side," Ken Brenn Sr. called up the memory. "I don't remember who won but the race was so good, they parked both of them on the start-finish line.

"When they interviewed Kenny on the frontstretch, they asked what he thought the difference was between him and Billy Pauch. He told 'em, 'He does it for a living and I do it for fun.' And that was probably very, very true."

When Mr. Ken Brenn talks, everyone listens. That's because the man has some colossal cred as a car owner: almost 20 years before he even gave stock cars a solitary thought, Brenn Sr. was providing quality rides in Midgets, Champ Cars and Sprints for champions like Indy 500 winners Rodger Ward, Mark Donohue and Bobby Unser.

"I always considered Kenny tougher when he was in his father's car. Because his father always had top-notch stuff," Billy noted, confessing, "When I first started racing, I used to be so jealous of Ken Brenn! But how can you be jealous of somebody who has everything that *you* really want?"

Equipment aside, Brenn Sr.—with his legacy of national-level experience with more than 150 drivers—has no trouble sizing up who has it and who doesn't.

"They wanted it very badly. And they prepared themselves," Brenn said of the sport's biggest winners. "Y'know, once a guy gets good, you very seldom see him get in a bad race car. The good drivers attract the good race cars, and the good race cars attract the good drivers. And once you get past that learning curve, then it becomes easier for them.

"A guy like Billy Pauch didn't come to the track and put out 100 percent. He put out 110 or 120 percent every night. And I think that's true of the guys who win races— it takes more than 100 percent of their ability to do it.

"He came prepared," Brenn said of Billy. "I think that's one of the most important things in racing—to come prepared. And he came prepared both mechanically and psychologically.

"He's one of very few we're going to see in our lifetime like that. I've seen some good ones but Billy stands right up there. There's no question that he wanted to do it and he wanted to do it well. And he came there every night, not wanting to finish second or third. He was prepared to win."

JACK KROMER

Back in the '80s, at the height of their heated weekly tussle for top track honors at Flemington, the senior Brenn told Pauch just that.

"The biggest compliment I ever got was from Ken Brenn," Billy confided. "I was walking through the pits and he stopped me, said, 'You're the best driver I ever seen come through that back gate.' That was big for me, coming from him. 'Cause he'd never say much, and we didn't talk much. So for him to say that—that was big."

Friends and foes: Billy and Kenny held each other in high regard on both counts.

In 2015, when the Flemington Speedway Historical Society announced Kenny Brenn as the recipient of their Hall of Fame "Tas" Award, an honor bestowed on Pauch two years earlier, "Billy called them and asked if he could be the one to present it to Kenny," informed Brenn Sr., who was noticeably moved by Pauch's public salute to his son. "It was nice to see both of them get along so well and be such fierce competitors on the race track."

For Brenn, it's about much more than racing. "I think Billy Pauch is a good *person*—in the race car and out of the race car," is his opinion. "And you're out of the race car a lot longer than you're in it. So it's better to be good outside than inside! He worked hard enough at it to become good both ways.

"He's somebody we'll always remember. One in a million."

24.
Planning Ahead

The Pauch family farm in Stockton sits less than six miles from the outer perimeter of Lambertville—hometown of "The Old Master," Frankie Schneider, one of the greatest stock car drivers to ever grab the wheel.

Starting at Flemington Speedway in 1947, Schneider barnstormed all over the Northeast and into Canada, simply annihilating the competition along the way. He was the 1952 NASCAR National Modified champion, won a Grand National race at Old Dominion in '58, and took every big title that was worth taking throughout the 1950s and '60s. Langhorne. Nazareth National. Eastern States. Lebanon Valley's Opens. The All-Star Stock Car Racing League. An estimated 600 feature wins at 59 speedways in nine states. Inducted into both the Northeast Dirt Modified Hall of Fame and Eastern Motorsports Press Association Hall of Fame. At the end of the millennium, *Area Auto Racing News* bestowed on Schneider the lofty mantle "Driver of the Century."

Billy Pauch was just wrapping up his championship Sportsman career, moving up to Modified, when Frankie scored his final victory at Nazareth, on July 31, 1977. By then, Schneider's superiority and skills had slipped, eroded by time and technology. Yet, he continued to compete for another two decades—a fading shadow of his former self, to be remembered as an also-ran by an entire generation of fans who never had the privilege of witnessing his true power.

The falling-down chicken barn that Billy bought and transformed into a state-of-the-art race shop.

*Pauch sold both Tobias and Olsen cars with his signature stamp. Crewman Phil McCloughan remembered, "When Billy started selling Olsen chassis with his specs and bodies, he would help customers set them up and be on the phone giving them information. Roy asked him, 'Now what are **you** going to do to win? You're giving them your car...setting it up... explaining how to drive better— and they have better motors and more money!'"*

At the end of the day, one of the most celebrated stock car drivers on the planet had nothing. No money. A few trophies. A book of memories.

Growing up a stone's throw from Schneider, up County Route 523, Pauch had a front-row view of the drawn-out descent of the driver considered the greatest in his lifetime. It had to impact his perspective.

From the very beginning, Billy has been all about making money and investing it for the future; hedging his bets so he and his family would always have a cushion to fall back on.

"Back in the day, when I first started racing, I'd race all summer and then during the winter I'd always get a job. Worked for Asplundh Tree Trimmers one winter. Worked for Stover's Wells another winter. Worked as a union laborer, laying brick and mixing concrete. Worked building race cars for John Oldenburg in Flemington. Built Street Stocks, Late Models for a while. Did all kinds of stuff during the winter to try to make a living," Pauch described. "Then finally, I was good enough that I was making enough money racing that I didn't have to do that."

When he married Barbara Burns in 1984, her stepdad gave the couple a choice: a big wedding or a small wedding and money toward a house. They chose the second option, purchasing a little two-bedroom on Route 12 in Flemington. *Equity.* Billy was still running the race operation out of his father's barn—but he knew he needed to branch out.

"He worked in the main garage down home, what I built in '62 to work on race cars," Roy related. "Before that, we worked in the corn crib. He did good and then his mother run him out—told him, 'Get your stuff out to the barn! Timmy needs a place to work!' So he worked out of the barn until he moved up here."

Up here: the spread on Route 519, between Rosemont and Frenchtown, where Billy constructed an expansive 9,000-square-foot race shop—including a dedicated welding space, a high bay, an engine room, loft and kitchen—with help from the Liedl brothers.

In 1988, "I was driving by and I saw it was for sale. Four acres. I looked and it had this big building—an old chicken barn. Went in and checked it out and it was a mess. Falling down, junk in it," he remembered. But Billy could clearly see potential in the long-wasted land.

So he sold the place on Route 12 and bought the property, which included a house in addition to the collapsing outbuilding. "One of the reasons I could afford it was that the house was two-family. So we lived on the back side and rented out the front side," Pauch said. "I thought that was pretty cool: I could make money and pay the mortgage. And that kind of got me into rentals."

The neighboring property came up for sale in 1995—14 acres, featuring an old Victorian with a wrap-around porch. "At the time, I was doing pretty good racing so I bought it. It had two rentals on it—a little house plus the furniture barn. And then I put up the pole barn, and then more rental spaces. And that's how I survive now—on rentals."

And Billy kept on building. "In '99, I put up eight bays and I started renting them

MEL STETTLER

out for my kids' college. Sent both kids through college."

He is proud of the fact that Billy Jr. and Mandee "went through school and did good," both graduating from Rider University, he with a degree in accounting and she with a bachelor's in public relations. "When they were done, I figured that'd be my retirement," was always his plan for the future.

"I kinda figured it all out on my own. Nobody mapped this out for me. I probably got about 30 rentals now. Houses and rental bays and business rentals and garages and stuff," he calculated, noting, "It's hard to retire on a racer's 401K—*because there is none!*"

Billy illustrates the fast way around Flemington for students attending his driving school. A classroom session would precede actual track time.

DAVE PRATT

But the rental properties weren't the whole of Pauch's financial foundation. If there was any way to make money—he took advantage of the opportunity.

Once the race garage was built at the end of the '80s, Billy started up a speed shop business—Pit Stop Tire Service, selling McCreary tires and parts at both the shop and area tracks, with Barbara manning the tire truck and overseeing T-shirt sales while Billy raced.

"We made alotta money on T-shirts," said Pauch, who continually came out with new "must-have" designs.

Meanwhile, Barbara's long-time job as a school bus driver provided not only a steady income stream, but valuable health insurance for the whole family.

For a time, Billy even reengineered Olsen and Tobias cars, stamping them with his own signature suspension setups and selling everything from a bare frame to a complete roller direct to customers.

"That was the early '90s, when I started selling cars. I didn't think I'd ever do it," Pauch said of the endeavor. "But I figured it was a good business and I'd try it."

Pauch's three school cars are loaded up for action.

Billy had been winning big in Olsen cars, so he cut a deal with Doug Olsen to produce a chassis customized to his liking. "The way I wanted the torsion…the way I wanted the pickup points and all that. Those were the main differences. We had a good-handling car and I had Doug build 'em the way I wanted them and called them a Pauch-Olsen," he explained. "I did a lot of cars back then! I know in one year, I'd sell 25-30 cars. Not complete cars, usually—but I did frames and bodies and parts. I had a machine shop making me axle brackets and all kinds of stuff. I had my own style birdcages.

"If a guy would listen to me and do what I told him, put on what shocks I told him and all—those cars went good," he confirmed. "And if they brought it over and had us set it up? They'd go out and win races."

The profitable enterprise continued even after Pauch switched chassis builders. "After I left Faust I kinda left Olsen and went with Tobias. And then we were making Pauch-Tobias cars. I had a deal with Richie there, building cars, too."

In 1989, even before all the car-building began, the Billy Pauch Driving School was born.

To get that venture off the ground, Pauch put together a two-seater Late Model, a couple of school cars and a lesson plan. His wife rounded up a bunch of firesuits, helmets and safety gear and handled registrations. They were off and running.

Each spring, would-be racers could sign up for a three-hour classroom seminar followed by a dedicated day at the track in either their own cars or the school Modified or Sprint Car, with Billy offering guidance and feedback. Those just wanting a taste of the racing thrill could purchase a ride with Pauch in the two-seater.

Typically, they would schedule four school sessions each year at places like Flemington, Grandview, Bridgeport, New Egypt or Susquehanna, with 15-20 students per class. Even with the expense of equipment and track rental, it was a money-making side business. The added bonus? Billy really enjoyed doing it.

"I like to work with people, putting them in a race car for the first time and letting them experience it," he found out, coming to the realization that "I've learned more from teaching people, maybe, than what I've taught them! I listen to myself explain stuff out loud, stuff that I think about. And when I explain it and try to put it across to them, it sinks into me more. Maybe that made me a better driver, too."

Billy did a good job promoting the driving school and the racing simulator (below).

Always thinking: As a ploy to promote the driving school, Pauch figured out how to construct and program a racing simulator that mimicked the motion and experience of driving a Sprinter, using a crashed J&M car outfitted with all kinds of hydraulics. He debuted it at the annual Motorsports Racecar & Trade Show in 2001, charging five dollars for a four-minute ride, and posting a fast-time award for the weekend.

Fans were lined up to try it. "The year we brought it out, they ran it nonstop. It was wild! I knew it would be popular but I didn't know it would be *that* popular," Billy said. His latest—built without the hydraulics with his grandson in mind—is a racing simulator

patterned after the Zemco Sprint Car, his record-setting Syracuse ride.

"I had the driving school from 1989 to 2010. Did that for 20-some years. Sold tires, had the speed shop. We did a lot of things to make money," Billy said of his end goal, which was always centered on staying solvent. "So it wasn't just all racing—you had to be a little diversified, y'know? But you had to stay with stuff that was involved with racing. Because that's what I do."

Ray Carroll, who partnered with Pauch in his prime, is one who'll vouch for that. "He's *all* racing. His whole *life* has been racing. His whole *world* is racing, other than his children and his home," Ray assessed. "But he still had the wherewithal to build up his own business and plan for the future, invest his money properly. I do give him a lot of credit."

Fellow competitor Frank Cozze has known Billy a long time, knows what drives him. And yeah—the Frankie Schneider finale factors in.

"Listen, I know a lot of guys that's what they did: they raced for a living. And in the end, they didn't have anything," Cozze cogently observed. "Billy made sure he ended up with something. You gotta give a guy like that credit, because I saw an awful lot of those guys who ended up with nothing. Just the memories. They had nothing. They only planned for that day. They didn't plan ahead.

"But Billy planned ahead. You gotta give him credit for that."

As for the reality of making a livelihood racing, Pauch recalled a story Cozze had told him years earlier.

"Frank said he once came home from a road trip with a bunch of money, he'd won a couple races, and he told his father he was thinking about quitting the business and racing for a living," Billy recounted.

Dick Cozze—a successful salvage-yard entrepreneur and Hall of Fame race car owner—slyly knocked that notion right out of his son's head.

"Well, you've gotta pay for fuel," he said, taking some bills from Frank's money pile. "And you've gotta pay for tires. And motor maintenance. Motels. Pit fees." Cozze Senior kept ticking off expenses and peeling off bills.

When he was done, Frank was left with $50.

"I think you'd better keep your job," was Dick's tart advice.

25

Family

(Left) Roy and Anna Mae, Christmas 1956, expecting Billy. (Below) Their 1958 Christmas card. (Above) Billy at three, 1960.

a very ☀ merry ☀ Christmas ☀

Mr. & Mrs. Roy Pauch
and Family

LEROY

Roy Pauch would be the first to admit he had no business racing. "I was a farmer," he firmly stated. As the story goes, a friend of his was competing at Hatfield in the mid 1950s; that led another buddy to prod Roy into a partnership to build their own car.

"I didn't know nothing about racing, but this guy was a good mechanic and he could fabricate real good," he said. "So we proceeded. I got the car, got the motor block, and he showed me how to port and relieve it. It was about a week or two's work in getting one of them flatheads ready."

That was about how long the alliance lasted. "His wife and my wife determined that he wasn't going to help me anymore. And we separated," Roy indicated. "But I wasn't a quitter."

So with his farmer's ingenuity, he figured things out by trial and error. "It wasn't like anyone would help you much because everything was top secret," Roy pointed out. "It wasn't like you went to a speed shop and people would tell you what to do. You were on your own."

He started a few races back in 1957-8, and doggedly kept at it, throughout the 1960s and into the '70s, even though the results didn't match the effort. In all that time, Roy won

Roy loses the handle at Nazareth, as Frankie Schneider, Rags Carter and Sammy Beavers file past.

JOHN REILLY

a single feature event, at Nazareth in '72. By his own admission, he wasn't a great driver.

But those years of cut-and-try, cleverly turning junked pieces and parts into competitive components, made him a great mechanic. "Towards the end, I was getting on to it," Roy said of his knack for tuning a race car. "And then when Billy came along, I had a lot of things that were going. It wasn't what anybody else was doing but he dominated his two years in Sportsman with a lot of these ideas.

"He was getting good. Why hold him back? So I started helping him."

ANNA MAE

If you had assumed that Billy took after his father—you'd be wrong. Leroy was a racer, sure. But it was his tough-as-nails mother who was the *real* competitor in the Pauch family.

"I got pictures of her hung up in the shop, with her trophies and all," Billy said of his mom's racing endeavors in the mid to late '60s. Not only did Anna Mae race—this woman had a *ride.* "A guy by the name of Jimmy Hash. Real nice guy. He was a friend of the family who had a Sportsman car, and she would drive that in the Powder Puffs. Number 98," he specified.

"She was *into* it. She'd read the papers to find Powder Puffs. I remember one time she made the guy tow to one. They pulled up to the gate and said, 'We're here for the

Powder Puffs. Where do we go?' The official looked at the car, told her, 'I don't think you want to enter the Powder Puffs with that car.' It was a *demo derby!*"

The feisty Anna Mae was no slouch in the seat. "She got around pretty good. Won a bunch of Powder Puffs—six or seven, maybe more, mostly at Windsor but Flemington and Harmony, too," Billy strained to recall the details. "I don't know, I was a little kid. But I do remember carrying her trophies around after the races—that felt like a big deal to me, to carry the trophy."

ACE LANE JR.

But like everything in racing, it wasn't all accolades. "She drove Jimmy's car at Harmony one time—had it up on the fence!" Billy then segued into an incident that is still a sore point, some 47 years after the fact.

"The one and only time I let her drive my car, she wiped it out!"

In 1975, Pauch was kicking ass in Flemington's Rookie division, acing every race en route to his first championship in his home-built Mustang. And then—Anna Mae took the car out in a Powder Puff. And crashed it to smithereens.

"They pulled her out of the car and I could see she was OK. But the car was *destroyed.* That was my pride and joy!" Billy wailed. "I thought I was done for the year! Had to clip it from the cage forward, all new, and the rear was hung out.

"She tore it all up, pretty big time," he said, the sting of it still raw. "Somebody sent me pictures of the crashed car and I used to have them on my phone. She never thought it was funny." Billy pictured his prickly mother's outraged pique, which lasted decades. "She always swore the old man did something to the car and it broke on the last lap."

Anna Mae took it serious—on the track and on the street.

"She drag raced, too, I think at Harmony," Billy thought back. "I remember the car vaguely, from when I was little. My father bought a '58 Chevy, had a 348 with three twos on it. That was like a hot rod, back in the '50s. Then they traded that in on a '63½ Ford Galaxie with a 427 with two fours and a four-speed on the floor.

"She was a leadfoot," Billy appreciated. "Always go down the road 100 miles an hour…

"I remember one time, we were coming down River Road and little Frankie Schneider was with us, and he kept egging her on. *'Do 50!'* She'd do 50. *'Do 60! Do 70!'* She'd take it up to 70. *'Do 80!'* She'd get it up to 80 or 90."

Roy, Billy and Timmy with Anna Mae's hot Galaxie.

The kids were all squealing in the back seat. "You better not tell your mother!" Anna Mae warned Frankie.

"So she takes him home and the first thing he says is, 'She got up to 90 miles an hour with me in the car, Ma!'

"I think that was the last time his mother let him ride with us."

Anna Mae's dual-quad R-code Galaxie "was a pretty hot car," Billy granted. "She had that car through the '60s. Then she started working for the post office, delivering mail and stuff, and got calmer cars."

TIMMY

"My whole immediate family: everybody raced," informed Billy. That included his only sibling, Timmy, two and a half years his junior.

"Timmy was a pretty good driver. Probably more patient than I was," Billy maintained. "Then again, everyone's more patient than me. I'm not a patient person!"

If you asked Anna Mae about her two sons (or even if you didn't ask her, she'd still state her opinion), Timmy was by far the better race car driver. Blunt to the boundaries of hurtful.

The truth was that Timmy had the talent but he didn't have the temperament to be a top-tier driver.

ACE LANE JR.

"He just never liked to deal with people. He wasn't a people person. And he didn't like dealing with the crowds after the races," Billy said of his brother. "But as far as driving—he was a good driver. He won one or two Sportsman races at Flemington, then he ran Modified for a little bit. Then he just packed it in.

"He came back in the late '90s, when they were doing Enduro racing. It was more affordable, I guess. Running Modifieds was always an expensive proposition. Running Enduros was a lot cheaper. So he started running Enduros at Flemington. Ran there up until they closed, then he went to Grandview. Won a lot of races at both those tracks, championships and stuff. If you look at the record books, you'll see he had a lot of wins."

The Pauch brothers both pursued similar goals, but on different ends of the spectrum. Likewise, their personalities were polar opposites.

"Billy's more aggressive than Timmy. Timmy don't hurry nothing; he's just laid back. He has the most trouble with being depressed," revealed Roy, who also struggled with what he called "my crisis of nerves" for much of his life. "What I would say is Timmy has more feelings for people than Billy does." He thought about that. "Two kids: one's the direct opposite of the other."

Billy would agree with that assessment.

"Timmy took more after my father. I took more after my mother. My mother was a neat freak—everything had to be clean and organized. My father and brother were like,

Roy and his boys, 1979.

BOB YURKO

'There's the pile over there. It's in there somewhere.' Only they knew where anything was in the garage!" As opposed to Billy, whose spotless shop has, as Anna Mae would say, "a place for everything and everything in its place."

Regimented: that's the way Billy lives his life. Ray Carroll recognized that. "If you know Billy well, you know he's very, very robotic. He does everything on a schedule. He goes to lunch at a certain time, he goes to dinner, he comes back to the shop and works on the car at a certain time, he sets the car up on a certain day," Carroll took note. "He's so set in his ways! But I respect him for everything he does: he's very neat, orderly, organized, and he knows his business when it comes to racing."

Roy and Timmy knew their stuff, too—it's just that it was all over the place.

"Neither one of them were really driven. They just went along, y'know?" Billy considered. "My father was there helping me almost my whole career in Modifieds. But when he wanted to go, he went.

"He was like the weather—came and went when he wanted."

Following a stomach aneurysm and subsequent stroke, Roy Pauch made his final exit on March 7, 2016. Timmy took care of Anna Mae, who had her own health problems, as did he. She died at home, on the farm in Stockton, on August 6, 2020. Timmy passed there four and a half months later. He was 61.

The only family Billy has now is the one he created.

BARBARA

She was the prettiest girl at a house party in Flemington: that's where blonde, blue-eyed Barbara Burns caught Billy's eye, in '76. She had no idea who he was.

"When I met him, he was working at a gas station," said Barbara, who lived in the town of Flemington but had never been to the track. "My brother would always go to the races, was a big fan of Bill's. I really didn't know much about racing. I was just attracted to him, really. I didn't know how good he was. Not a clue."

She found out quickly. Later that year, Billy asked Barbara to accompany him to the Flemington Speedway awards banquet. "His Sportsman championship banquet," she reminisced. "That was probably one of our first real dates."

By the time she was a senior in high school, they were inseparable.

"When I turned 17, we went to Florida on a vacation, drove down." Barbara termed that trip a turning point in their relationship. "Then we came back and I had my car accident.

"I was leaving Bill's shop and the roads were icy," she described. A car coming in the opposite direction hit her head-on.

"I heard people passing me, yelling to me. I just kept saying, 'Go get Bill...Go get

A celebratory kiss after a big win at Flemington in 1985.

ACE LANE JR.

Bill!' Somebody finally went down to the shop and got him. Then they took me to the hospital."

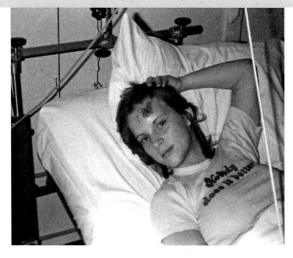

She was good and banged up, but the worst injury was a fractured femur. "Back then, they put you in traction. So I was in the hospital, in traction, for 49 days," Barbara said. In those seven weeks, "Bill didn't miss more than two days, coming to see me."

They were there for each other during the dark days: the year before Barbara's accident, in 1977, Billy had made the move up to Modified, with backing from Raceway Speed Center, expecting to set the world on fire. Although he knocked back three Sportsman wins in his own car early in the season, and was scored second in the year-end Daniel Boone 200 at Reading, Pauch went winless in the Modified.

"That was devastating to him," Barbara confided. "It was very hard on him that he didn't win a Modified feature that year."

Barbara stood by as Billy beat himself up about it all winter. "It didn't matter that it was his rookie year. He's very competitive," was her broad understatement. "Take him skiing, he's gonna go right to the top. He doesn't start on bunny hills."

Billy and Barb were married in Sandy Ridge Church in 1984. Billy Jr. wed Michelle Dysart there in 2012.

They'd been together for eight years when Billy slipped an engagement ring on Barbara's finger; they were married six months later, on November 16, 1984 in the little Sandy Ridge Church in Stockton, taking up Barb's stepdad's offer of a down payment on a house in lieu of a big wedding.

"We had about 85 people in a very small place, just a buffet, nothing fancy. But we had a good time," Barbara said of the wedding reception. "We didn't go on a honeymoon until the following year."

Their first Christmas as a married couple was spent in their first house, on Route 12 in Flemington. They were still living in that little two-bedroom when Billy Jr. was born in 1987. By the time Mandee was born, five years later, the Pauches had moved to the first of two adjacent properties they'd purchase in Frenchtown.

Another championship to enjoy at the 1987 Flemington banquet.

Barbara was a racer's wife and business partner—selling T-shirts, tires, hard parts—while trying to raise children who grew up in the grandstands, amidst the taunts and trash-talk unfeeling fans unleashed on their father and her husband.

"You don't want them to have to hear that stuff," she said of the vitriol aimed at any big winner. "I constantly told the kids that it's *not* OK to clap or boo. Just sit still and be quiet, and ignore those people. I think they learned that well."

It was easier said than done on her end—but she always bit her tongue.

"When I sold tires, I would go up in the grandstands to watch Bill's race and there would be people there booing him, hoping that he crashed into the wall, and this and that," Barbara stewed. "Then I would go back down to the tire trailer—and those *same exact people* would come and buy tires from me, and ask me to let them go…not pay me until the following week."

She would be incredulous. "You just wished my husband would crash into the wall, and now you're asking for him to give you credit until next week? I mean, *how crazy is that?*

"But I was always told to swallow it. To keep the business separate from your personal feelings." Barbara was the perennial peacemaker, avoiding confrontation or controversy at all costs, although it took a toll on her. "I usually let them go, let them pay me the following week. But then they'd still be the same people in the grandstands, clapping when he hit the wall…when he spun…booing. *The same people.*

"'Can I pay you next week?'"

Her pacifism carried over to her family interactions and philosophies. Like the fights Roy and Billy had "all the time," she said of their frenzied father-son battle of wills. "It made it very hard on me. I'm not a good person with that stuff. I'm not a fighter. I don't like competition," she noted the irony, "but here I am."

Smack in a lifestyle centered on cutthroat competition.

All these years, Barbara has kept a lot bottled up. "The worst thing you can do is fight with a race car driver at the track. I tell that to Mandee and little Billy all the time! You never fight with your loved one before they go out on the race track—because then they're thinking about everything else and not concentrating on their racing," she laid it out.

"So that's why I always walked on thin ice, tried to cause as little static as possible, tried to avoid confrontation, so Bill could be successful in racing. I think I supported him 100 percent," Barbara contended. "Now, I'm dealing with some health challenges, so I don't go to the track as much as I did. After all these years, it's time to put my health front and center."

Billy and Barbara were out for a ride on his Suzuki road bike through the town of Lambertville about eight years ago, when a car turned left into them, crushing her foot under the downed 'cycle. Multiple operations were performed to put the shattered bones back together, but healing was delayed and complicated by Barbara's diabetes. Still coping with that slow progress, she's undergone open heart surgery and was hospitalized more than once with pneumonia in recent years.

Barbara has always been the backbone of this family, standing offstage, her quiet and steadfast support making

Tooling around Williams Grove on the scooter in 2020.

JACK KROMER

it possible for her husband and her son and her daughter to go out and grab their dreams, live in the limelight of their ambitions. And now, she is exhausted.

"There are people who think I just don't want to do it anymore, that I have no interest in what Bill does," Barbara said of her absence at the race tracks. "That's not what it is. I'm just tired. When did you not know me to care about things? I care about things I shouldn't care about! I help everybody that I shouldn't be helping."

For the first time in her adult life, Barbara is worrying about…Barbara.

"I enjoy staying home. It's relaxing. I spend a couple hours with my mom, come back home and put Flo on, watch all their races on TV," she said of her newfound time away from the tracks.

"I always put myself to the side. I always was second," Barbara recognized. "Now, it's time for me to step back and take care of myself."

BILLY JR.

Billy Pauch's sole son and namesake: the life burden doesn't get any bigger than dragging around that mantle, with its ponderous weight of expectation.

"You were a local rock star if you were winning—especially in the late '80s and '90s, when our crowds in racing were the biggest," said Billy Jr. As the son of one of the region's most celebrated winners, "You couldn't turn the corner without someone knowing who you were. There were alotta eyes on you."

Little Billy's destiny was decided before he was born. "Between his grandfather and his father, I don't think I had a choice in the matter," Barbara surrendered. "I just wanted him to do what he enjoyed doing—it didn't matter to me what that was.

"I went to all his wrestling matches and basketball games in school, when his dad was working

DAVE PRATT

on the race cars. I went through all that with him. Then he said, 'No Mom, I want to race.'" Barbara sighed. "So out the door went the sports and in the door went the racing. And that was about it."

That's one big helmet to grow into.

Big Bill quickly laid down the ground rules. "I remember when I was nine, coming back from basketball. And he said to me, 'If you wanna race, I'll get you a car. But you've gotta work for it—an hour each day at the shop.' That taught me a lot. I wasn't *given*. I *earned*."

Young Billy started Quarter Midget racing in 1999, piecing together a part-time midweek schedule around his father's packed-to-the-rafters racing calendar. Remember: Senior was racing to put food on the table and pay the monthly bills. It was straight-up business, the family's livelihood, and necessitated his full attention.

"My dad would try to go. But he didn't get to many races," Billy Jr. admitted. "Both of my grandfathers, Bosh and Leroy, took me racing a ton when I was a kid."

From Quarter Midgets, he stepped up to Slingshots. "Ran Phoenixville every Wednesday, because my dad could go on Wednesday nights. I never really got to run every week because of his schedule, but I was able to start racing," he offered. "Moved from there to the Slingshots at Borger's Speedway for '01 and '02. We could do that because it was Tuesday nights: could never go racing on the weekends because that was when Dad raced."

Unlike his father, Junior was not an out-of-the-box phenom.

"I was OK, won a race or two, wasn't no superstar or nothin' like that," he accepted. "I was racing against kids who were running two-three days a week."

And the chant began: "Well, this is Billy Pauch's kid—*why isn't he winning every week?*"

It took a long time for little Billy to find his own feet.

He was just turning 16 in 2003 when he leapfrogged over the Sportsman ranks and landed in a Modified. "Dad took the ride in the 114 and Buddy Biever gave me an older car to run Big Diamond." Young Billy maintained the car himself while Roy attended to the motor. "I didn't set the world on fire. Ran 22 races and I broke in 12 of 'em. Because I was 15, 16, trying to race a Modified. My father's and grandfather's idea was that I had to screw up in order to learn.

"It does beat you down: you start thinking, *Should I be doing this? Do I not have it?*"

But the Kid's Kid got some encouragement from an unlikely source at the opening day race that year at Hagerstown in February. "In the heat race, I ran second to last. Tom Hager finished last and pulled in behind me," Billy Jr. said, remembering Hager's words at the end of the race. "There's only 24 cars here and I was slow, so I let you go, just to see if you'd be any good," Tom told Junior. "You'll be all right. It's gonna be a few years but you'll be fine."

Hager had him pegged.

"About 2012 or '13, it started clicking. Since that time, I don't think I've won less than six races a year."

Bosh with Billy Jr. and Mandee (in her brother's Slingshot).

BOSH

Sebastian Bronnhuber wasn't Barbara's father by birth or by name—but he was the only father she ever knew.

"He was a friend of my dad," Barbara explained. "When my dad died in a fire, my mom was pregnant with me and he took care of her. Once I was born, he took care of me, and my mom and my brother."

Bronnhuber—"Bosh" to everyone who knew him—married Mary Burns and raised her two kids as his own. He was beaming when he walked Barbara down the aisle to wed Billy Pauch, who became like a second son.

"My mother's father helped him a lot, with advice on the rentals and the outside business world," Billy Jr. acknowledged. "Bosh did all the wiring in my dad's first building—he did a lot around here for my father, especially when he first got started."

And later on, he did the same for his grandson. "Roy didn't go with little Billy that much—he was racing with big Bill," Barbara said of her son's start in the sport. "It was my dad and Ronnie Totten who went with little Billy, until he got older and could drive his own truck. Until then, my dad went with him most of the time."

As irascible as Roy in his own way, with a ribald sense of humor and the remnants of a Germanic accent, Boshy wasn't a born-and-bred racer nor a bona fide wrench. But he had his own fan following: his pit barbecue chicken was famous throughout the county.

Senior (114) and Junior race each other at Big Diamond in 2003.

MEL STETTLER

His mother knew what had to happen. "I kept telling Billy, 'You can't drive like your father. You have your own driving style.' Little Billy used to like it around the bottom; big Bill always ran up top, always full blown out. Little Billy had patience—he'd run along the bottom and pick 'em off gradually, one by one by one. Where big Bill hadda pass 'em all in one lap," Barbara dissected the dichotomy of their driving styles.

"Once he got settled and figured out his own driving ability, then he started to do good. Because he was finally being himself, and not trying to fill his father's shoes."

With the Pauch name came opportunities for Billy Jr.—ARCA at Pocono, the NASCAR pavement Mod tour in Connecticut, Oklahoma's Chili Bowl. But it was too much, too soon. He wasn't ready.

"I was trying to do too much—I tried to drive everything I possibly could and didn't focus on one thing," he said in hindsight. "I tried to be like him."

A pivotal turning point for Billy Jr. was teaming up with Rick Holsten in '14. In the past eight years, he and Holsten have connected for 44 wins and three Modified track championships—two at New Egypt and one at Georgetown. He also took the 2015 Big Diamond title in his own car. In the bigger picture, little Billy hit the 100 career win mark on May 19, 2021, picking them off in small- and big-block Modifieds, Midgets, 305 Sprints, SpeedSTRs and 600 Micros at 11 tracks in four states to reach that milestone.

More than 100 victories add up to a very respectable career. True, it's not in the otherworldly realm of 740+. But Billy Jr. is not his father. He never purported to be.

Outside the race track, he's got a solid everyman's life as a financial consultant for MetLife, sitting at the computer pricing insurance. His wife Michelle is a schoolteacher. They have two beautiful kids, and in recent years built a house on a piece of property purchased from his parents.

Billy Jr. is joined in the winner's circle by wife Michelle, son BP3 and daughter Avery.

"I'm at the point…the only drivers with more wins than me each year are guys who do this for a living. I'm OK with winning my 10-15 a year and having another job. Because I realize if you're gonna win 20-40 a year like Sheppard and Friesen and my dad did—that's all you do!" Billy Jr. deliberated. "I've got such a good job I couldn't move off it. Hopefully, I end up with 200-300 wins in my career. Not 700, but that's who I am. I'm satisfied with that."

When Pauch Jr. started out, "there were three of us racing together—Cozze's son, Jimmy Horton IV, and me"—all offspring of big-name Modified drivers. "Out of the three of us, I'm the only one who's still racing Modifieds.

"So I must've been good enough to keep it going," he concluded.

 **Born five years after her brother,** Mandee laments that she missed a lot of her father's biggest moments.

"I look back to 1994. Dad set the world record. Where was I? I asked Mom: *Where was I??*"

"You weren't even two! You were home with the babysitter," Barbara told her.

Nonetheless, "I'm now learning that definitely affected me a lot. I know I have triggers—not abandonment issues, but I have a fear of missing out on a lot of stuff," Mandee admitted.

So she's been on a mission not to miss a minute of racing.

"I know in middle school, high school—my parents always pushed me to do sports, to go to parties, to go to prom." The plea fell on deaf ears. "I had my prom dress bought, all ready and everything. And I told my date, 'Listen, I'm not going unless it rains.'"

It didn't rain. And her father raced. And Mandee was there, most likely celebrating one of his 10 wins at New Egypt that season, while the hopped-up Pauch haters in the crowd hurled catcalls and beer cans.

By that time, she had grown a tough skin, insulating herself from the insults.

But it wasn't always that way.

"I will always remember one 76er at Grandview." Mandee got serious. "You know how they line the cars up on the frontstretch, and the drivers get out and they wave when they do the introductions? I know Dad was starting towards the back because he was down in turn four. I remember running down there, trying to wave to my dad…standing up against the fence, trying to get his attention. And the people behind me in the grandstands were all yelling and cursing him.

"I remember just falling into tears. Lori Totten— she was there with me, babysitting me—was rubbing my back, telling me, 'Don't listen to 'em, don't listen…' I could not understand how people could talk bad about *my dad*. Of course, the older I got, the more I understood. But at the time, it was *heartbreaking*. As a child—and I was definitely younger than 10—to hear people say those things about my father, it broke me."

Barbara did her best to protect the kids.

DAN CULHANE

How can people be that hateful?

"The next day, we were sitting at the house, on the porch, and I said something to my dad," Mandee broached the subject. "He explained to me that he works hard, he puts in all the effort. But the fans in the stands don't understand all that goes into it—they just see what happens on the track, they see us winning races. They don't see what happens behind the scenes to get us to this level."

Reluctantly, she came to grips with the grim realities. "It made me more respectful of the drivers who win. Between my dad and my brother, I see all the work they put into it. And I see that it's an incredible thing that they're able to dominate and make a name

DAN SCHAFER

for themselves," Mandee said, getting emotional. "People just want to downgrade them. It's…God, I just started crying, talking about it."

From that pain came a purpose: educating and entertaining fans with weekly behind-the-scenes vlogs on her wildly popular YouTube channel, *Dirt Track Untold*.

From helping to promote her father's racing school program and marketing T-shirts at the tracks and on social media, Mandee transitioned into freelance public relations, working with area speedways and other race teams.

"The more I worked with clients, the more tracks I worked with—I realized that I actually had a voice! For the longest time, it was Billy Pauch, 'The Kid,' and then it was 'The Kid's Kid.' I'm Billy Pauch's *other* kid over here! He's got *another* one!" she laughed. "And since I started doing my own thing, it's so incredible."

Billy Sr. gave her the idea to videotape their racing experiences around the circuit in 2017. "He pulled out the oldest camcorder I could possibly imagine. And he wanted me to walk around Volusia for a week with this old-school camcorder, and I felt so embarrassed," she confessed.

She was surprised at the response. "I thought, *who would want to know what the heck I have to talk about?*—and it just went over so well!" Mandee marveled. *"This is what Dad had to say at lunch…We saw Frank Cozze and Janice at Peach Valley…We went to the track early and washed the car…This happened, that happened…* People really enjoyed it!"

Focused on his job, Dad did his damnedest to stay out of camera range in the beginning, but that has changed. "He's gotten so much better. He'll turn to me now, give me a smile," Mandee enthused. "And what I love so much: when he finally warmed up to me videotaping, people saw another side of Billy Pauch. Before that, people only ever saw him in race mode. Now when I'm videotaping after the races, over dinner, he's having a drink or two—he's goofy and happy and smiling and explaining what's going on. And that is a whole new world.

"I want people to have a better appreciation and understanding of all that we go through. All that we put into it: all the sweat, all the tears, all the time, to go out there and win those races," she outlined her intent. "The fans in the stands, who never worked on a car or raced a car in their lives—they love to see accidents, they love to see crashes, all that drama, the adrenaline, the excitement of it. They don't realize how much a tire costs—when that blows, it's $225. When you wreck a car, it's thousands of dollars. And there's a *human* in that race car."

Over the years, Mandee has honed her craft, adding multi-angle in-car camera footage, live Q&As, tech tips, stories from the shop and the road, all centered on her immediate family: her father, her brother, and now her husband.

On January 29, 2022, Mandee married Modified touring series regular Mike Mahaney who also descends from winning lineage: he is the son of 1988 Fulton Speedway co-champion and '89 Southern Tier 100 winner Jim Mahaney.

With the Mahaney operation based in upstate New York, and her close-knit family collected on the Pauch compound in New Jersey, the new Mrs. Mahaney has done a lot of bouncing around in recent years. That will probably continue to be the case.

"I travel back and forth," Mandee obliged, admitting, "It's still very hard for me to miss my father's races."

Mandee and Mike.

BRADY HOUSER

MANDEE ON MAKING IT...

"Mom and Dad were invited to Ray Evernham's induction into the NASCAR Hall of Fame. At the very last minute, my mom got pneumonia and my parents couldn't go, so Dad asked me to fill in. Mike and I went. We sat at a table with Don 'The Snake' Prudhomme—a table with all big names. It was jaw-dropping! It was incredible to be in a room with so many accomplished people.

There was an after-party, but I was honestly hesitant to go. I told Mike, 'Who are we going to know? Who are we going to talk to? We're just filling in for my parents, we're not even technically supposed to be here!'

So we kinda sit in the corner, eating and drinking. And Ryan Newman waves us over. I'm looking over my shoulder. 'Mike, is he waving to *us*?'

So we sit down with Ryan Newman. He goes, 'Do you know who I am?' *Of course.* Do you know who I am? And he says, 'You're Billy Pauch's daughter. You're Mandee. I watch your YouTube videos.' I was so struck. *Get the heck out!?!*

We sat there until the party closed out. And Ryan Newman gave me so many tips and advice. Still to this day, he'll text me once in a while. 'That was a great video.'

He has two young daughters—maybe that's how he came across my videos. And he's told me, 'You have to focus on the kids.' Gosh, he sounds just like my father! 'The kids are the future.'

At the time, BP3 was so young. But I told him I had plans to do something with my nephew. And about a year ago, I started involving my nephew more and more. Ryan texted me, 'I see you're doing what I told you to do!'

Yes, and it's working!"

TEAMWORK:

*"I was with good teams. That's what makes you shine—**good teams.** Like I always say: you can equate a race team to a football team. You can be the best quarterback in the league, but if you ain't got a front line to hold 'em up so you can pass the ball and make touchdowns—you're lying on your back."*

DOLLARS & SENSE...

Kevin Bifulco—who created a prosperous excavating business with his bare hands; who had kicked around in Street Stocks at Windsor and New Egypt in the '90s and early 2000s—understood, finally, that success is all about *need*.

"I didn't have the *need* to win on the race track," he accepted in 2004. "I was worrying about topsoil, stone, mulch, demo. If somebody calls me for a backhoe at three o'clock in the morning, I'm getting up." And while driving a race car was fun, "I always kept my priorities straight."

Watching Billy Pauch wheel a Modified from the sidelines, Bifulco saw the same unconditional commitment that had propelled his business hustle to its heights. *The need.* He could certainly get onboard with that.

Nicky Lombardi knew Kevin, set up a meeting with Billy at the Amwell Valley Diner after the 2004 season. "He's sizing me up, I'm sizing him up," Bifulco recalled. "I mean, we're both *old*—in our late 40s, pushing 50 at the time. So we're eating lunch, and I said to him, 'I'd like to get a car.'"

One thing about Kevin: he doesn't do anything half-measure. "I think he thought I was gonna offer to sponsor a motor or something."

Instead, Bifulco told Billy, "I'm gonna buy two brand-new cars and two new Feil motors."

Pauch was floored. "TWO? I don't think we need all that."

Kevin was committed. "I think we do. When we go to the track we wanta have *the goods*. We gotta win! We're getting old—we can't jerk around!"

Right away, Bifulco found out how frugal Pauch is. "He's very thrifty...very calculated in his planning," he discovered. "Me? If I want something, I'm going for it. I'm not waiting 'til tomorrow—I gotta have it *today!*"

In a direct reversal of most driver-owner dynamics, Billy tries to rein in Kevin, to keep him from spending too much money.

"He's a smart man. He wants to try this and that. But if the car's not winning? JUNK IT! JUNK IT!" Kevin declared, exasperated with their struggles the past season. "It's like a guy trying to shoot a deer and he stays on his trail for too long, too long. And he chases the deer into somebody else's property. That car was *no good*. Cut it up! Being a little tight, he lets the cost interfere with it. Me, I'd do away with it. I got a dump truck that's burning oil, costing me too much money—I sell it! Get rid of it!

Kevin and Billy bank a big one at Bridgeport in 2016.

RICK SWEETEN

"We wasted a year on that car, spinning his wheels," Kevin claimed. "I'm not mad about it. But he worked hard. And it brought him down. And we had a brand new weapon in the garage! When we finally brought it out he tells me, 'Wow, that car is so much better!' *No shit.*"

Kevin shook his head. "Sell it to some kid running Sportsman and let him beat his brains out with it! But he don't give up."

Billy has been with Bifulco longer than any other car owner—17 years and counting, which is an eternity in this business. Together, they've won 96 times, more than with anyone else in his career, other than himself. It's not over yet, but it's getting close. Billy just turned 65; Kevin is not far behind him. When Pauch decides to finally call it quits, it will be carrying Kevin's colors. They will go out together.

"Y'know, it upsets ya a little bit," Bifulco wistfully reflected. "I think to myself now, if I coulda got this guy and had him when we were both a little younger..." The thought drifts off—no need to finish it.

"I'm not sponsoring no young kid. They don't have the *need*...they don't have the *want*...they don't have the *work ethic*," Kevin guaranteed. "Y'know what I mean?"

26.
Winding Down

More than a decade ago—in the pits at New Egypt on August 30, 2011, to be exact—Billy slid into the cockpit and buckled up, just like he'd done on every other race night, thousands of times before. But for the first time in his life, he did not feel like he was one with the car.

That was the last time he ever sat in a Sprint Car.

"When you're a kid, you think you're going to live forever," Roy put forth that falsehood, recalling his son's moment of epiphany. "He's getting up there. He beat everybody in a Sprint Car—he beat Rahmer, he beat 'em all. But his last time in a Sprint Car, at New Egypt, he finished third in his heat, went out in the feature, took a couple laps and pulled off. I asked him, 'What happened to the car?' He said, 'I felt uncomfortable.'

"You don't feel comfortable, you get out."

But Billy only abandoned the Sprint Car, the more dangerous animal. On that very same night, as a matter of fact, he won the companion Modified race. And since then, has added another 61 wins—and five more championship titles—to his body of work through 2021.

The family, minus Mike who was off racing: Billy Jr. with BP3 and wife Michelle holding Avery, Mandee with Speedy, Barbara and Billy.

Yet, it's inevitable: at 65, he knows his career is winding down.

"There was a time, when I was in my 30s, I had the advantage of youth. Well, I don't have that advantage anymore," Billy accepts. "Youth's big. But experience is big, too. That's all I've got now: experience. I don't have youth anymore."

Now, when car owner Kevin Bifulco asks him, "Whadda we need to win?"—Billy gives him the God-given reality: "Thirty years of youth, where I can hold onto the wheel for 30 laps and drive every lap like it's the last lap."

For sure, the adrenaline's still flowing on race-day mornings. "But I'm not 18 no more. It takes a while for everything to wake up and start moving," Pauch yields to the years. "Once I'm in the car, and I'm out there and I'm racing—then I'm 18 again."

There's no reason to keep doing this. "His hearing's getting bad; he's got a short fuse. If he quit tomorrow, it ain't like he's got no money coming in," his father bottom-lined as far back as 2013. His physical body is held together by pins and plates and screws from all the injuries he's suffered in the sport—Pauch pushes through all those aches and pains to stay in the seat.

What's the motivation?

"Everybody asks me, 'How the heck can you do this so long?' I never really thought about it but it's *winning*. If I didn't win, I wouldn't want to be doing it," Billy stated. "That's what keeps me

Even as late as 2021, it was usually big Bill giving advice to Junior, educating him on what'll work and what won't. Then, the roles were suddenly reversed.

"He really got me straightened out there at the end of the year," Billy said of his son. "He's gotten really good. I can't get over how much understanding and how many insights he had."

On a roll of late, Billy Jr. is happy to return the favor.

"It's finally taken me 'til I'm 30-something to be able to give back to him and help him. Time catches up to all of us. But the guy can still drive! He doesn't want to do it as much as he used to, the work part of it—which is 95 percent of it. And to be honest, I don't think I'd want to still be doing it at 65. I always tell Michelle I'll never make it past 55, because I want to do other things in life and don't want this to be the only thing I've ever done."

motivated, keeps me going. 'Cause it sure ain't the money any more. And the work? *Whew!* These cars are just so much work these days—all these panels…everything so little and light…you touch, you bend something. It's just so much maintenance anymore."

Which brings up the issue of hands-on help—or rather, the lack thereof.

"When he was a kid, everybody came to the garage," Roy had made note.

But that's no longer the case. Kevin Bifulco acknowledges the problem. "His driving capability is still good—but you need the help! And these young kids—they don't wanta help an old guy. They wanta help their friends."

It doesn't further the cause that Billy can sometimes be demanding, intolerant of mistakes that cost him a good finish.

Back in the day, "I was with good teams. All I had to do was *drive*. I didn't have to do everything like I do now, where I have to set the car up, and load the car up, and drive it to the track, and then race it," Billy said of the current situation. He has crew chief Phil Cox, and a few others. Yet, it's not like 20 years ago when the shop was overrun with volunteers.

Billy Jr,, BP3, Mandee and Billy sign hero cards at the Motorsports Trade Show in January 2022.

JOHN MELOLING

"You know how many guys help me to load up on a Saturday? *Nobody*," Pauch pronounced. "I'm mounting tires, loading the car, filling the coolers…

"That's what's killing me. I'm lucky that Jimmy Stryker down the road comes and takes the body off the car and washes it every week, puts it back on. That's big."

At this place in his career, Billy's priorities are changing. "I drove all kinds of stuff. I don't know why. I just did," he mused. "Now, I'm getting so picky that I don't want to drive *nothing*."

The next generation: BP3 scored his first win in a pedal car race at the 2021 Hunterdon County Fair last August.

And while his car owner is still gung-ho—Pauch, in a lot of ways, is not. "Kevin wants to buy a 440 to run the series," he groaned. "I said to him: I don't want to drag around to all these shows, at this point in my life. I want to live *slower*, not *faster*."

So Billy's judiciously picking and choosing. When DIRTcar series director Dean Reynolds called him last year, to extend an invite to a special race at Bristol, Pauch turned it down. "It woulda been kinda neat, to say you run Bristol. But—*aah*, I'm cutting back! Screw it."

What gets him going these days are more pedestrian pursuits.

As his friend Fred Rahmer cheekily commented, "Billy's mellowing. He's starting to calm down. He's actually close to where you could almost recognize him as a human being!"

He might not get fired up about that 440, but he'll talk all day about the new camper he and Barb just bought. Or his grandkids—Billy Pauch III or BP3, as he's called, and his little sister, Avery.

"Me and the little guy are camping out tonight at Fort Tick, the little cabin I built back in the woods, with bunk beds," Billy informed, then turned to the six-year-old, assuring his grandson that their boxer, Speedy, would tag along for protection. "I'm really looking forward to it."

It's probably a given that BP3 will race. But not this year. His granddad has still got some unfinished business on the race tracks—even though, as everyone points out, he's got nothing left to prove.

"It's hard to give up that limelight when you live in the racing world. But everybody's day comes," reckoned Ray Carroll, now a tech inspector at Bridgeport Speedway, where Billy spends his Saturday nights.

In the '90s, when Pauch and Carroll were a team, it was all about making money.

"The end product today is Billy races for the glory. And the money's not that important. Now, it's about winning. He wants to win so bad!" Ray recognized, fairly startled by that fact. "When he won that race last year, and I saw him get so emotional—I thought, *omigod, he really does want to win that much.*"

In its new configuration, shortened to four-tenths of a mile, with all that banking carrying speed, Bridgeport is now a young man's track. You need to be up on the wheel, elbows out for the distance, with no break in the action to even draw a breath.

The only Modified event he won there in 2021 went nonstop for 30 laps: hard on any driver, but doubly demanding for a guy well into his 60s.

RICK SWEETEN

"I'm drained a little bit here," Billy admitted as he exited the car, catching his breath. "I was watching the board and seen the 31 was hanging in there pretty good, and I knew I was better than him. Then I guess the Krachun kid got second there. He drives hard, but I was driving hard, too.

"I started third, it went nonstop—I'll take it."

Having done this close to 750 times in his life, Pauch knows the drill: brandish the flag, pose for the photographers, hoist the trophy and wave to the fans.

Then, the victory lane interview.

Win #742 on June 26, 2021 at Bridgeport Motorsports Park.

"Last year, we had a pretty good setup and then they kinda threw that out the window on me, putting 50 pounds on my car," Billy said of the track's rule changes. "So we changed the coils, and we were kinda behind on that. But that's racing. You gotta go home, figure it out. I'm lucky I've got Phil Cox as my crew chief. We think a lot alike— sometimes that's good, sometimes that's bad. We make the same mistakes together, too!

"But tonight, we got it right. And I sat up in the seat there and cowboyed it out. For an old guy, I think I did pretty good."

He is the lion in winter: weary of the hunt but still keen for the kill.

As the crowd cheered his accomplishment this night, Pauch turned to give a final wave, savoring their response.

"I'm thankful for those of you who come to watch me," he told the fans, emotion clouding his voice, "and still remember my name."

BILLY PAUCH CAREER WIN LIST

compiled by Fred Voorhees ARRA
Auto Racing Research Associates
Documenting Racing History

YEAR	DATE	#	TRACK	DIVISION	LAPS	CAR
1975	4/12/75	1	Flemington	Rookie	10	Pauch 15
	4/19/75	2	Flemington	Rookie	10	Pauch 15
	4/26/75	3	Flemington	Rookie	10	Pauch 15
	5/3/75	4	Flemington	Rookie	10	Pauch 15
	5/10/75	5	Flemington	Rookie	10	Pauch 15
	5/17/75	6	Flemington	Rookie	10	Pauch 15
	5/18/75	7	Nazareth	Sportsman	15	Pauch 15
	5/23/75	8	Statewide	Sportsman	15	Pauch 15
	5/24/75	9	Flemington	Rookie	10	Pauch 15
	5/31/75	10	Flemington	Rookie	15	Pauch 15
	6/7/75	11	Flemington	Sportsman	15	Pauch 15
	6/8/75	12	Nazareth	Sportsman	15	Pauch 15
	6/29/75	13	Nazareth	Sportsman	15	Pauch 15
	7/4/75	14	Statewide	Sportsman	15	Pauch 15
	7/12/75	15	Flemington	Sportsman	15	Pauch 15
	8/17/75	16	Nazareth	Sportsman	15	Pauch 15
Total 1975 Wins (16)						
1976	3/28/76	17	Nazareth	Sportsman	15	Pauch 15
	4/23/76	18	East Windsor	Sportsman	15	Pauch 15
	4/24/76	19	Flemington	Sportsman	15	Pauch 15
	5/2/76	20	East Windsor	Sportsman	15	Pauch 15
	5/8/76	21	Flemington	Sportsman	15	Pauch 15
	5/22/76	22	Flemington	Sportsman	15	Pauch 15
	5/28/76	23	East Windsor	Sportsman	15	Pauch 15
	6/4/76	24	East Windsor	Sportsman	15	Pauch 15
	6/5/76	25	Flemington	Sportsman	15	Pauch 15
	6/11/76	26	East Windsor	Sportsman	15	Pauch 15
	6/20/76	27	East Windsor	Sportsman	15	Pauch 15
	6/25/76	28	East Windsor	Sportsman	15	Pauch 15
	6/27/76	29	East Windsor	Sportsman	15	Pauch 15
	7/2/76	30	East Windsor	Sportsman	15	Pauch 15

	7/3/76	31	Flemington	Sportsman	15	Pauch 15
	7/4/76	32	East Windsor	Sportsman	15	Pauch 15
	7/10/76	33	Flemington	Sportsman	15	Pauch 15
	7/17/76	34	Flemington	Sportsman	15	Pauch 15
	7/18/76	35	East Windsor	Sportsman	15	Pauch 15
	7/25/76	36	East Windsor	Sportsman	15	Pauch 15
	8/20/76	37	East Windsor	Sportsman	15	Pauch 15
	8/25/76	38	Reading	Sportsman	20	Pauch 15
	8/28/76	39	Flemington	Sportsman	100	Pauch 15
	9/3/76	40	East Windsor	Sportsman	15	Pauch 15
	9/11/76	41	Flemington	Sportsman	15	Pauch 15
	9/12/76	42	East Windsor	Sportsman	20	Pauch 15
	9/18/76	43	Flemington	Sportsman	15	Pauch 15
	10/10/76	44	East Windsor	Sportsman	20	Pauch 15
	Total 1976 Wins (28)					
1977	3/27/77	45	Nazareth	Sportsman	15	Pauch 15
	4/3/77	46	Nazareth	Sportsman	15	Pauch 15
	4/17/77	47	Nazareth	Sportsman	15	Pauch 15
	Total 1977 Wins (3)					
1978	4/9/78	48	East Windsor	Sportsman	15	Pauch 15
	6/4/78	49	East Windsor	Modified	25	Pauch 15
	6/10/78	50	Flemington	Modified	30	Pauch 15
	7/1/78	51	Flemington	Modified	100	Dornberger 99
	8/19/78	52	Flemington	Modified	20	Pauch 15
	10/15/78	53	East Windsor	Modified	20	Pauch 15
	Total 1978 Wins (6)					
1979	5/5/79	54	Flemington	Modified	20	Norcia 81
	5/11/79	55	East Windsor	Modified	20	Pauch 15
	6/2/79	56	Flemington	Modified	30	Pauch 15
	6/30/79	57	Flemington	Modified	20	Pauch 15
	7/7/79	58	Flemington	Modified	30	Pauch 15
	8/13/79	59	Albany-Saratoga	Modified	79	Pauch 15
	8/24/79	60	Acella	DIRT Modified	100	Pauch 15
	9/28/79	61	Acella	Modified	30	Pauch 15
	10/20/79	62	Flemington	Modified	100	Pauch 15
	11/4/79	63	Flemington	Modified	20	Pauch 15

First win in New York: Albany-Saratoga's 1979 Super Shootout.

DAVE MOULTHROP

Total 1979 Wins (10)

1980	3/16/80	64	Acella	Modified	35	Scamardella 121
	4/11/80	65	Acella	Modified	35	Scamardella 121
	4/25/80	66	Acella	Modified	35	Scamardella 121
	5/26/80	67	Flemington	Modified	200	Scamardella 121
	6/1/80	68	Flemington	Late Model	12	Michalenko 15
	6/28/80	69	Flemington	Modified	100	Scamardella 121
	7/25/80	70	East Windsor	Modified	35	Scamardella 121
	7/26/80	71	Flemington	Modified	30	Scamardella 121
	8/9/80	72	Flemington	Modified	30	Scamardella 121
	8/15/80	73	East Windsor	Modified	20	Scamardella 121
	8/16/80	74	Flemington	Modified	20	Scamardella 121
	8/16/80	75	Flemington	Modified	20	Scamardella 121
	8/16/80	76	Flemington	Modified	20	Scamardella 121
	8/23/80	77	Flemington	Modified	30	Scamardella 121
	8/29/80	78	East Windsor	Modified	50	Scamardella 121
	8/30/80	79	Flemington	Modified	30	Scamardella 121
	9/21/80	80	East Windsor	Modified	35	Scamardella 121

Total 1980 Wins (17)

1981	5/25/81	81	Flemington	Modified	20	Liedl L
	6/13/81	82	Flemington	Modified	20	Liedl L
	6/20/81	83	Flemington	Modified	30	Liedl L
	8/8/81	84	Flemington	Modified	30	Liedl L
	8/15/81	85	Flemington	Modified	20	Liedl L
	8/22/81	86	Flemington	Modified	20	Liedl L
	8/22/81	87	Flemington	Modified	20	Liedl L
	8/22/81	88	Flemington	Modified	20	Liedl L
	8/22/81	89	Flemington	Modified	30	Liedl L
	8/29/81	90	Flemington	Modified	30	Liedl L
	9/5/81	91	Flemington	Modified	30	Liedl L
	9/7/81	92	Flemington	Super Mod	30	Liedl L
	9/12/81	93	Flemington	Modified	100	Liedl L
	9/20/81	94	Albany-Saratoga	Modified	50	Liedl L
	9/20/81	95	Albany-Saratoga	Small Block	50	Arnold 57

	10/3/81	96	Bridgeport (5/8ths)	Small Block	40	Arnold 57
	10/24/81	97	Flemington	MODCAR Modified	50	Liedl L
Total 1981 Wins (17)						
1982	5/8/82	98	Flemington	Modified	30	Liedl L
	5/9/82	99	Penn National	Small Block	20	Arnold 57
	5/16/82	100	Flemington	MODCAR Modified	50	Arnold 57
	5/21/82	101	East Windsor	Small Block	25	Arnold 57
	5/31/82	102	Flemington	Modified	20	Arnold 57
	6/11/82	103	East Windsor	Small Block	20	Arnold 57
	6/11/82	104	East Windsor	Small Block	20	Arnold 57
	6/26/82	105	Flemington	Modified	30	Liedl L
	7/17/82	106	Flemington	Modified	20	Liedl L
	7/31/82	107	Flemington	Modified	30	Liedl L
	8/1/82	108	Penn National	Small Block	20	Arnold 57
	8/1/82	109	Penn National	Small Block	20	Arnold 57
	8/12/82	110	East Windsor	Small Block	50	Arnold 57
	8/22/82	111	Penn National	Small Block	20	Arnold 57
	8/22/82	112	Penn National	Small Block	20	Arnold 57
	8/22/82	113	Penn National	Small Block	20	Arnold 57
	9/4/82	114	Flemington	Modified	30	Liedl L
	9/11/82	115	Flemington	Modified	100	Liedl L
	9/17/82	116	East Windsor	Small Block	25	Arnold 57
	9/26/82	117	East Windsor	Small Block	20	Arnold 57
	10/24/82	118	Flemington	Modified	200	Pauch 15
Total 1982 Wins (21)						
1983	6/18/83	119	Flemington	Modified	30	Sesely 15
	9/1/83	120	Albany-Saratoga	Modified	25	Pauch 15
	9/1/83	121	Albany-Saratoga	Modified	25	Pauch 15
	9/3/83	122	Flemington	Modified	30	Sesely 15
	9/5/83	123	Flemington	Modified	30	Sesely 15
Total 1983 Wins (5)						
1984	6/9/84	124	Flemington	Modified	20	DeBlasio 5
	7/11/84	125	Flemington	DIRT Modified	84	DeBlasio 5
	7/14/84	126	Flemington	Modified	20	DeBlasio 5
	7/14/84	127	Flemington	Modified	20	DeBlasio 5
	7/14/84	128	Flemington	Modified	20	DeBlasio 5

	7/28/84	129	Flemington	Modified	30	DeBlasio 5
	8/25/84	130	Flemington	Modified	30	DeBlasio 5
	9/1/84	131	Flemington	Modified	30	DeBlasio 5
	9/2/84	132	Flemington	Modified	30	DeBlasio 5
	9/22/84	133	Flemington	Modified	100	DeBlasio 5
	9/23/84	134	Nazareth	Small Block	20	Pauch 15
	9/23/84	135	Nazareth	Small Block	20	Pauch 15
	9/30/84	136	Flemington	Modified	30	DeBlasio 5
Total 1984 Wins (13)						
1985	2/11/85	137	Volusia	Modified	30	DeBlasio 5
	2/13/85	138	Volusia	Modified	30	DeBlasio 5
	2/15/85	139	Volusia	Modified	30	DeBlasio 5
	4/26/85	140	Flemington	Modified	100	DeBlasio 5
	6/1/85	141	Flemington	Modified	30	DeBlasio 5
	6/22/85	142	Flemington	Modified	30	DeBlasio 5
	6/22/85	143	Flemington	Modified	30	DeBlasio 5
	7/19/85	144	East Windsor	Small Block	20	Van Varick 15
	7/20/85	145	Flemington	Modified	20	DeBlasio 5
	7/20/85	146	Flemington	Modified Sprint	15	Pauch 15
	7/21/85	147	Penn National	Small Block	25	Hanson 134
	7/27/85	148	Flemington	Modified	30	DeBlasio 5
	7/28/85	149	Penn National	Small Block	25	Hanson 134
	8/2/85	150	East Windsor	Small Block	25	Van Varick 15
	8/3/85	151	Flemington	Modified	30	DeBlasio 5
	8/10/85	152	Flemington	Modified	20	DeBlasio 5
	8/10/85	153	Flemington	Modified	20	DeBlasio 5
	8/10/85	154	Flemington	Modified	20	DeBlasio 5
	8/20/85	155	Fonda	Modified	100	DeBlasio 5
	9/1/85	156	Penn National	Small Block	100	Hanson 134
	9/15/85	157	Penn National	Small Block	30	Van Varick 15
	9/21/85	158	Flemington	Modified	100	DeBlasio 5
	9/28/85	159	Fonda	Modified	50	DeBlasio 5
	10/5/85	160	Flemington	Modified	30	DeBlasio 5
Total 1985 Wins (24)						
1986	5/17/86	161	Flemington	Modified Sprint	15	Van Varick 15
	5/24/86	162	Flemington	Small Block	20	Van Varick 15

5/26/86	163	Flemington	DIRT Modified	86	DeBlasio 5
5/26/86	164	Flemington	Modified Sprint	15	Van Varick 15
5/31/86	165	Flemington	Modified	30	DeBlasio 5
6/7/86	166	Flemington	Modified	20	DeBlasio 5
6/20/86	167	East Windsor	Small Block	20	Van Varick 15
6/22/86	168	Penn National	Small Block	25	Becker 41a
6/27/86	169	East Windsor	Small Block	50	Van Varick 15
6/29/86	170	Penn National	Small Block	25	Becker 41a
7/3/86	171	Grandview	Small Block	40	Becker 41a
7/13/86	172	Penn National	Small Block	25	Becker 41a
7/19/86	173	Flemington	Modified	20	DeBlasio 5
7/27/86	174	Penn National	Small Block	25	Becker 41a
8/3/86	175	Penn National	Small Block	25	Becker 41a
8/8/86	176	East Windsor	Small Block	20	Van Varick 15
8/8/86	177	East Windsor	Small Block	20	Van Varick 15
8/9/86	178	Flemington	Modified Sprint	15	Van Varick 15
8/24/86	179	Penn National	Small Block	25	Becker 41a
8/30/86	180	Flemington	Modified	30	DeBlasio 5
8/30/86	181	Flemington	Modified Sprint	15	Van Varick 15
10/4/86	182	Flemington	Modified	30	DeBlasio 5
10/6/86	183	Fulton	Small Block	200	Becker 41a

Total 1986 Wins (23)

1987	3/20/87	184	Port Royal	Small Block	25	Keystone 126
	3/22/87	185	Bridgeport (5/8ths)	Modified	50	Keystone 126
	5/8/87	186	Bridgeport (5/8ths)	Modified	30	Keystone 126
	5/9/87	187	Flemington	Modified	30	Keystone 126
	5/10/87	188	Penn National	Small Block	25	Keystone 126
	5/17/87	189	Penn National	Small Block	25	Keystone 126
	5/23/87	190	Flemington	Modified	20	Keystone 126
	5/23/87	191	Flemington	Modified	20	Keystone 126
	5/24/87	192	Penn National	Small Block	25	Keystone 126
	6/6/87	193	Flemington	Modified	20	Keystone 126
	6/13/87	194	Flemington	Modified	30	Keystone 126
	6/14/87	195	Penn National	Small Block	25	Keystone 126
	6/17/87	196	Flemington	Modified	100	Keystone 126
	6/20/87	197	Flemington	Modified	30	Keystone 126

6/20/87	198	Flemington	Small Block	20	Keystone 126
7/3/87	199	Bridgeport (5/8ths)	Modified	25	Keystone 126
7/4/87	200	Flemington	Modified	30	Keystone 126
7/5/87	201	Penn National	Small Block	20	Keystone 126
7/11/87	202	Flemington	Modified	20	Keystone 126
7/12/87	203	Penn National	Small Block	25	Keystone 126
7/17/87	204	Bridgeport (5/8ths)	Modified	25	Keystone 126
7/18/87	205	Flemington	Modified	30	Keystone 126
7/25/87	206	Flemington	Modified	30	Keystone 126
7/31/87	207	Bridgeport (5/8ths)	Modified	12	Keystone 126
7/31/87	208	Bridgeport (5/8ths)	Modified	12	Keystone 126
7/31/87	209	Bridgeport (5/8ths)	Modified	12	Keystone 126
7/31/87	210	Bridgeport (5/8ths)	Modified	12	Keystone 126
8/15/87	211	Flemington	Modified	30	Keystone 126
8/21/87	212	Bridgeport (5/8ths)	DIRT Modified	25	Keystone 126
8/29/87	213	Flemington	Modified	30	Keystone 126
9/2/87	214	Albany-Saratoga	Small Block	40	Keystone 126
9/27/87	215	Fulton	Small Block	200	Keystone 126
10/10/87	216	Syracuse NYSF	DIRT Small Block	30	Keystone 126

Total 1987 Wins (33)

1988	2/8/88	217	Volusia	Modified	30	Keystone 126
	3/13/88	218	Nazareth	Modified	30	Keystone 126
	3/27/88	219	Bridgeport (5/8ths)	Modified	40	Keystone 126
	4/10/88	220	Nazareth	Modified	20	Keystone 126
	4/16/88	221	Flemington	Modified	30	Keystone 126
	4/17/88	222	Nazareth	Modified	30	Keystone 126
	4/30/88	223	Flemington	Modified	20	Keystone 126
	5/7/88	224	Flemington	Small Block	20	Keystone 126
	5/15/88	225	Penn National	Small Block	25	Keystone 126
	5/21/88	226	Grandview	Small Block	25	Keystone 126
	5/22/88	227	Penn National	Small Block	25	Keystone 126
	5/28/88	228	Flemington	Modified	30	Keystone 126

	5/29/88	229	Penn National	Small Block	20	Keystone 126
	5/29/88	230	Penn National	Small Block	20	Keystone 126
	6/3/88	231	Bridgeport (5/8ths)	Modified	20	Keystone 126
	6/10/88	232	Bridgeport (5/8ths)	Modified	25	Keystone 126
	6/11/88	233	Flemington	Modified	30	Keystone 126
	6/18/88	234	Flemington	Modified	20	Keystone 126
	6/21/88	235	Williams Grove	DIRT Modified	50	Keystone 126
	6/30/88	236	Grandview	Small Block	40	Keystone 126
	7/1/88	237	Bridgeport (5/8ths)	Modified	40	Keystone 126
	7/3/88	238	Penn National	Small Block	20	Keystone 126
	7/5/88	239	Ransomville	Modified	76	Keystone 126
	7/10/88	240	Penn National	Small Block	35	Keystone 126
	7/15/88	241	Bridgeport (5/8ths)	Modified	12	Keystone 126
	7/24/88	242	Penn National	Small Block	25	Keystone 126
	7/30/88	243	Flemington	Modified	20	Keystone 126
	7/31/88	244	Penn National	Small Block	25	Keystone 126
	7/31/88	245	Penn National	Small Block	25	Keystone 126
	8/5/88	246	Bridgeport (5/8ths)	DIRT Modified	40	Keystone 126
	8/12/88	247	Bridgeport (5/8ths)	Modified	20	Keystone 126
	8/14/88	248	Penn National	Small Block	25	Keystone 126
	8/21/88	249	Penn National	Small Block	25	Keystone 126
	8/28/88	250	Penn National	Small Block	25	Keystone 126
	9/5/88	251	Flemington	URC Sprint	25	Fiore 8
	9/10/88	252	Grandview	Small Block	76	Keystone 126
	9/11/88	253	Penn National	Modified	35	Keystone 126
	9/25/88	254	Fulton	Small Block	200	Keystone 126
	10/16/88	255	Bridgeport (5/8ths)	Modified	12	Keystone 126
	10/23/88	256	Hagerstown	Modified	100	Keystone 126
	10/29/88	257	Flemington	Small Block	100	Keystone 126
	10/29/88	258	Flemington	URC Sprint	40	Fiore 8
	Total 1988 Wins (42)					
1989	3/26/89	259	Penn National	Small Block	35	Keystone 126
	4/2/89	260	Bridgeport (5/8ths)	Modified	25	Barker Bus 76
	4/16/89	261	Hagerstown	Modified	20	Barker Bus 76
	4/16/89	262	Hagerstown	Modified	20	Barker Bus 76
	4/22/89	263	Grandview	Small Block	25	Keystone 126

4/23/89	264	Penn National	Small Block	25	Keystone 126
4/28/89	265	East Windsor	Small Block	20	Barker Bus 76
4/28/89	266	East Windsor	Small Block	20	Barker Bus 76
5/21/89	267	Penn National	Small Block	25	Keystone 126
5/27/89	268	Flemington	Small Block	20	Keystone 126
5/27/89	269	Flemington	Modified	20	Barker Bus 76
5/28/89	270	Penn National	Small Block	25	Keystone 126
6/3/89	271	Flemington	Modified	20	Barker Bus 76
6/11/89	272	Penn National	Small Block	25	Keystone 126
6/17/89	273	Flemington	Modified	20	Barker Bus 76
6/17/89	274	Flemington	Modified	20	Barker Bus 76
6/25/89	275	Penn National	Small Block	25	Keystone 126
6/30/89	276	East Windsor	Small Block	50	Barker Bus 76
7/8/89	277	Flemington	URC Sprint	25	Fiore 8
7/9/89	278	Penn National	Small Block	35	Keystone 126
7/15/89	279	Flemington	Modified	20	Barker Bus 76
7/15/89	280	Flemington	Modified	20	Barker Bus 76
7/27/89	281	Flemington	DIRT Modified	89	Barker Bus 76
7/28/89	282	East Windsor	Small Block	20	Barker Bus 76
7/28/89	283	East Windsor	Small Block	20	Barker Bus 76
7/29/89	284	Flemington	Modified	30	Barker Bus 76
8/4/89	285	East Windsor	Small Block	25	Barker Bus 76
8/22/89	286	Williams Grove	DIRT Modified	89	Barker Bus 76
8/23/89	287	Grandview	DIRT Modified	89	Barker Bus 76
8/25/89	288	East Windsor	Small Block	25	Barker Bus 76
8/26/89	289	Flemington	Small Block	20	Keystone 126
8/27/89	290	Penn National	Small Block	25	Keystone 126
9/1/89	291	East Windsor	Small Block	20	Barker Bus 76
9/1/89	292	East Windsor	Small Block	20	Barker Bus 76
9/3/89	293	Penn National	Small Block	100	Keystone 126
9/10/89	294	Penn National	Modified	35	Barker Bus 76
9/15/89	295	East Windsor	Small Block	20	Barker Bus 76
9/15/89	296	East Windsor	Small Block	20	Barker Bus 76
9/24/89	297	Fulton	Small Block	200	Keystone 126
9/29/89	298	East Windsor	Small Block	20	Barker Bus 76
9/29/89	299	East Windsor	Small Block	20	Barker Bus 76

Date	#	Track	Class	Laps	Car
9/30/89	300	Flemington	Modified	20	Barker Bus 76
11/4/89	301	Georgetown	Modified	30	Barker Bus 76
11/11/89	302	Delaware Int'l.	Small Block	50	Barker Bus 76
11/11/89	303	Delaware Int'l.	Modified	50	Barker Bus 76

Total 1989 Wins (45)

Year	Date	#	Track	Class	Laps	Car
1990	4/13/90	304	East Windsor	Small Block	25	Barker Bus 76
	4/14/90	305	Flemington	Modified	30	Barker Bus 76
	4/20/90	306	East Windsor	Small Block	20	Barker Bus 76
	4/27/90	307	East Windsor	Small Block	25	Barker Bus 76
	5/5/90	308	Flemington	URC Sprint	25	Keystone 126
	5/11/90	309	East Windsor	Small Block	25	Barker Bus 76
	5/12/90	310	Flemington	Modified	20	Barker Bus 76
	5/18/90	311	East Windsor	Small Block	20	Barker Bus 76
	5/18/90	312	East Windsor	Small Block	20	Barker Bus 76
	5/19/90	313	Flemington	Modified	30	Barker Bus 76
	5/27/90	314	Penn National	Small Block	20	Barker Bus 76
	6/1/90	315	East Windsor	Small Block	25	Barker Bus 76
	6/15/90	316	East Windsor	Small Block	20	Barker Bus 76
	6/16/90	317	Flemington	Modified	30	Barker Bus 76
	6/24/90	318	Bridgeport (5/8ths)	URC Sprint	12	Keystone 126
	6/24/90	319	Bridgeport (5/8ths)	Modified	25	Barker Bus 76
	6/27/90	320	Flemington	DIRT Modified	90	Barker Bus 76

MEL STETTLER

I raced with Billy pretty much all my life. Probably raced against Billy more than anybody in my career. Everybody thinks we're arch enemies. But he's a friend. We both look out for each other, and we do care about each other. There were times when I was hurt, he was usually the first one to call. And the same when he was hurt: I'm hopefully the first one to call him. We both respect each other, at the end of the day.

JIMMY HORTON

Date	#	Track	Type	$	Sponsor
6/29/90	321	East Windsor	Small Block	50	Barker Bus 76
6/30/90	322	Flemington	Modified	20	Barker Bus 76
6/30/90	323	Flemington	Modified	20	Barker Bus 76
6/30/90	324	Flemington	Modified	20	Barker Bus 76
7/7/90	325	Flemington	Modified	30	Barker Bus 76
7/15/90	326	Bridgeport (5/8ths)	URC Sprint	25	Keystone 126
7/21/90	327	Flemington	Modified	30	Barker Bus 76
7/27/90	328	East Windsor	Small Block	25	Barker Bus 76
7/28/90	329	Flemington	Modified	20	Barker Bus 76
7/29/90	330	Susquehanna	PA Sprint	25	Keystone 126
8/4/90	331	Flemington	Modified	30	Barker Bus 76
8/17/90	332	East Windsor	Small Block	25	Barker Bus 76
8/25/90	333	Flemington	Modified	30	Barker Bus 76
8/30/90	334	Flemington	Modified	100	Barker Bus 76
8/31/90	335	East Windsor	Small Block	20	Barker Bus 76
9/2/90	336	Penn National	Small Block	100	Barker Bus 76
9/9/90	337	Bridgeport (5/8ths)	Small Block	20	Barker Bus 76
9/14/90	338	East Windsor	Small Block	20	Barker Bus 76
9/14/90	339	East Windsor	Small Block	20	Barker Bus 76
9/15/90	340	Fulton	Small Block	200	Barker Bus 76
9/16/90	341	Utica-Rome	Small Block	50	Barker Bus 76
9/17/90	342	Grandview	Open Comp. Sprint	35	Keystone 126
9/28/90	343	East Windsor	Small Block	20	Barker Bus 76
10/13/90	344	Delaware Int'l.	Modified	100	Barker Bus 76
10/14/90	345	Bridgeport (5/8ths)	Small Block	20	Barker Bus 76
10/19/90	346	East Windsor	Small Block	20	Barker Bus 76
10/19/90	347	East Windsor	Small Block	20	Barker Bus 76
10/27/90	348	Flemington	Open Comp. Sprint	25	Keystone 126
11/3/90	349	Delaware Int'l.	Small Block	50	Barker Bus 76
11/3/90	350	Georgetown	Modified	30	Barker Bus 76
11/4/90	351	East Windsor	Small Block	25	Barker Bus 76

Total 1990 Wins (48)

Year	Date	#	Track	Type	$	Sponsor
1991	4/19/91	352	East Windsor	Small Block	25	Tabloid Graphics 15
	4/26/91	353	East Windsor	Small Block	20	Tabloid Graphics 15
	5/11/91	354	Flemington (asphalt)	Small Block	20	Scheer 1a
	5/24/91	355	East Windsor	Small Block	25	Tabloid Graphics 15

	5/31/91	356	East Windsor	Small Block	50	Tabloid Graphics 15
	6/2/91	357	Bridgeport (5/8ths)	Small Block	20	Tabloid Graphics 15
	6/7/91	358	East Windsor	Small Block	25	Tabloid Graphics 15
	6/8/91	359	Flemington (asphalt)	Small Block	20	Scheer 1a
	6/14/91	360	East Windsor	Small Block	20	Tabloid Graphics 15
	7/3/91	361	Grandview	Modified	40	Tabloid Graphics 15
	7/6/91	362	Flemington (asphalt)	Modified	20	Scheer 1a
	7/19/91	363	East Windsor	Small Block	25	Tabloid Graphics 15
	7/28/91	364	Bridgeport (5/8ths)	Modified	25	Tabloid Graphics 15
	8/3/91	365	Grandview	Small Block	40	Tabloid Graphics 15
	8/4/91	366	Bridgeport (5/8ths)	Modified	25	Tabloid Graphics 15
	8/11/91	367	East Windsor	Small Block	50	Tabloid Graphics 15
	8/17/91	368	Flemington (asphalt)	Modified	30	Scheer 1a
	8/23/91	369	East Windsor	Small Block	25	Tabloid Graphics 15
	8/24/91	370	Flemington (asphalt)	Modified	20	Scheer 1a
	8/24/91	371	Flemington (asphalt)	Modified	20	Scheer 1a
	9/6/91	372	East Windsor	Small Block	25	Tabloid Graphics 15
	9/7/91	373	Grandview	Small Block	76	Tabloid Graphics 15
	9/8/91	374	Penn National	Modified	35	Tabloid Graphics 15
	9/13/91	375	East Windsor	Small Block	20	Tabloid Graphics 15
	9/13/91	376	East Windsor	Small Block	20	Tabloid Graphics 15
	9/14/91	377	Grandview	Small Block	35	Tabloid Graphics 15
	9/20/91	378	East Windsor	Small Block	25	Tabloid Graphics 15
	9/22/91	379	Utica-Rome	Small Block	50	Tabloid Graphics 15
	9/27/91	380	East Windsor	Small Block	20	Tabloid Graphics 15
	9/27/91	381	East Windsor	Small Block	20	Tabloid Graphics 15
	10/4/91	382	East Windsor	Small Block	25	Tabloid Graphics 15
	10/18/91	383	East Windsor	Small Block	20	Tabloid Graphics 15
	10/18/91	384	East Windsor	Small Block	20	Tabloid Graphics 15
	Total 1991 Wins (33)					
1992	4/10/92	385	East Windsor	Small Block	25	Tabloid Graphics 15
	4/12/92	386	Big Diamond	Small Block	25	Tabloid Graphics 15
	5/1/92	387	East Windsor	Small Block	25	Tabloid Graphics 15
	5/3/92	388	Penn National	Small Block	25	Tabloid Graphics 15
	5/3/92	389	Penn National	Small Block	35	Tabloid Graphics 15
	5/10/92	390	Penn National	Small Block	25	Tabloid Graphics 15

Date	No.	Track	Type	Purse	Sponsor
5/15/92	391	East Windsor	Small Block	20	Tabloid Graphics 15
5/15/92	392	East Windsor	Small Block	20	Tabloid Graphics 15
5/22/92	393	East Windsor	Small Block	20	Tabloid Graphics 15
5/23/92	394	Grandview	Small Block	25	Tabloid Graphics 15
5/31/92	395	Penn National	Small Block	25	Tabloid Graphics 15
6/12/92	396	East Windsor	Small Block	20	Tabloid Graphics 15
6/13/92	397	Flemington (asphalt)	Late Model	25	Trenton Mack 704
6/14/92	398	Penn National	Small Block	25	Tabloid Graphics 15
6/20/92	399	Grandview	Small Block	20	Tabloid Graphics 15
7/4/92	400	East Windsor	Small Block	20	Tabloid Graphics 15
7/4/92	401	East Windsor	Small Block	25	Tabloid Graphics 15
7/5/92	402	East Windsor	Small Block	25	Tabloid Graphics 15
7/11/92	403	Grandview	Small Block	25	Tabloid Graphics 15
7/18/92	404	Grandview	Small Block	25	Tabloid Graphics 15
7/19/92	405	Penn National	Small Block	25	Tabloid Graphics 15
7/25/92	406	Grandview	Small Block	25	Tabloid Graphics 15
8/2/92	407	Penn National	Small Block	25	Tabloid Graphics 15
8/6/92	408	Grandview	Small Block	35	Tabloid Graphics 15
8/7/92	409	East Windsor	Small Block	25	Tabloid Graphics 15
8/9/92	410	Penn National	Small Block	25	Tabloid Graphics 15
8/19/92	411	Grandview	Modified	35	Tabloid Graphics 15
8/25/92	412	Grandview	PA Sprint	50	Zemco 1
9/11/92	413	East Windsor	Small Block	25	Tabloid Graphics 15
9/12/92	414	Grandview	Small Block	76	Tabloid Graphics 15
9/18/92	415	East Windsor	Small Block	25	Tabloid Graphics 15
10/3/92	416	Grandview	Small Block	100	Tabloid Graphics 15
10/16/92	417	East Windsor	Small Block	20	Tabloid Graphics 15
10/16/92	418	East Windsor	Small Block	20	Tabloid Graphics 15
10/18/92	419	Bridgeport (5/8ths)	Small Block	20	Tabloid Graphics 15
10/25/92	420	Hagerstown	Modified	100	Tabloid Graphics 15
11/7/92	421	Delaware Int'l.	Small Block	50	Tabloid Graphics 15

Total 1992 Wins (37)

Year	Date	No.	Track	Type	Purse	Sponsor
1993	4/11/93	422	Penn National	Small Block	35	Tabloid Graphics 15
	4/25/93	423	Penn National	Small Block	25	Tabloid Graphics 15
	5/9/93	424	Penn National	Small Block	25	Tabloid Graphics 15
	5/12/93	425	Grandview	CRA Sprint	30	Zemco 1

	5/30/93	426	Penn National	Small Block	20	Tabloid Graphics 15
	5/30/93	427	Penn National	Small Block	20	Tabloid Graphics 15
	6/11/93	428	Williams Grove	PA Sprint	25	Zemco 1
	6/19/93	429	Grandview	Small Block	35	Tabloid Graphics 15
	6/19/93	430	Grandview	Small Block	35	Tabloid Graphics 15
	7/17/93	431	Bridgeport (5/8ths)	Modified	25	Tabloid Graphics 15
	7/24/93	432	Bridgeport (5/8ths)	Modified	20	Tabloid Graphics 15
	7/31/93	433	Susquehanna	Small Block	20	Tabloid Graphics 15
	8/7/93	434	Grandview	Small Block	40	Tabloid Graphics 15
	8/24/93	435	Grandview	PA Sprint	50	Zemco 1
	8/27/93	436	Williams Grove	PA Sprint	25	Zemco 1
	8/29/93	437	Penn National	Small Block	25	Tabloid Graphics 15
	9/5/93	438	Penn National	Small Block	100	Tabloid Graphics 15
	9/19/93	439	Utica-Rome	Small Block	50	Tabloid Graphics 15
	10/3/93	440	Hagerstown	PA Sprint	50	Zemco 1
	10/17/93	441	Penn National	Small Block	50	Tabloid Graphics 15
	10/24/93	442	Flemington (asphalt)	NASCAR Modified	250	Fiore 44
	11/13/93	443	Delaware Int'l.	Small Block	50	Tabloid Graphics 15
	11/14/93	444	Delaware Int'l.	Modified	50	Tabloid Graphics 15
	Total 1993 Wins (23)					
1994	2/18/94	445	East Bay	All Star Sprint	25	Zemco 1
	4/16/94	446	Williams Grove	PA Sprint	25	Zemco 1
	4/18/94	447	Penn National	Small Block	35	Tabloid Graphics 15
	4/23/94	448	Williams Grove	PA Sprint	25	Zemco 1
	4/24/94	449	Selinsgrove	PA Sprint	25	Zemco 1
	4/25/94	450	Penn National	Small Block	25	Tabloid Graphics 15
	5/14/94	451	Selinsgrove	PA Sprint	25	Zemco 1
	5/22/94	452	Penn National	Small Block	25	Tabloid Graphics 15
	6/17/94	453	Williams Grove	PA Sprint	20	Zemco 1
	6/25/94	454	Selinsgrove	PA Sprint	25	Zemco 1
	7/4/94	455	Selinsgrove	PA Sprint	30	Zemco 1
	7/16/94	456	Bridgeport (5/8ths)	Small Block	94	Tabloid Graphics 15
	10/8/94	457	Syracuse NYSF	WoO Sprint	35	Zemco 1
	Total 1994 Wins (13)					
1995	2/17/95	458	East Bay	All Star Sprint	25	Zemco 1
	3/25/95	459	Selinsgrove	PA Sprint	25	Zemco 1

ACE LANE JR.

Date	No.	Track	Class	Laps	Car
3/26/95	460	Williams Grove	Small Block	25	Faust M1
4/15/95	461	Bridgeport (5/8ths)	Modified	25	Faust M1
4/29/95	462	Bridgeport (5/8ths)	Modified	25	Faust M1
5/6/95	463	Bridgeport (5/8ths)	Modified	25	Faust M1
5/13/95	464	Bridgeport (5/8ths)	Modified	20	Faust M1
5/13/95	465	Bridgeport (5/8ths)	Modified	20	Faust M1
6/3/95	466	Bridgeport (5/8ths)	Modified	25	Faust M1
6/4/95	467	Penn National	Small Block	25	Faust M1
6/10/95	468	Bridgeport (5/8ths)	Modified	20	Faust M1
6/17/95	469	Bridgeport (5/8ths)	Modified	25	Faust M1
6/18/95	470	Penn National	PA Sprint	30	Zemco 1
6/28/95	471	Path Valley	PA Sprint	25	Zemco 1
7/7/95	472	Williams Grove	PA Sprint	25	Zemco 1
7/17/95	473	Grandview	PA Sprint	25	Zemco 1
7/22/95	474	Bridgeport (5/8ths)	Modified	12	Faust M1
7/22/95	475	Bridgeport (5/8ths)	Modified	12	Faust M1
8/5/95	476	Bridgeport (5/8ths)	Modified	25	Faust M1
9/9/95	477	Bridgeport (5/8ths)	Modified	20	Faust M1
9/9/95	478	Bridgeport (5/8ths)	Modified	20	Faust M1
9/16/95	479	Bridgeport (5/8ths)	Modified	25	Faust M1
10/1/95	480	Hagerstown	Modified	100	Faust M1

Total 1995 Wins (23)

Year	Date	No.	Track	Class	Laps	Car
1996	4/14/96	481	Penn National	Small Block	25	Faust M1
	4/26/96	482	Williams Grove	PA Sprint	25	Zemco 1
	6/4/96	483	Rolling Wheels	WoO Sprint	25	Zemco 1
	6/16/96	484	Penn National	PA Sprint	30	Zemco 1
	6/26/96	485	Fulton	Modified	50	Faust M1

	7/7/96	486	Susquehanna	PA Sprint	30	Zemco 1
	7/8/96	487	Selinsgrove	PA Sprint	30	Zemco 1
	7/16/96	488	Bridgeport (5/8ths)	BOSS/PA Sprint	25	Zemco 1
	7/20/96	489	Flemington (asphalt)	NASCAR Modified	20	Barney 15
	7/23/96	490	Bridgeport (5/8ths)	DIRT Modified	96	Faust M1
	8/9/96	491	Williams Grove	PA Sprint	25	Zemco 1
	8/10/96	492	Flemington (asphalt)	NASCAR Modified	30	Barney 15
	8/18/96	493	Knoxville	Sprint	20	Zemco 1
	8/23/96	494	Williams Grove	PA Sprint	20	Zemco 1
	8/30/96	495	Williams Grove	PA Sprint	25	Zemco 1
	9/7/96	496	Bridgeport (5/8ths)	Modified	25	Faust M1
	9/13/96	497	Williams Grove	USAC Sprint	30	Zemco 1
	9/14/96	498	Grandview	Small Block	76	Faust M1
	9/27/96	499	Williams Grove	PA Sprint	25	Zemco 1
	10/1/96	500	Bridgeport (5/8ths)	Modified	50	Faust M1
	11/10/96	501	Hagerstown	Modified	100	Trenton Mack 704

Total 1996 Wins (21)

1997	2/12/97	502	East Bay	All Star Sprint	25	Zemco 1
	3/9/97	503	Williams Grove	PA Sprint	25	Zemco 1
	3/29/97	504	Selinsgrove	PA Sprint	25	Zemco 1
	5/10/97	505	Flemington (asphalt)	NASCAR Modified	30	Barney 15
	6/7/97	506	Bridgeport (5/8ths)	Modified	25	Trenton Mack 704
	7/25/97	507	Port Royal	All Star Sprint	30	Zemco 1
	8/30/97	508	Flemington (asphalt)	NASCAR Modified	50	Barney 15
	10/5/97	509	Fulton	Small Block	200	Pauch 1P
	10/19/97	510	Susquehanna	KARS Sprint	40	Chesson 76
	10/25/97	511	Delaware Int'l.	Sprint	30	Zemco 1

Total 1997 Wins (10)

MEL STETTLER

1998	2/10/98	512	East Bay	All Star Sprint	30	Zemco 1
	4/18/98	513	Bridgeport (5/8ths)	Modified	25	Trenton Mack 704
	5/16/98	514	Bridgeport (5/8ths)	Modified	25	Trenton Mack 704
	8/15/98	515	Bridgeport (5/8ths)	Modified	25	Trenton Mack 704
	8/21/98	516	Williams Grove	PA Sprint	20	Zemco 1
	8/25/98	517	East Windsor	Small Block	50	Trenton Mack 704
	8/26/98	518	Grandview	All Star Sprint	40	Zemco 1
	8/29/98	519	Bridgeport (5/8ths)	Modified	12	Trenton Mack 704
	9/12/98	520	Grandview	Small Block	76	Pauch 1
	10/24/98	521	Williams Grove	PA Sprint	40	Zemco 1
	11/1/98	522	Hagerstown	PA Sprint	50	Zemco 1
Total 1998 Wins (11)						
1999	2/6/99	523	Volusia	All Star Sprint	20	Zemco 1
	2/11/99	524	East Bay	All Star Sprint	25	Zemco 1
	4/3/99	525	New Egypt	Modified	30	Hanson 1
	4/17/99	526	New Egypt	Modified	20	Hanson 1
	4/24/99	527	New Egypt	Modified	30	Hanson 1
	5/15/99	528	New Egypt	Modified	30	Hanson 1
	6/16/99	529	New Egypt	PA Sprint	30	J&M 55
	6/22/99	530	New Egypt	Modified	50	Hanson 1
	6/26/99	531	New Egypt	Modified	30	Hanson 1
	7/24/99	532	New Egypt	Modified	30	Hanson 1
	7/31/99	533	New Egypt	Modified	50	Hanson 1
	8/7/99	534	New Egypt	Modified	30	Hanson 1
	8/21/99	535	Bridgeport (5/8ths)	Modified	25	Hanson 1
	9/4/99	536	New Egypt	Modified	30	Hanson 1
	9/12/99	537	New Egypt	Modified	30	Hanson 1
	9/18/99	538	New Egypt	Modified	25	Hanson 1
	9/19/99	539	Albany-Saratoga	Small Block	50	Hanson 1
	9/25/99	540	New Egypt	Modified	30	Hanson 1
	10/16/99	541	New Egypt	Modified	50	Hanson 1
	10/31/99	542	Hagerstown	PA Sprint	50	J&M 55
	10/31/99	543	Hagerstown	Small Block	100	Schmidt 5
Total 1999 Wins (21)						
2000	4/1/00	544	New Egypt	Modified	30	Hanson 1
	4/29/00	545	New Egypt	Modified	25	Hanson 1

	6/3/00	546	New Egypt	Modified	30	Hanson 1
	6/16/00	547	East Windsor	Small Block	25	Hanson 1
	6/17/00	548	New Egypt	Modified	30	Hanson 1
	6/23/00	549	East Windsor	Small Block	50	Hanson 1
	6/24/00	550	New Egypt	Modified	20	Hanson 1
	6/24/00	551	New Egypt	Modified	20	Hanson 1
	7/1/00	552	New Egypt	Modified	30	Hanson 1
	7/1/00	553	New Egypt	Modified	30	Hanson 1
	7/18/00	554	Grandview	PA Sprint	25	J&M 55
	7/21/00	555	East Windsor	Small Block	20	Hanson 1
	7/21/00	556	East Windsor	Small Block	20	Hanson 1
	7/22/00	557	New Egypt	Modified	30	Hanson 1
	7/29/00	558	New Egypt	Modified	30	Hanson 1
	8/2/00	559	New Egypt	DIRT Modified	100	Hanson 1
	8/19/00	560	New Egypt	Modified	30	Hanson 1
	8/26/00	561	New Egypt	Modified	30	Hanson 1
	9/3/00	562	Big Diamond	Small Block	100	Pauch 1P
	9/9/00	563	Grandview	Small Block	76	Pauch 1P
	9/16/00	564	New Egypt	Modified	30	Hanson 1
	9/22/00	565	East Windsor	Small Block	50	Hanson 1
	10/14/00	566	New Egypt	Modified	50	Hanson 1

Total 2000 Wins (23)

2001	4/7/01	567	New Egypt	Modified	30	Pauch 1
	4/21/01	568	New Egypt	Modified	30	Pauch 1
	5/5/01	569	New Egypt	Modified	30	Pauch 1
	5/26/01	570	New Egypt	Modified	30	Pauch 1
	6/24/01	571	Grandview	PA Sprint	35	J&M 55
	6/30/01	572	New Egypt	Modified	40	Pauch 1
	7/6/01	573	East Windsor	Small Block	25	Pauch 1
	7/13/01	574	East Windsor	Small Block	25	Pauch 1
	7/18/01	575	Grandview	PA Sprint	25	J&M 55
	7/21/01	576	New Egypt	Modified	20	Pauch 1
	7/28/01	577	New Egypt	Modified	30	Pauch 1
	8/3/01	578	East Windsor	Small Block	25	Pauch 1
	8/18/01	579	New Egypt	Modified	30	Pauch 1
	8/25/01	580	New Egypt	Modified	30	Pauch 1

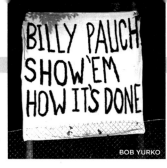

	9/1/01	581	New Egypt	Modified	30	Pauch 1
	9/7/01	582	East Windsor	Small Block	25	Pauch 1
	9/29/01	583	New Egypt	Modified	30	Pauch 1
	10/14/01	584	New Egypt	Modified	50	Pauch 1
Total 2001 Wins (18)						
2002	3/25/02	585	Bridgeport (5/8ths)	Modified	25	Pauch 1
	4/13/02	586	New Egypt	Modified	30	Pauch 1
	4/26/02	587	East Windsor	Small Block	25	Pauch 1
	5/4/02	588	New Egypt	Modified	30	Pauch 1
	6/1/02	589	New Egypt	Modified	30	Pauch 1
	6/8/02	590	New Egypt	Modified	30	Pauch 1
	6/21/02	591	East Windsor	Small Block	20	Pauch 1
	6/28/02	592	East Windsor	Small Block	25	Pauch 1
	8/9/02	593	East Windsor	Small Block	25	Pauch 1
	8/11/02	594	Grandview	SCRA Sprint	30	J&M 55
	9/2/02	595	Big Diamond	Small Block	100	Biever 114
	10/20/02	596	New Egypt	Modified	50	Biever 114
Total 2002 Wins (12)						
2003	4/19/03	597	New Egypt	Modified	30	Biever 114
	5/10/03	598	New Egypt	Modified	25	Biever 114
	7/11/03	599	Big Diamond	Small Block	25	Biever 114
	7/12/03	600	New Egypt	Modified	30	Biever 114
	7/16/03	601	New Egypt	Modified	30	Biever 114
	7/25/03	602	Big Diamond	Small Block	25	Biever 114
	8/20/03	603	New Egypt	Modified	100	Biever 114
	10/18/03	604	New Egypt	Modified	30	Biever 114
Total 2003 Wins (8)						
2004	4/10/04	605	New Egypt	Modified	30	Biever 114
	6/9/04	606	New Egypt	Modified	50	Biever 114
	7/2/04	607	Bridgeport (5/8ths)	Modified	25	Biever 114
	7/16/04	608	Bridgeport (5/8ths)	Modified	25	Biever 114
	7/24/04	609	Bridgeport (5/8ths)	Modified	25	Biever 114
	8/28/04	610	New Egypt	Modified	30	Biever 114

Total 2004 Wins (6)

2005	4/9/05	611	New Egypt	Modified	30	Bifulco 1
	4/16/05	612	New Egypt	Modified	30	Bifulco 1
	5/6/05	613	Bridgeport (5/8ths)	Small Block	25	Pauch 1
	6/4/05	614	New Egypt	Modified	30	Bifulco 1
	6/10/05	615	Bridgeport (5/8ths)	Small Block	25	Pauch 1
	6/22/05	616	New Egypt	DIRT Modified	100	Bifulco 1
	7/9/05	617	New Egypt	Modified	30	Bifulco 1
	8/6/05	618	New Egypt	Modified	30	Bifulco 1
	8/9/05	619	Big Diamond	Modified	75	Hansell 357

Total 2005 Wins (9)

2006	4/15/06	620	New Egypt	Modified	30	Bifulco 1
	5/26/06	621	Georgetown	Modified	25	Pauch 1
	6/6/06	622	Big Diamond	Modified	75	Hansell 357
	7/21/06	623	Georgetown	Modified	25	Brown 1W
	8/4/06	624	Georgetown	Modified	25	Brown 1W
	8/5/06	625	New Egypt	Modified	30	Bifulco 1
	8/18/06	626	Georgetown	Modified	30	Brown 1W
	8/22/06	627	Grandview	PA Sprint	25	Hamilton 77
	9/29/06	628	Georgetown	Modified	30	Brown 1W
	11/18/06	629	Bridgeport (5/8ths)	Modified	40	Schmidt 5

Total 2006 wins (10)

2007	6/2/07	630	Bridgeport (5/8ths)	Modified	25	Bifulco 1
	6/9/07	631	Bridgeport (5/8ths)	Modified	25	Bifulco 1
	6/22/07	632	Georgetown	Modified	25	Brown 1W
	6/30/07	633	Bridgeport (5/8ths)	Modified	20	Pauch 1
	7/14/07	634	Bridgeport (5/8ths)	Modified	30	Bifulco 1
	8/1/07	635	New Egypt	Modified	50	Bifulco 1
	8/11/07	636	Bridgeport (5/8ths)	Modified	12	Bifulco 1
	10/12/07	637	New Egypt	Small Block	40	Brown 1W

Total 2007 wins (8)

2008	2/13/08	638	Volusia	DIRT Modified	30	Brown 1W
	4/19/08	639	New Egypt	Modified	30	Bifulco 1
	4/26/08	640	New Egypt	Modified	30	Bifulco 1
	6/7/08	641	New Egypt	Modified	30	Bifulco 1
	6/28/08	642	New Egypt	SpeedSTR	20	Evernham 98

	7/12/08	643	New Egypt	Modified	30	Bifulco 1
	7/19/08	644	New Egypt	Modified	30	Bifulco 1
	9/13/08	645	New Egypt	Modified	35	Bifulco 1
	9/13/08	646	New Egypt	Modified	35	Bifulco 1
	11/22/08	647	Georgetown	Modified	30	Hyneman 126
Total 2008 wins (10)						
2009	1/16/09	648	AC Convention Ctr.	3/4 Midget	25	Ingalls 8
	4/25/09	649	New Egypt	Modified	30	Bifulco 1
	5/2/09	650	New Egypt	Modified	30	Bifulco 1
	5/30/09	651	New Egypt	Modified	30	Bifulco 1
	6/6/09	652	New Egypt	Modified	30	Bifulco 1
	7/18/09	653	New Egypt	Modified	30	Bifulco 1
	7/25/09	654	New Egypt	Modified	30	Bifulco 1
	8/1/09	655	New Egypt	Modified	40	Bifulco 1
	8/15/09	656	New Egypt	Modified	30	Bifulco 1
	9/19/09	657	New Egypt	Modified	30	Bifulco 1
	10/3/09	658	New Egypt	Modified	40	Bifulco 1
Total 2009 wins (11)						
2010	4/24/10	659	New Egypt	Modified	30	Bifulco 1
	5/15/10	660	New Egypt	Modified	30	Bifulco 1
	5/29/10	661	New Egypt	Modified	30	Bifulco 1
	8/14/10	662	New Egypt	Modified	30	Bifulco 1
	8/31/10	663	New Egypt	Modified	40	Bifulco 1
	9/25/10	664	New Egypt	Modified	20	Bifulco 1
	9/25/10	665	New Egypt	Modified	20	Bifulco 1
	10/10/10	666	Georgetown	Modified	25	Brown 1W
	10/16/10	667	New Egypt	Modified	40	Bifulco 1
	10/22/10	668	Delaware Int'l.	Small Block	50	Pauch 1
	10/23/10	669	Delaware Int'l.	Modified	50	Brown 1W
Total 2010 wins (11)						
2011	4/9/11	670	New Egypt	Modified	30	Bifulco 1
	4/16/11	671	New Egypt	Modified	30	Bifulco 1
	5/28/11	672	New Egypt	Modified	30	Bifulco 1
	6/2/11	673	New Egypt	Modified	30	Bifulco 1
	6/4/11	674	New Egypt	Modified	30	Bifulco 1
	6/18/11	675	New Egypt	Modified	30	Bifulco 1

	6/25/11	676	New Egypt	Modified	30	Bifulco 1
	7/2/11	677	New Egypt	Modified	30	Bifulco 1
	7/9/11	678	New Egypt	Modified	30	Bifulco 1
	7/16/11	679	New Egypt	Modified	30	Bifulco 1
	8/6/11	680	New Egypt	Modified	30	Bifulco 1
	8/23/11	681	New Egypt	Modified	40	Bifulco 1
	8/30/11	682	New Egypt	Modified	30	Bifulco 1
	10/15/11	683	New Egypt	Modified	20	Bifulco 1
	10/21/11	684	Delaware Int'l.	Small Block	50	Bifulco 1
	Total 2011 wins (15)					
2012	3/17/12	685	Selinsgrove	Modified	40	Bifulco 1
	4/7/12	686	New Egypt	Modified	30	Bifulco 1
	4/14/12	687	New Egypt	Modified	30	Bifulco 1
	5/12/12	688	New Egypt	Modified	30	Bifulco 1
	7/21/12	689	New Egypt	Modified	30	Bifulco 1
	8/30/12	690	Bridgeport (5/8ths)	Modified	40	Bifulco 1
	9/29/12	691	New Egypt	Modified	25	Bifulco 1
	11/10/12	692	Bridgeport (5/8ths)	Modified	40	Bifulco 1
	Total 2012 wins (8)					
2013	4/14/13	693	New Egypt	Small Block	30	Bifulco 1
	6/4/13	694	Kutztown	SpeedSTR	40	Sinibaldi 9
	6/22/13	695	New Egypt	Small Block	30	Bifulco 1
	7/13/13	696	New Egypt	Small Block	30	Bifulco 1
	7/28/13	697	Path Valley	SpeedSTR	25	Sinibaldi 9
	8/20/13	698	New Egypt	Modified	30	Bifulco 1
	9/7/13	699	New Egypt	Small Block	30	Bifulco 1
	9/28/13	700	New Egypt	Small Block	20	Bifulco 1

10/18/13	701	Delaware Int'l.	Small Block	50	Bifulco 1
10/20/13	702	Delaware Int'l.	Modified	50	Bifulco 1

Total 2013 wins (10)

2014	4/5/14	703	New Egypt	Small Block	30	Bifulco 1
	4/12/14	704	New Egypt	Small Block	30	Bifulco 1
	4/19/14	705	New Egypt	Small Block	30	Bifulco 1
	5/3/14	706	New Egypt	Small Block	30	Bifulco 1
	5/14/14	707	Kutztown	SpeedSTR	30	Sinibaldi 9
	5/28/14	708	Kutztown	SpeedSTR	30	Sinibaldi 9
	6/18/14	709	Kutztown	SpeedSTR	17	Sinibaldi 9
	6/21/14	710	New Egypt	Small Block	30	Bifulco 1
	7/26/14	711	New Egypt	Small Block	30	Bifulco 1
	8/19/14	712	New Egypt	Modified	30	Bifulco 1
	9/6/14	713	New Egypt	Small Block	30	Bifulco 1
	10/11/14	714	Five Mile Point	SpeedSTR	30	Sinibaldi 9
	11/2/14	715	Grandview	SpeedSTR	35	Sinibaldi 9

Total 2014 wins (13)

2015	5/27/15	716	Kutztown	SpeedSTR	30	Heffner 27
	6/17/15	717	Kutztown	SpeedSTR	17	Heffner 27
	8/8/15	718	New Egypt	Modified	30	Bifulco 1
	10/10/15	719	Five Mile Point	SpeedSTR	30	Heffner 27
	11/13/15	720	Bridgeport (5/8ths)	Small Block	30	Bifulco 1

Total 2015 wins (5)

2016	4/23/16	721	New Egypt	Modified	30	Bifulco 1
	5/18/16	722	Kutztown	SpeedSTR	30	Heffner 27
	5/25/16	723	Kutztown	SpeedSTR	30	Heffner 27
	6/15/16	724	Kutztown	SpeedSTR	17	Heffner 27
	8/17/16	725	Kutztown	SpeedSTR	30	Heffner 27
	8/27/16	726	New Egypt	Modified	30	Bifulco 1
	9/24/16	727	Bridgeport (5/8ths)	Modified	50	Bifulco 1

Total 2016 Wins (7)

2017	No wins

2018	5/5/18	728	Bridgeport (5/8ths)	Modified	25	Bifulco 1
	6/23/18	729	Bridgeport (5/8ths)	Modified	25	Bifulco 1
	8/4/18	730	Bridgeport (5/8ths)	Modified	25	Bifulco 1
	8/22/18	731	Grandview	Small Block	30	Bifulco 1

Total 2018 Wins (4)

2019	3/30/19	732	Bridgeport (5/8ths)	Modified	44	Bifulco 1
	5/18/19	733	Bridgeport (3/8ths)	Modified	25	Bifulco 1
	6/1/19	734	Bridgeport (3/8ths)	Modified	25	Bifulco 1
	6/8/19	735	Bridgeport (3/8ths)	Modified	25	Bifulco 1
	7/13/19	736	Bridgeport (5/8ths)	Modified	25	Bifulco 1
	8/31/19	737	Bridgeport (5/8ths)	Modified	25	Bifulco 1

Total 2019 Wins (6)

2020	7/18/20	738	Bridgeport (4/10ths)	Modified	30	Bifulco 1
	7/25/20	739	Bridgeport (4/10ths)	Modified	30	Bifulco 1
	9/5/20	740	Bridgeport (4/10ths)	Modified	30	Bifulco 1

Total 2020 Wins (3)

2021	5/4/21	741	Bridgeport (4/10ths)	SpeedSTR	20	Rodota R7
	6/26/21	742	Bridgeport (4/10ths)	Modified	30	Bifulco 1
	9/25/21	743	Bridgeport (4/10ths)	SpeedSTR	20	Rodota R7

Total 2021 Wins (3)

CAREER STATS...

Winning Tracks: 33 in 7 states (NJ, PA, NY, MD, DE, FL, IA)

Winning Car Owners: 33

Winning Divisions: 13

BILLY PAUCH CAREER ACHIEVEMENTS

TRACK TITLES...

Flemington: 1 Rookie (1975), 1 Sportsman (1976), 8 Modified (1979, 1981, 1985, 1986, 1987, 1988, 1989, 1990), 1 Modified Sprint (1986), 1 Small Block (1991)

East Windsor: 1 Sportsman (1976)

Bridgeport 5/8ths: 4 Modified (1987, 1988, 2007, 2019)

Bridgeport 4/10ths: 1 Modified (2020)

Penn National: 3 Small Block (1988, 1989, 1992)

New Egypt: 6 Modified (1999, 2000, 2002, 2008, 2011, 2013)

Kutztown/Action Track: 1 SpeedSTR (2016)

SERIES TITLES...

New Jersey State Sportsman Championship: 1976

New Jersey State Modified Championship: 1984

Dirt Modified Florida Tour: 1982, 1985, 2008

Thunder on the Hill Sprint Series: 1990, 1992, 1993, 1995, 2001

In 2021, the record-setting Zemco Sprint car was installed in the National Sprint Car Hall of Fame & Museum in Knoxville, Iowa. (L to R) Crew chief Tommy Carl, Pee Wee Zemaitis, driver Billy Pauch, car owner John Zemaitis and crewman Don Jobe.

CAREER HIGHLIGHTS...

All-time Fulton Victoria 200 Winner: 1986, 1987, 1988, 1989, 1990, 1997

All-time Thunder on the Hill Sprint Feature Winner: 11

Six-time Grandview Freedom 76 Winner: 1988, 1991, 1992, 1996, 1998, 2000

14 Super DIRT Series Wins: East Windsor (1979), Flemington (1984, 1986, 1989, 1990), Bridgeport (1987, 1988, 1996), Williams Grove (1988, 1989), Grandview (1989), New Egypt (2000, 2005), Volusia (2008)

Two-time World of Outlaws Sprint Winner: Syracuse NYSF (1994), Rolling Wheels (1996)

All-time Speed Record on the Syracuse Mile: 144.590 mph in the Zemco Sprint Car (1994)

DIRT 320/358 Modified Nationals at Syracuse NYSF: 1987

Summer Nationals at Ransomville: 1988

NASCAR Race of Champions Modified 250 at Flemington: 1993

Williams Grove National Open: 1998

Octoberfest at Hagerstown: Mod (1988, 1992, 1995, 1996), Sprint (1993, 1998, 1999), Small Block (1999)

Delaware State Dirt Track Championships: Mod (1989, 1993, 2010, 2013), Sprint (1997), Small Block (1989, 1990, 1992, 1993, 2010, 2011, 2013)

Big Diamond Coalcracker: 2000, 2002

Over 100 Wins: Flemington, East Windsor, New Egypt

HONORS...

EMPA Driver of the Year: 1987, 1992

AARN Winningest Driver in the Northeast: 1987, 1988, 1989, 1990, 1991, 1992

Flemington Speedway Historical Society "Tas" Award: 2013

Northeast Dirt Modified Hall of Fame: 2016

York County Hall of Fame: 2017

He has a knack for carrying a car—over the years, I'd say he probably carried the car at least 50 percent of the time. That's a big percentage.

ROY PAUCH

DAVE PRAT

ACKNOWLEDGMENTS

*A huge debt of gratitude to everyone who contributed to this project, but especially to **Fred Voorhees**, who compiled and documented Billy's career win stats and spent countless hours combing through old publications to check facts; and also **Lenny Sammons**, for very generously opening the **Area Auto Racing News** photo archives to me.*

Thanks to:

Jeff Ahlum
Dave Argabright
Ted Arnold
Steve Barrick
Kevin Bifulco
Ken Brenn
Tommy Carl
Ray Carroll
Pete Chesson
Frank Cozze
Al and Dave DeBlasio
Jim Donnelly
Jay Dugan
Kevin Eckert
Ray Evernham
Bob Faust
Tony Feil
Mario Fiore
Gene Franckowiak
Dave Garboski
D.A. Hanson
Davey Hoffman
Jimmy Horton
Glenn Hyneman
Rick Kuhl
Roger Laureno
Rich Lavalette
Leon Liedl
Nick Lombardi
Joe Macfarlan/
3widespicturevault.com
Phil McCloughan

Bob McCreadie
Bob Miller
Donnie Miller
Doug Olsen
The Pauch Family
Bob Pickell Jr.
Stan Ploski
David Quier
Fred Rahmer
Bruce Schell
Tom Schmeh

Tony Sesely
John Sine
Tony Siscone
John Skistimas
Chuck Snyder
Jeff Strunk
Lenny Swider
Rich Tobias Jr.
Craig Von Dohren
John Zemaitis
Doug Zupan

*Billy is grateful to all the photographers who captured the important moments in his career, including **Jack Kromer** and **Mel Stettler** (pictured with him and Kenny Brenn, above). In addition, the following shooters also went out of their way to locate and contribute specific images:*

Bob Armbruster
Ken Dippel
Mike Feltenberger
Ace Lane Jr.

Harry Meeks Sr.
Dave Pratt
Rick Sweeten
Bob Yurko

About the Author...

Buffy Swanson attended her first stock car race in 1968 at Weissglass Stadium in Staten Island, where she fell in love with the sport and her future husband, Jim (not necessarily in that order). She went on to cover the Northeast dirt Modifieds for *Area Auto Racing News*, *Speedway Scene*, *Stock Car Racing*, *Circle Track*, *Trackside* and *Speedway Illustrated*. Honored by the Northeast Dirt Modified Hall of Fame in 2010, Buffy's award-winning work has been recognized by the Eastern Motorsports Press Association, American Auto Racing Writers & Broadcasters Association, and the New Jersey Press Association. She resides in Jackson, New Jersey.